D1044959

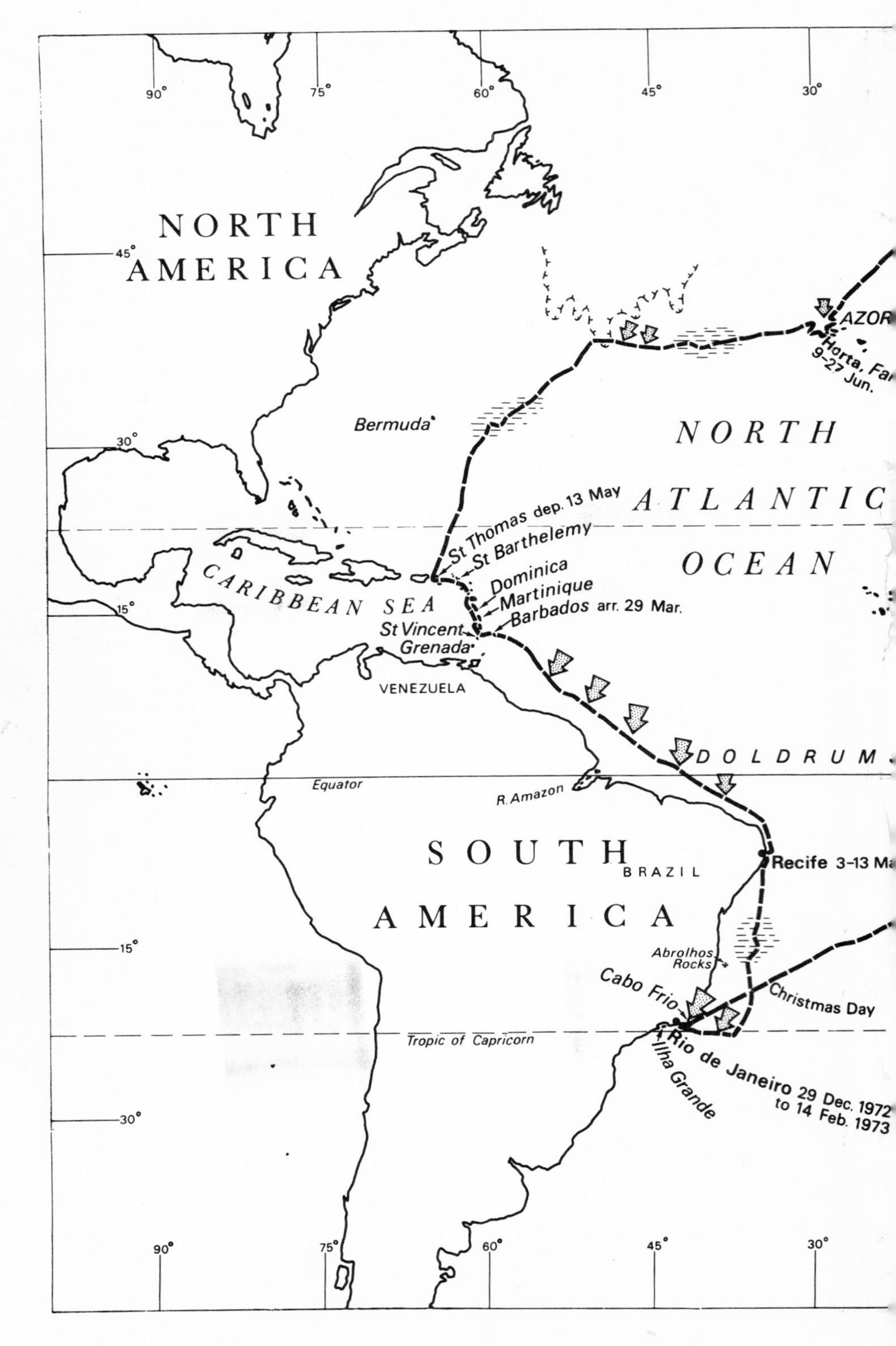
90°
75°
60°
45°
30°
NORTH
AMERICA
45°
AZOR
Horta, Fa
9–27 Jun.
Bermuda
30°
NORTH
ATLANTIC
OCEAN
St Thomas dep. 13 May
St Barthelemy
Dominica
Martinique
Barbados arr. 29 Mar.
CARIBBEAN SEA
St Vincent
Grenada
15°
VENEZUELA
DOLDRUM
Equator
R. Amazon
SOUTH
AMERICA
BRAZIL
Recife 3–13 M
15°
Abrolhos Rocks
Cabo Frio
Christmas Day
Tropic of Capricorn
Rio de Janeiro 29 Dec. 1972
to 14 Feb. 1973
Ilha Grande
30°
90°
75°
60°
45°
30°

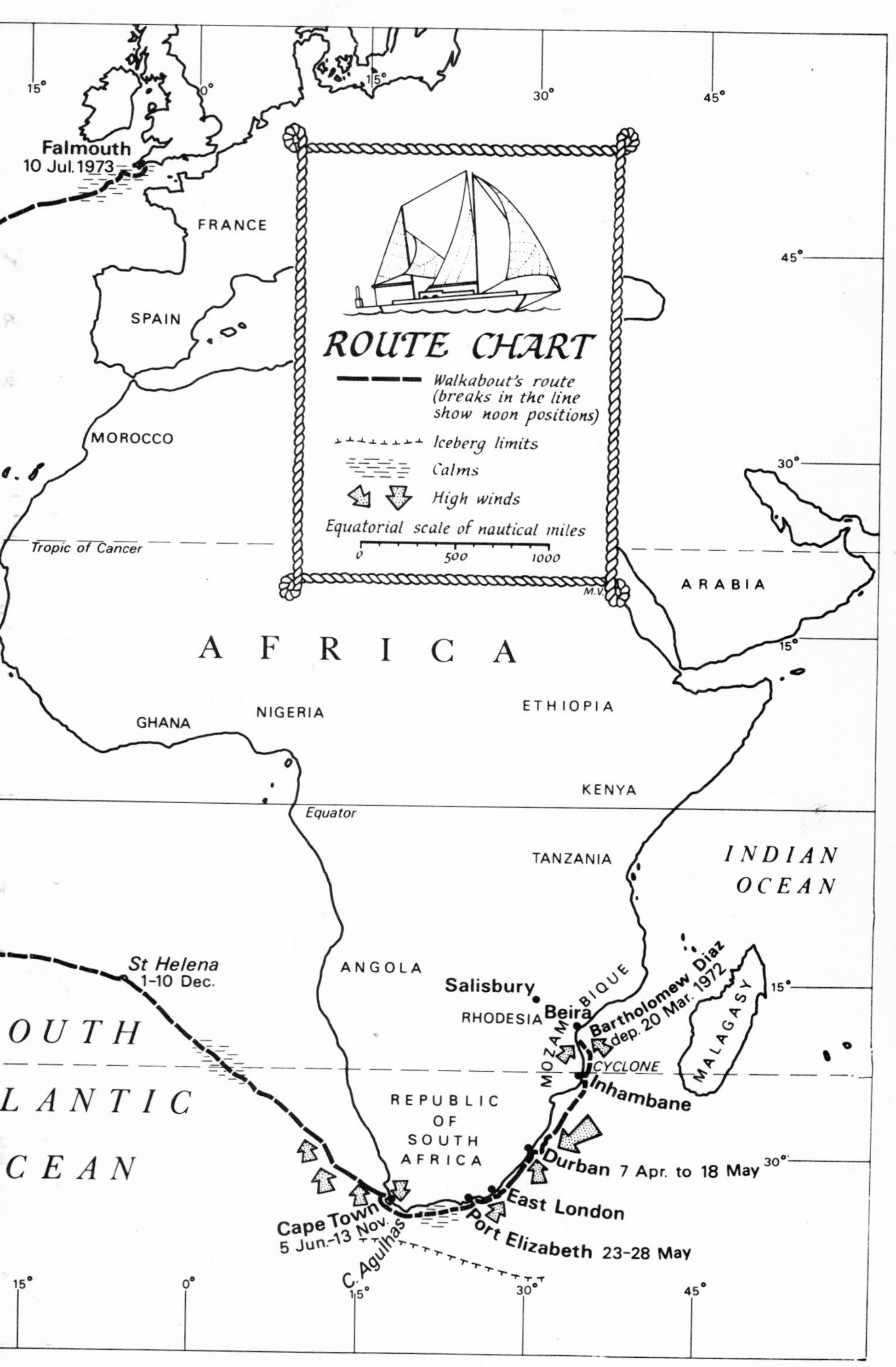

ROUTE CHART
Walkabout's route (breaks in the line show noon positions)
Iceberg limits
Calms
High winds
Equatorial scale of nautical miles
0
500
1000
M.V.
Falmouth
10 Jul. 1973
FRANCE
SPAIN
MOROCCO
Tropic of Cancer
ARABIA
AFRICA
GHANA
NIGERIA
ETHIOPIA
KENYA
Equator
TANZANIA
INDIAN OCEAN
ANGOLA
St Helena
1-10 Dec.
Salisbury
RHODESIA
Beira
MOZAMBIQUE
Bartholomew Diaz
dep. 20 Mar. 1972
CYCLONE
MALAGASY
Inhambane
OUTH
LANTIC
CEAN
REPUBLIC OF SOUTH AFRICA
Durban 7 Apr. to 18 May
East London
Port Elizabeth 23-28 May
Cape Town
5 Jun.-13 Nov.
C. Agulhas
15°
0°
30°
45°

THE WALKABOUTS

A Family at Sea

by

MIKE SAUNDERS

STEIN AND DAY/*Publishers*/New York

First published in the United States of America in 1975

Printed in the United States of America
Stein and Day/*Publishers*/Scarborough House,
Briarcliff Manor, N.Y. 10510

Library of Congress Cataloging in Publication Data

Saunders, Mike, 1940-
The walkabouts.

1. Walkabout (Yacht) 2. Voyages and travels—
1951- I. Title.
G530.W274S28 910′.41 [B] 75-9849
ISBN 0-8128-1820-2

ACKNOWLEDGEMENTS

For the sailing photographs I am much indebted to Colin Harrington, and for the majority of drawings to Dick Everitt; a number of drawings in Appendix I first appeared in *Practical Boat Owner*, whose editor has kindly given permission for them to be re-published.

My thanks also to several publishers who kindly gave permission to quote from their publications: Messrs Faber and Faber for lines from *The Love Song of J. Alfred Prufrock* (T. S. Eliot, *Collected Poems, 1909–1962*), the Oxford University Press for excerpts from *Cruising under Sail* by Eric Hiscock, and the Hydrographer of the Royal Navy for excerpts from *The Africa Pilot* and *The Mariner's Handbook.*

The medical list was drawn up with the generous aid of Dr Robert Fynn and Bertie Friedlander, pharmacist.

It would take a supplementary volume to thank by name all those who helped us in a hundred ways, from unstinting hospitality to sweat on the slipway. Persuaded by my publishers of the sales limitations of such a volume, I content myself with thanking them unnamed; they and I know who they are.

M. S.

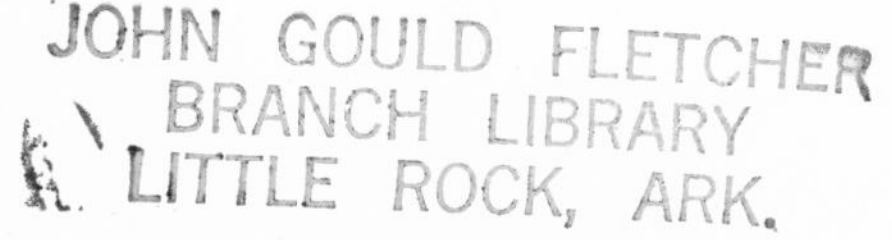

For Liz,
who makes all things possible

LIST OF ILLUSTRATIONS

I

WHEN AN AUSTRALIAN aborigine suddenly throws up his job and takes to the bush for anything from a few weeks to several years, people say he has "gone walkabout". He may have no particular destination, but that does not necessarily mean that he has no purpose. He goes walkabout to get away from it all, to cleanse the soul or possibly just to satisfy a yearning for adventure.

In the end we became walkabouts for much the same reasons, I suppose, though at first there were motives of a far more respectable sort. This is hardly surprising, because we were a family leading a suburban life of a more or less respectable sort, complete with mortgage nicely matched to a career as a consulting engineer in mechanical and chemical fields. The mortgage was attached to a rambling colonial-style house set in an acre and a half of garden and orchard which were no real trouble to look after because the servants attended to them. Which does not mean that we had money, but simply that we were living in Salisbury, Rhodesia. It was an easy life in the regular sunshine, and, one would have said, an ideal place to raise a boisterous brood of children.

There were four of them.

Kevin, the eldest, a handsome lad of ten, was the most reserved, almost secretive, though one would hardly have thought so during those occasions when he abandoned his books to hurtle shrieking through the flower-beds on his bicycle like a plundering Hun. Mark, nine, who carried a bonny head of curls and could produce either a ready grin or a flash of temper, liked this sort of thing better than his brother. He rather avoided his books, however, in favour of making things with his hands, and was known in the neighbourhood as a fixer of toys and soapbox-carts and the like. The youngest boy, Bruce, just six, made up in determination and imagination for what he lacked in looks, and ruthlessly ensured that he came first in everything he attempted. He was interested in any living thing, plant or creature, and was generally regarded by the family as a budding Gerald Durrell. The baby of the family was Rachel, though at three years of age she was already emerging from babyhood and becoming a very feminine little girl. A dog, two cats and five guinea-pigs completed the menagerie which my wife, Liz, ruled with serene competence.

One day early in July the telephone rang. "Hullo! Mr Saunders?" A man's voice introduced its owner. "I hear you're looking for a yacht."

"That's right. The word certainly gets around quickly."

"That's hardly surprising when you consider there are only a handful of salt-water sailors in Rhodesia. Less than a score of boats, in fact, and I know them all. There is really only one for sale in Rhodesia—unless you have money outside the country. You haven't? I thought not. Same as the rest of us. Only villains and politicians can get their money out these days."

"You're absolutely right. But—er—the boat?"

"Well, it isn't actually in Rhodesia, of course. Not the sort of boat you could bring inland. She's lying in a swamp near Paradise Island in Mozambique. A strong sea boat, take you anywhere you want to go. At least, she could. But she hasn't been sailed for some years now, so I don't know what her condition is. Go and see the owner. He lives near Salisbury." He gave me the details.

"That's terrific. Thanks very much. Oh, by the way, what's her name?"

"Her name? *Walkabout.*"

From that moment we were lost. Naturally we were not properly aware of this, and continued to weigh decisions as gravely as though they really meant something. But the fact that we were seriously looking for a boat meant that the main decision had already been taken, and the reasons stretched back to Rhodesia's Unilateral Declaration of Independence, shortly after we had returned to settle in the country after living for some years in England.

U.D.I. turned Rhodesia from an attitude of hopeful tolerance and set it on the road to racial nationalism, adopted by nearly all African countries in the last couple of decades. It was distressing to see how the whites became increasingly obdurate and the blacks progressively more bitter, and in 1968, after a friend had been summarily deported for no discoverable reason, we helped to start the Centre Party, a multi-racial party that aimed at a settlement of the U.D.I. dispute between Britain and Rhodesia. We acted, we all realised, more from a wish to attempt to do something positive than in the conviction that we should succeed.

We did not succeed. A referendum on the republican issue and an election made that plain, not to mention repeated failures to reach a settlement. International sanctions cut Rhodesia off from the world and made people smug and parochial. And finally the unanswerable question of security, with all its complex ramifications, hung over the future. We reluctantly decided in the end to leave Rhodesia and return to England.

But that was not a simple matter. Because of sanctions and the severe shortage of foreign exchange, the government had barricaded the country with monetary restrictions. Emigrants' bank accounts were frozen, and they were permitted to take out less money than holiday makers—hardly a sound basis on which to build a new life. We thought of various ways to get our savings out in uncut gems or Persian carpets, before hitting on the plan to fit out a motor caravan and drive to England. While this seemed an exciting way of doing things, it had to be dropped completely when we found that our journey north would be barred by red tape if not, indeed, by machine-guns.

At this point a friend said, "If you want to do it the adventurous way, why not buy a boat and sail there? You've been talking about sailing round the world ever since you were so high."

Quite true, and why not? I had in fact just built a 20ft trimaran as a first testing step, but I suddenly knew that, unless I plunged into the deep-end now, my dreams would slowly crumple in disappointment at my lack of courage in this moment of decision.

"I don't want to end up like J. Alfred Prufrock," I told Liz—

"'For I have known them all already, known them all,
Have known the evenings, mornings, afternoons,
I have measured out my life with coffee spoons.'"

Liz nodded slowly and understood. Quoting T. S. Eliot meant serious business.

Barely a week later we were discussing *Walkabout* with her Owner. She was a 33ft ketch, far too small for six of us, and she only had one cabin. She sounded as though she needed fitting out and re-rigging, and the Owner was asking more than we could afford to pay. Worst of all, it was incredibly difficult to see the boat.

She was lying in a remote lagoon near a small island called Bartholomew Dias, 100 miles south of Beira off the coast of Mozambique. We should have to mount an expedition to reach the place. Stage I would be a car journey of 500 miles, the first half over good tarred roads but the second half over a road so bad that it amounted to no more than a pavement of rumours; in fact, the authorities would not admit that it was there at all. Stage II would be from the coastal village of Inhassoro, driving 30 miles along a deserted beach at low spring tide to the end of a long spit. Stage III would call for a boat to carry us 5 miles over to the island itself. But, as not a soul inhabited the region, a boat had to be either carried from Salisbury or kept near the island. Bartholomew Dias itself was also uninhabited, except for a few holiday cottages, one of which belonged to *Walkabout*'s Owner.

It was altogether a daunting business just to inspect the boat, let alone fit out for an ocean voyage. And as the Owner pointed out, there was virtually no other suitable place along that swamp-infested coast to keep her. Anyone with the least grain of sense would have rejected the whole idea at once.

I decided forthwith to buy her, but not without dutifully explaining to Liz why we should not. For, whatever the drawbacks, it was instantly obvious that here was a boat made to cross oceans. She was built in Fremantle, Australia, in the early fifties, and had sailed to South Africa, had sailed up the Mozambique Channel, had sailed to the Comora Islands. She had been designed by the late John Alden, the celebrated

Boston designer, and was a sister ship of the famous *Svaap*. In this yacht W. R. Robinson circumnavigated the world in the thirties. *Walkabout* is also cited by Eric C. Hiscock in *Voyaging under Sail*, the cruising man's bible and handbook. In short, she was a professional.

The story runs—and it is probably apocryphal—that she was built at first for the Sidney–Hobart race. The Driscoll brothers, who built her, lavished on her all their love, and ultimately all their money, so they finished up with a beautiful boat, complete in every detail on the outside, but with not so much as a hathook in the cabin. The Sidney–Hobart race had long since passed and they reckoned then that if they did not leave without delay they never would. They leaped aboard and sailed away. They slept in hammocks and cooked over a paraffin stove on the floor, and had a pretty thin time of it by all accounts. When they reached South Africa they leaped off again, kissed the soil, and then found more lively objects for their affections. The second folly had to be paid for with the boat, for one got married. They sold *Walkabout* and settled down.

We left the Owner and drove home in a state of excitement, minds racing with problems and solutions. Liz sounded the only sober note.

"Mike, when we agreed to give up our home and take the children to sea we didn't have such a small boat in mind, did we? With this lot aboard, I just hope we keep our sanity. And you know nothing about sailing, really. Oh, I know you've been messing around in boats along the Mozambique coast half your life. But little ones, and mostly motor boats. No yachts or long cruises, no navigation. Are you happy about inspecting *Walkabout* and making sure she's sound?"

"Of course not. I'm terrified of everything, but you have to start somewhere. Are *you* happy to start now and tackle it together?"

She nodded. "On that basis, I'm happy."

Weeks of frustration followed when we put the house up for sale and tried to plan while the Owner blew hot and cold over arranging an inspection, let alone concluding a sale. At last he agreed to meet me in Inhassoro at a certain low tide and get me to Bartholomew Dias. To Liz's great disappointment she could not come because of the children, but a friend of mine came instead. Brian Gough was an enormous square-jawed fellow, and he had done a lot of sailing, which was a great comfort, though he disclaimed any ability to survey yachts.

"I'll leave that side to you," he said. "I hope you've been able to mug up something on it."

"Not much," I replied. "I combed this wretched landlocked country looking for a yacht surveyor, and of course couldn't find one. The best I could do was a retired marine engineer who used to look after a fleet of government boats on the Nile. The old boy was a bit vague, but suggested I should look for wood rot by poking with a steel spike. So I bought a couple of spikes."

We set off one lunch-time in my old American station wagon, and drove over the hot tarmac with the noon sun burning behind us. Rhodesian roads are usually too good to be of much interest, and for hours you can roar over the undulating savannah, peeling off hundreds of miles of black road with your mind as sluggish as a sun-baked toad. That evening we reached the border at Machipanda, and wound down the escarpment towards Portuguese territory; the air became warmer and the vegetation thicker. A hundred miles later we came to a second escarpment and dropped down to the sweaty plains of the Pungwe flats. Here we left the tarmac of the main Beira–Salisbury road and turned south on to a dirt track marked by a hand-painted board nailed to a tree saying, optimistically and probably inaccurately, "Lourenco Marques, 750 km.".

From here on, the journey was hard and we pounded slowly forward, twisting to miss the potholes which looked like black puddles in the headlights. The fine dust which settled thickly on every surface upset Brian, but I liked it. The smell and taste of it are the essence of Africa, and it felt soft and cool underfoot. Occasionally a small head of antelope would canter out of the headlights, their eyes shining a bright white, but we saw no sign of people.

We drove through the night without encountering any serious difficulties. On a couple of occasions we got stuck and had to dig ourselves out, and once we hit a small tree that lay across the track. We slewed down a bank and for one nasty moment I thought it was the work of Frelimo guerrillas, but the tree had simply fallen over. We jacked the car back on to the road, repaired the damaged gear-linkage and pressed on, stopping only for a quick breakfast by the side of the road shortly after dawn.

It was nearly noon when we arrived at Inhassoro five minutes after the appointed hour, fatigued nearly to indifference. The Owner was waiting for us. He was a trifle testy.

"Hello, there! You're a little late, aren't you? I was about to leave."

I apologised, and Brian and I picked up our camping gear and climbed into a natty red beach buggy. The Owner drove at a reckless pace down the steep, sandy track leading to the beach, and we started on Stage II of the journey. The beach was several hundred yards wide and swept off into the distance, until it disappeared over the curve of the horizon. We drove for nearly 30 miles along the edge of the surf, deep blue sea to our right and desolate low scrub on our left. A glance at the map in Chapter IV will show that we were driving up a long, thin peninsula which separates a lagoon, lying unseen behind the scrub, from the open sea. Towards the end of this peninsula the beach narrows and steepens, and the stumpy remnants of a petrified forest studs the sands and finally bars the way. Here we stopped and Brian and I climbed out. The Owner hurled the beach buggy at an opening in the scrub and scrambled out of sight with a fearful clatter, while we followed on foot.

The lagoon lay on the other side, barely 100 yards away, a postcard picture of crystal blue water set about with white beaches. Anchored near the shore was a modest Atlantic liner, the Owner's 65ft motor yacht—*Janet Susan*. An African mariner rowed us aboard in the dinghy, and the twin diesels thrust the big white yacht towards B.D.

The first we saw of the island were evergreen casuarina trees, which grew thickly along parts of the shore. In that barren place they gave me a sharp twang of pleasure. The Owner was discussing *Walkabout*. I shook with excitement.

"I hadn't really looked at her for some time, so we cleared her out, took her to pieces, really. Good news and bad. The water-tanks and a couple of other things have rusted away, but basically she's as sound as a bell. Anyway, you can see for yourself—there she is."

Through the haze of heat and fatigue I saw *Walkabout* high and dry in a little cove, shored up with four stout poles. She looked wonderful. Solidity stood about her like a halo, and strength flowed from every timber. Her rudder looked like a vault door. And yet her lines flowed as sweetly from stem to stern as water over a dolphin's back. I felt already that the Fates had disposed without consulting me, but I had to make some show of independence, so I got out the shiny spikes and began to dig with a will.

Walkabout showed a splendid indifference to the probings, for she was built of jarrah, an iron-hard Australian wood. The spikes curled back in defeat. I hunted for corrosion under the new paint, but found that every fastening and structural piece of metal was either copper or bronze. Brian was greatly impressed, but wondered how easy it would be to handle her heavy gear. I was frankly frightened by the weight and size of her tackle.

After the boat had been refloated on the tide and towed back to moorings I sat inside, on the bare wooden seats, and soaked up the atmosphere. This was more than the faintly drain-like smell of bilgewater. It included the sight of heavy timbers and bronze kneebraces, the paraffin lamps and brass ship's clock, the steady pendulum motion as one sat below the water-line. But the cabin was as stark as I had feared. Everything was painted a uniform industrial grey, there were no shelves or nets, there were no cabin partitions and no galley. From its central position the toilet—which was defective—commanded the cabin like decayed royalty. It would be no easy matter to convert this boat to a home for a family of six. I began to draw up schemes on how it might be done.

That night Brian and I camped in the ruins of an old house. Bartholomew Dias had once been a port of some local importance and, it was rumoured, a secret retreat for German submarines during World War II. That was when it had been part of the mainland; but one year massive seas raised by a cyclone had driven through the peninsula and turned it into an island. Now all that remained were a couple of ruined houses, a few holiday cottages and a derelict hotel that was, in fact, new but had never been finished.

At sunrise the next day I was back on *Walkabout*, scheming

and dreaming. There was also much practical work to be done. Brian and I were hard at it all day, inspecting, measuring and checking. I measured and sketched virtually every item connected with the boat, noting every single thing that might have to be done. Once we were back in Salisbury, another expedition would have to be mounted to check even a single dimension.

By that evening I had worked out a scheme for refitting and had estimated costs. It could be done, I was sure, but much depended on the first cost of the boat. I would tell the Owner that I was, in principle, most interested. So interested, in fact, that I would agree to buy if the price was right. Then I could go back to Salisbury, discuss the matter with Liz, plan, dream, and then—who knows?

The Owner knows. Using some sixth business sense he homes in on a sale, naming the maximum price I had agreed with myself.

"If you like, we can draw up a rough contract and sign before you leave, Mike."

I nod soundlessly and try to speak. Eventually a sound emerges like a saw drawn over a nail. It resembles the syllable "Yes".

The next day we returned to Inhassoro in *Janet Susan*, steaming out of the lagoon through the narrow, treacherous gap gouged by the cyclone. On our way down the coast a contract was drawn up which stated that I had four months in which to find the purchase price, after which time both the deposit and the boat would be forfeit. Meanwhile, the boat would remain in B.D. in the Owner's custody and at my expense.

The journey home was as boneshaking as the journey out. We drove continuously, and after a time it seemed that I had been grafted to the jolting steering column. Only one incident occurred, when Brian was unlucky enough to be driving. A family of warthogs suddenly rushed squealing from the ditch and hurled themselves between the wheels of the car. There was no missing them. Mother and one piglet escaped with a good fright, but the second piglet was killed instantly.

Brian was shattered. Despite his formidable appearance, he hated killing and could not bear the sight of blood. He wanted to bolt from the scene of the crime immediately, but I said that it was a pity to leave the tasty victim to the hyenas, and I slung one piglet in the back while Brian stared fixedly ahead.

And so it was that when we finally rolled into Salisbury in the early hours of the following morning I had two gifts for Liz —a dead warthog and a 12-ton yacht. She could never decide which had disturbed her more.

II

THE UNFORTUNATE WARTHOG was easily disposed of—he tasted delicious pot-roasted in beer—but there was nothing we could do about *Walkabout* except press on with all possible speed.

There was a daunting amount to be done in a very short space of time, but these situations somehow develop their own momentum which sweeps one forward willynilly. It was now September, and we had to sell up and prepare everything for the voyage by the end of December. The plan after that was to fit out while camping on B.D., and set out towards the end of January. We would sail down the Mozambique Channel and round South Africa into the South Atlantic. It became evident from textbooks that the classical sailing ship route from the Cape of Good Hope to England described a curve bowing westwards in the middle—sufficiently far westwards to make it worthwhile calling in at the West Indies, where, I learnt, because of the hurricane season, it was advisable to leave before July. I reckoned that the whole voyage would take about six months, and that was the most our finances would stretch to in any case.

The greatest problem would be fitting out. Sanctions had been in force against Rhodesia for seven years, and many common or garden materials were difficult to come by. Yacht gear was virtually unobtainable, apart from a few dinghy fittings. And everything, even food, had to be assembled before we left Rhodesia, for nothing at all was available on B.D.

We started drawing up lists: lists of every single thing needed, lists of the things needed from abroad, lists of priorities, lists of costs, and finally a list to classify all the lists. The first priority was a sextant. I had already established that there was no such instrument for sale in Rhodesia, and could not find a second-hand one in South Africa. Eric, my father-in-law, who lived in England, agreed to buy one in Britain and send it out, together with safety harnesses and certain vital engine spares. The goods would be sent out as gifts, thus surmounting the first obstacle with delightful ease—or so it seemed at the time.

A new compass was also needed, but nothing suitable was available in Rhodesia. It was my sister who came to the rescue this time. She lives in South Africa, and she said that if I could smuggle the money to her in Durban she would buy a compass and try to send it to Salisbury as a gift. This was done, and at the same time I took the opportunity to get a few more vital items which were not available in Rhodesia, such as blocks and bottle screws, items which are commonplace in the scruffiest of chandlers abroad. All this gear came through the mail with as little fuss as a postcard. But a tin of antifouling paint—an unknown commodity in Rhodesia—was seized by the customs and held for six weeks. During this period tortuous negotiations were conducted with several government departments. I had to declare that no foreign currency had left the country, that no equivalent material was manufactured within the country, and that if the antifouling was allowed into the country its use would not involve expenditure of foreign currency at a future date. The final problem of a tariff category was solved when I persuaded them to classify the paint as an insect repellant. My instinctive dislike of officialdom began to assume new dimensions.

As soon as we started to buy gear a new difficulty arose—how was the stuff to be paid for? The only way was to sell our furniture and personal effects. So a programme for selling as well as for buying had to be worked out, disposing of the non-essentials first and keeping the necessities, such as stove and beds, until the last.

Liz and I had decided at the outset on a policy of ruthless elimination. Every single thing which was not essential to shipboard life would be sold or given away regardless of its sentimental or material value. The voyage was to be more than an adventure: it was to be a spring-cleaning in our lives. In practice the shedding of our worldly goods was a slow and dreary business, and the house was gutted by a deliberate process of hara-kiri until Liz and I were left sitting on the floor assuring each other dismally that we were "doing the right thing".

In the end, though, the catharsis did work. When we were finally stripped to basic essentials we felt a wonderful sense of freedom, and realised for the first time how tyrannical material possessions, posing as bastions of comfort and security, can become.

The house itself took a long time to sell, for people were jittery over a new round of secret settlement negotiations being conducted by Lord Goodman. Throughout the preparations we were obliged to keep fairly quiet about our activities and intentions, for fear that the government would step in with some ruinous restriction.

The children seemed hardly affected by the turmoil, for important things like pets, friends and family remained unchanged. We were worried about their formal education at sea, and Liz's stepmother, who is a headmistress in England, went to some lengths to get books and information.

Meanwhile the procurement of gear proceeded with great speed and intensity but with a host of difficulties. We had realised at the outset that with four children to look after a self-steering device was essential. Using photographs of the boat as well as measurements that had been taken, I designed a self-steering gear that could be bolted on to *Walkabout* as a complete working unit without interfering with anything already on the boat. I opted for a horizontally pivoted wind vane for simplicity, although I was a little doubtful of its power. The quotations by a couple of firms for construction were far too high, so I made the thing myself for about £10. When it was complete we decided that the obvious emblem for *Walkabout*'s self-steering was feet—real feet. Liz stepped into a pot of black paint and then walked over the wind vane, and the job was done. We could not agree on a name for it, so we left it to reveal its own name (and nature)—which it did in due course in a series of destructive incidents.

I also realised that a small boat would be needed to carry us over to B.D. from the mainland, a boat light enough to be carried on a roof-rack and one that would also serve later as a sailboat for Kevin and Mark. We decided on an Optimist plywood dinghy, an 8ft single-sprit sail pram. I built the boat with enthusiastic assistance from Mark. Because of this, and because the Optimist was his birthday present, it made the voyage come alive for him in a way that the unseen *Walkabout* could never have done. We painted the pram vile shades of blue and yellow and dubbed her *Puffabout.*

Many other things had to be designed and made because they could not be bought. A galley stove using ordinary paraffin primus stoves was welded up by my father out of angle iron. It was as sturdy as a girder bridge and was fitted with a drip tray more suited to catching molten metal than spilled stew. If it ever broke loose it would probably kill every occupant of the cabin. Another item that had to be built locally was an anchor. I was obsessed with the need for strength, and designed a 60 pounder.

The new rigging was also a headache. No suitable wire, stainless or galvanised, was to be had, so I settled on a type of galvanised wire rope used for supporting telegraph poles, and properly treated it never gave the slightest trouble. For the running rigging, though, I had to make do with manila rope, which subsequently gave much trouble, for it has a short life at sea. A thousand and one other things detailed in the, by now, copious lists had to be researched and bought. Each had to be suited to the aggressive environment of the sea, where severe corrosion and harsh wear could be expected. Few things were so suited. Everything from sleeping-bag zips to locker hinges seemed tailored to Rhodesia's dry and equable climate.

I took to prowling round with a magnet in my pocket. Running to earth some likely-looking catches I would say to the shop assistant, "Are those genuine brass catches?"

"Yes, sir."

"Right through?"

"But of course, sir."

I would whip out the magnet and the catches would leap towards it eagerly. The ecstatic click as they closed with the magnet would be followed by an embarrassed silence.

"Well, that's very odd, sir. I could have sworn that they were brass. Must be brassed steel, I suppose. Ha! ha!"

"I suppose so. You wouldn't know where I could get real brass ones, would you?"

"I'm afraid not, sir. Shouldn't think there are any in the country."

This scene would be re-enacted a dozen times a week, and

the man with the magnet must have become a pretty unpopular figure.

But perhaps the most nagging equipment problem at the time was something to replace *Walkabout*'s main water tanks, which would have been impossible to reproduce accurately and difficult to carry down to B.D. Flexible bags holding about 4 gallons each seemed the best solution. They could be stowed in all the oddly shaped corners, they would be easy to carry, and I felt that many small containers would be safer than one large one. I experimented endlessly with a whole range of flexible materials and different sealing techniques available in Rhodesia, but none of them stood up to the fiercely destructive tests to which we subjected them.

Finally I designed a bag that did not break or leak. But the water in it tasted awful and I began to think of double-skinned bags. The final bag was made of double-skinned vinyl plastic welded together, the outer skin a very tough heavy gauge material and the inner skin a clear tasteless P.V.C. The full bag was left on the gravel drive and everyone passing it had to kick or roll it. After surviving a week of this punishment it was declared fit to survive the savage sea and the rest were ordered. These bags gave not the slightest problem throughout the whole voyage.

During my spare time I learnt navigation. Liz was chronically concerned about navigation, and I was more than uneasy. But we were lucky. The Salisbury Polytechnic had just started an extra-mural course on navigation for those lonely deep-sea sailors who, even if they never put to sea and would never own a sextant, could at least derive some vicarious satisfaction from wrestling with a position line in the roaring forties. A friend of mine, Brendan Conway, had also started a private course of his own. I attended both courses.

In practice the navigator's art is not a specially difficult one, but to the beginner it is pure witchcraft. Navigation is rich in archaic jargon, and the novice is immediately cowed by Zenith Distances, Celestial Spheres, Ecliptics and Meridian Passages: his mind tends to drift to more delectable topics when Heavenly Bodies are under discussion, and he is startled when the instructor suddenly demands to know how he would handle his Prime Vertical. He has to unlearn all those spatial concepts of the universe carefully instilled into him at school. The navigator grandly regards the earth as the centre of the universe and all the celestial bodies as marks on a great plastic sphere that revolves around the earth at a constant speed to conform to Greenwich Mean Time. Having mastered the basics and confusedly grasped the concept of Spherical Triangles and their solution with Haversines, the student is stunned to discover that he cannot find out where he is unless he *knows* where he is.

"It's quite simple," the instructor tells him. "First you assume where you are. Then you find out what your sextant should have read had you been there, or rather where you are by what your sextant did read, as compared with what it should have read."

Only those students who firmly keep their eyes on distant horizons and great voyagers like Sir Francis Drake and Vasco da Gama survive the course. I was fortunate, for Brendan Conway was an ordained priest and secretary to the Archbishop himself. I could not have wished for more professional guidance in celestial navigation.

One day the practical aspect of my navigation received a sharp setback. Eric telephoned from England to say that the British Department of Trade and Industry had refused to grant an export permit to a sextant destined for Rhodesia. He could not be party to any circumvention of the law, so what should he do? I asked him to send the instrument to South Africa and gave him the address of a friendly firm in Johannesburg. It would be my responsibility to get it from there into Rhodesia.

It was now nearing the end of October, and things were rapidly coming to a head. We had decided that it was essential to visit *Walkabout* before December so that she could be beached and antifouled against the dreaded toredo worm. Tropical waters are infested with this worm, which can destroy a wooden boat in a few months. To keep them out it is necessary to cover the undersides with toxic paint every four months or so. I felt that it was also essential that Liz should see *Walkabout* before committing herself to an irrevocable departure from Salisbury. There was a good deal of preliminary fitting out to be done aboard, and much heavy gear to be carted down. The first week of November was chosen for the second expedition to B.D.

Again we faced the problem of how to travel up the beach and cross the straits to the island. My cousin provided a solution by generously lending us his 18ft motor-boat and trailer. The motor-boat was stoutly constructed and would do duty as a trailer truck en route as well as carrying us across the straits. The owner of the Inhassoro petrol pumps agreed to tow us in his Land-Rover up the beach, and a friend of ours, Gerald Lewin, was shanghaied into joining the expedition. He himself was one of the disconsolately landlocked deep-sea sailors of Rhodesia, and was building a 35ft fibreglass boat in his shed. We determined to take *Walkabout* 50 miles out into the Mozambique Channel for a trial sail.

The last few days passed in a blur of crises, arising principally from the fact that, though the house had at last been sold, we could not get the purchase money to pay for *Walkabout*, and without payment the Owner would not let us board the boat. Things like insurance policies which restricted *Walkabout* to inland waterways and specified that she should be pulled out of the water every night did nothing to ease matters.

The night before we left, Eric telephoned from England again to say that he still could not dispatch the sextant because this time the South African authorities had intervened. They would not allow it in without an import permit, obtainable only by personal application to the Department of the Interior in Pretoria. What should he do now? Against my better judgement and certain knowledge of Portuguese officialdom, I asked him to send it to a shipping agent in Beira. I wondered bitterly whether I should ever see it at all.

We planned to set off for B.D. at midday next day. The car had been packed to the roof-linings, the motor-boat loaded to the gunwales, the necessary visas wrung from the leisurely Portuguese Consulate, and the children sent to some obliging friends. I had taken a week's leave from the office and everything was ready—except that *Walkabout* remained elusively out of legal reach. As soon as the offices opened I was running from one to another persuading, perspiring, cajoling and explaining, until, with the help of a lawyer friend, I raised a surety at eleven o'clock. The letter of authorisation to board *Walkabout* was finally secured from the Owner at 11.30.

I went back to the house to find Liz and Gerald bouncing

with excitement and eager to be off. Just seventy days after my first sight of *Walkabout* we headed east.

As we left the hot, hazy city behind us the frustrations and oppressive anxieties of the past two months fell away, infecting us with a bubbling gaiety. Both car and trailer were monstrously overladen and we had to drive very slowly, but the journey over the difficult road merely added spice to the expedition. And the four shrill trebles incessantly piping demands and complaints were blissfully absent. We became as exuberant as children released from school on an excursion.

Gerald, rotund and black-bearded, was specially jovial.

"I see no ships," he cried as we crossed a desiccated river-bed.

"You fool," I shouted, shading my eyes against the glare of the parched Rhodesian landscape. "Can't you see the tide is out?"

"Relentless tide," he said. "We are about to become 'old salts', so we've got to speak in clichés all the time. Remember it's always 'the relentless tide' on this expedition."

"You mean hazardous expedition," said Liz.

"Fraught with danger," agreed Gerald.

"But we shall win through," she chanted, "despite the tyranny of the tiller. The winds are blowing Force 1 gusting 2 over the rolling seas, but the captain's steady hand is on the helm and his calm, weatherbeaten face makes our hearts grow strong."

"I bet you both get seasick," I said.

We rolled merrily along in this fashion till we reached the first town in Mozambique. Here we stopped for dinner and ate a garlic-drenched meal on the pavement outside the restaurant, enjoying the warm evening.

As we were drinking our coffee Liz said, "You know, this is the first time we've been away from the kids. Let's make a real holiday of it. How about some wine?"

"Okay," I said, "wine it is. Three gallons of red Dão."

"And two thousand millimetres of stinky sausage," said Gerald.

"One thousand grams of black olives," added Liz.

"And a couple of thousand of those black cigarettes for my pipe," I suggested.

"No," they both said together.

"To keep the insects at bay," I explained.

The extra provisions were loaded on to car and trailer, which sagged fractionally closer to the surface of the road with slight groans. We piled aboard and drove on through the night.

It was a pleasant surprise to find that since our last trip the road had been much improved. Because the rains were so late even the rough stretches presented no serious difficulty, and I was emboldened to speed up a little. This proved our undoing.

At two o'clock in the morning the car suddenly began to weave tipsily between the ruts. I looked behind and was horrified to see a trail of smoke and sparks apparently streaming from the trailer. One of the wheels had caught fire and filthy, acrid smoke was billowing out from the tyre. The fire was hurriedly quenched and the spare tyre fitted. A poor, much-used thing this time, that bulged unhealthily even when stationary. The rest of the journey was conducted at the comfortable pace of a hackney carriage, with frequent halts to pat the ailing tyre and feel its temperature.

We did not reach Inhassoro till the following day. As always, the sight of the sea from the top of the final ridge was balm to dust-rimmed eyes. As soon as the car stopped we plunged joyfully into the water and emerged soon after festooned with clinging brown seaweed, the harsh dust on our bodies replaced with a sticky powdering of warm salt. The bathing at Inhassoro is more attractive in prospect than in reality. After lunch the load in the car was transferred to the hired Land-Rover, and with the owner at the wheel we waddled heavily along the beach.

When we reached the petrified forest it was already late in the afternoon and the tide was creeping up the beach again. More than a ton of gear was tumbled rapidly out on to the sand. The motor boat was launched with some difficulty in the surf, and anchored with *Walkabout*'s heavy new anchor and chain. Then the Land-Rover hurtled off down the sunset-tinted beach with the trailer bounding behind it. A sense of pleasurable isolation stole over the spit. In the deepening dusk Gerald and I dragged everything above the high tide mark while Liz lit a fire among the dunes and prepared supper. The menu was the finest kind when you are tired and hungry—

crisp bacon, fried eggs, tomatoes, toast washed down with wine. We ate appreciatively.

"Liz, you're fantastic," said Gerald contentedly. "How about some coffee?"

"I can't find any water. Mike, where are the water-cans?"

"They're over by . . . No, wait, they're . . . hmm," I said thoughtfully.

Rope and wire I had remembered, also fuel, oil, self-steering, compass, rigging fittings, all manner of tools and sixty different sizes of screws to meet all eventualities. But the water-cans had been left at Inhassoro.

"But I thought *you* had . . . " I tailed off.

The crew sucked oranges to quench their thirst and stared hard at me. I gazed at the dark sea and invited them to enjoy the scintillating phosphorescence in the surf. Water supplies or not, that night we slept in peace under the star-studded tropical sky.

The next morning found us lugging gear from the high tide mark down the beach into the motor-boat, wading through the surf up to the armpits.

"I see no ships," said Gerald somewhat peevishly as he emerged from a large wave, the iron galley held high over his head.

"I begin to see what yachting is all about," said Liz. "It's carrying stuff from the land to the high tide mark, from the high tide mark to the dinghy, from the dinghy to the yacht, from the yacht to the jetty. . . . When am I going to be able to lie on the sun-drenched deck in a bikini sipping martinis, then?"

"You two do realise that mutiny is the most heinous of all crimes on the high seas? It is even more heinous than barratry," I said significantly.

"Mutiny is justified," roared Gerald, who was struggling against the undertow, "when the skipper is a totally deranged bloody sea-crazed dippy lunatic."

When the boat was full we clambered aboard, and after much futile cursing and wrenching at the starter-cord, the outboard motor started. It was the first and only occasion it did so. It was a fine, calm day, and we experienced no difficulty in getting through the gap in the breakers. In the little cove at B.D. *Walkabout* was rolling gently in the long swell. To my enormous relief she looked exactly the same as before.

We climbed aboard and Liz looked about uncertainly, a little unbelievingly. Yachts were totally outside her experience, and she had no yardstick whatever to judge them by. A man confronted for the first time by an electronic microscope might well say, for want of anything more perceptive, "So this is an electronic microscope". "So this is *Walkabout*!" said Liz. At that moment she did not take our plan to cross an ocean in the boat in the least seriously.

After we had each drunk several pints of water, Gerald and I returned to the spit to collect the rest of the gear. By the time all the tackle had been stowed aboard and the cabin had been made generally habitable, it was sunset. It had taken three days and two nights of strenuous labour to transport three people and the gear from Salisbury to *Walkabout*. We were all totally fatigued. The first night aboard was passed in uneasy sleep in strange rolling beds, boxed about with bulkheads.

The next morning we rose with the dawn eager to be up and about—for more than one reason. The defective toilet had been worked over the night before, but it continued to act capricious and sullen in turn. Eventually it was taken back to Salisbury for repair. In the meantime a routine was evolved. Gerald, lying closest to the main hatch, would be up at first light and rowing furiously to the nearest land in the tender, only too aptly named *Crawlabout*, he said. If the relentless tide was out he could be seen running heedlessly over the sharp rocks and into the first patch of bush. Liz and I managed as modestly as we could over the bowsprit. For all the inconvenience we were at least at work by sun-up every morning.

There was a great deal to be done. Assisted by the Owner's African mariners, Lampião and Manueri, *Walkabout* was beached and antifouled. New safety lines were fitted, the echo-sounder and compass were installed, the self-steering was mounted, part of the electric wiring was replaced, and, with Liz to advise, the proposed refitting of the cabin was refined and all necessary dimensions and material schedules were worked out. The cooker was a disaster. In our kitchen at home the three primus burners standing beside the electric cooker had looked minimal; in the cabin they looked monstrous. So the cooker too had to be taken back to Salisbury, and cut down to two burners.

Not for the first time Liz wondered how we were going to manage when Kevin, Mark, Bruce and Rachel were aboard. Could the regular, hot meals the children needed be prepared on two paraffin burners?

"I don't know, Liz," I said. 'That's for you to say."

"I think it's possible. But I'll have to work out a system and try it when we move into a caravan in Salisbury."

"Apart from that—what's your verdict?"

"Well, it does seem so cramped, and nothing keeps still even at anchor. But I think we can manage. After all, it won't be for more than a few months."

"So it's all systems go, then! Great! Not that I believe we'll ever actually get away."

"Neither do I."

Meanwhile *Walkabout* had yet to be sailed, a distinctly awesome prospect to all of us. But we agreed that our original plan to sail 50 miles out into the Mozambique Channel was too ambitious. There was simply not enough time, for we had to return to Salisbury at the weekend. We decided instead on a day sail, and prepared the boat to that end.

On Thursday morning we slipped our moorings and sailed northwards out of the lagoon in a brisk easterly wind. Lampião —who had been a deck hand on *Walkabout* for years—was aboard to hold my hand. As we sailed out from the protection of the island, the decks began a slow dance and a few small waves lapped aboard. After the trimaran *Walkabout* seemed ponderous, but she rode through the water with wonderful ease, and the heft of the helm was lovely in the hand.

At lunchtime we came about and headed back to B.D. in a freshening wind that was beginning to whip a little spray into the cockpit. *Walkabout*'s dance was more lively. I looked anxiously at Liz and Gerald, both now silent. Seasickness, the sailor's scourge, was plainly written on their set faces. For Liz it was double misery; she had hoped so much that the motion of the yacht would not affect her as badly as the trimaran had. But here she was on the first sail feeling as rotten as ever.

"Nearly everyone feels sick for the first couple of days," I

Walkabout beached at B.D. Gerald and I fit the self-steering while Lampião antifouls the hull

Muncher is mounted at low tide. Gerald waving vaguely

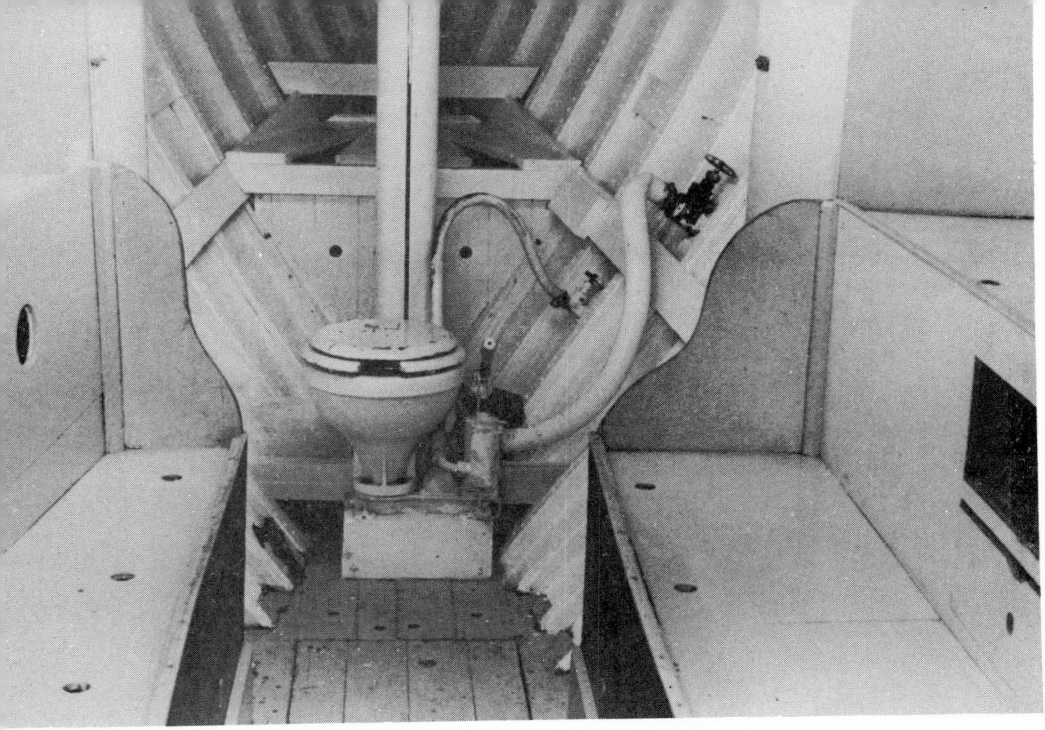

Above:
The defective toilet commanded the barren cabin like decayed royalty

Left:
Kevin, Liz and Bruce proudly display a fine barracuda. Pyjamas were regulation wear in fierce sunshine

said. "All the books say that. But it disappears after a bit."

She just nodded. You cannot convince anyone who is seasick that death is not imminent. Many would even welcome it.

"Never mind, love, in less than an hour we'll be lying snugly at anchor," I said.

At that moment the main sail blew out. In a single spectacular motion it unzipped itself from corner to corner. All I could say as we bundled the tatters on to the deck was, "What a shame, oh, what a shame!"

"Better now than halfway to Durban, skipper," said Gerald as we motored back to moorings.

"What does it mean, Mike?" asked Liz.

"It means a new sail. The old one is too rotten to mend. It means more smuggling and currency problems, and it's going to make a nasty dent in the budget. I just hope we can get one in time." I felt very low, and said that it would need only one more setback of this kind to scupper the whole voyage.

The next day we returned to Inhassoro in *Walkabout*, towing the motor-boat by the nose. We had to motor all the way, for there was not a breath of wind, and Liz and Gerald again looked green, this time because of the diesel fumes and the heat.

When we reached the village we discovered with no surprise whatever that the new tyre for the trailer, which I had ordered before we set off for B.D. and which had been promised for Monday, had not yet arrived from Beira. Lampião took *Walkabout* back to B.D., and we settled down on the beach to wait. The tyre turned up at the end of the day, delivered by the one-engined fish-plane which was the normal means of transport, and which shuttled erratically to and fro, landing on suitable beaches when the tide was right. That evening we started back, and reached home late the following afternoon.

Once more the endless stream of problems pressured us. We studied our lists and tried to estimate how long the rest of the preparations would take. It was provisionally decided to leave in mid-January 1972.

A few days after returning from B.D. we moved out of the house and into a hired caravan, which we parked in my father's backyard. Two tents were also erected; one was used as a general overflow area and the other as the children's bedroom.

The children adapted to their new surroundings with little emotion. They regretted leaving the house, but it was pleasantly exciting to be camping during term-time. In fact, their lives were not greatly affected.

We settled down in our transit camp as best we could. For a whole month we simulated shipboard conditions in the galley. Liz cooked only on the paraffin stove, and all our bread was baked in a tin oven that sat on top of one burner. To check the food lists we carefully measured our consumption of everything we ate and drank, and also kept a record of how much paraffin and methylated spirits we used. We tried all the tinned stuffs locally available, and on this score we had no problems, for Rhodesia produces an excellent range of foodstuffs at low prices. In this way we were able to refine our stores lists and check them roughly by working out the calories consumed.

A few days after camp had been set up the rainy season swept in with a will. The site became a quagmire of clinging red mud. Our standard of living plummeted, and one day I remarked to Liz that this was a good apprenticeship for boat-bums. She was struggling to bake bread over a flaming paraffin stove and did not reply—at least audibly.

"At least our lists are going well," I said weakly.

She looked at me darkly. I knew that she was thinking of one list in particular headed "Safety Equipment". We had discussed this list a great deal right from the start, and Liz hated these discussions. They always revolved around disasters. What do we need in the event of fire, sinking, broken limbs? How many calories and how many ounces of water a day would each member of the family survive on? We still had no life-raft, and although I was not convinced that a rubber life-raft was the ideal life-saver, it seemed the best insurance policy with four children aboard. So I had managed to get money into South Africa for my sister to buy a six-man life-raft in a canister. It then transpired that it could not be imported into Rhodesia. It was not a question of duty: the authorities would simply not allow it across the border at all, on the grounds that life-rafts were not essential to Rhodesia's survival in the sanctions war. I could not but agree with them. It took a fortnight of fruitless interviews and study of regulations before the solution suddenly came to me. It was not necessary to import anything at all!

The goods were in transit to Mozambique and could simply pass through Rhodesia in bond. The problem was thus solved in a perfectly legal if rather laborious fashion. *Walkabout*'s new mainsail was also handled in this way.

The safety list contained one other difficult item, and that was a radio. I had steadfastly refused to consider a transmitter, as I thought it too costly, too heavy, too unreliable, and, worst of all, psychologically harmful. If one puts to sea in a small boat it should be in the full knowledge that one is (or should be) totally self-reliant. It is unfair to involve others. Moreover, a small transmitter is a poor thing to rely on in a crisis; it may not work or it may not be heard.

This refusal to equip with radio shocked many of our friends, who invariably assumed that it was essential. It certainly distressed my father. He had already contributed to the cost of the life-raft, and now he offered to buy us a radio. However, there was nothing to be had for love nor money in the country, so we were saved the embarrassment of outright refusal. A radio receiver is essential, though, for time signals for navigation. Many erudite people said that nothing but a proper marine radio would do, but in the end we had to fall back on what was available and what we could afford. I bought a Rhodesian-made portable receiver of the type that the Africans carry around on their bicycles. It was one of the few things that never gave a moment's trouble.

The medical kit was another list that provoked much anxious thought. David Lewis gives a great deal of useful information in his books, and this provided a sound basis for the kit. A doctor and a pharmacist, both of them friends, polished it still further. We ended up with an impressive chest of drugs and appliances.

These protracted preparations for disaster had their effect on me as well as on Liz. For six nights in succession I was visited by nightmares of storms at sea. They were fearfully real, and when I awoke I still felt the foam about my waist and tasted the salt in my throat. The nightmares were worse than any conditions we experienced subsequently at sea, and I was thankful when they vanished as abruptly as they had come.

The political scene was distressing too. The British Foreign Secretary, Sir Alec Douglas Home, had come to Salisbury for summit settlement talks, and when he and his lady were photographed hugging African babies in the townships, it seemed clear that a settlement would be reached which the Africans would find it difficult to swallow. This indeed proved eventually to be the case; but initially it appeared as if they might raise no objection to the settlement. Liz and I began to feel remarkably silly now that one of the main reasons for leaving Rhodesia looked like vanishing into thin air.

But after a few weeks I realised that virtually every African would say no to a settlement, on the unthinking grounds that, if the whites wanted it, it must be bad for the blacks. There is so little real communication between the races in Rhodesia that the whites had no idea of this attitude. In the event, not only did the Africans say "no" to the Pearce Commission which was investigating acceptability, but there were riots and several deaths.

On the list front, things were at last falling into place, and a satisfactory pile of gear was accumulating in the garage. Oilskins, which were not available in Rhodesia, were made specially for us by a local firm; the galley stove and the toilet were mended; the mainsail was being made in South Africa; and the pile of charts and navigational books—smuggled in, of course—began to look quite workmanlike.

By mid-December only two serious problems remained unsolved. One was the enduring worry about the sextant, which had vanished into the doubtful postal system between England and Mozambique. The other was connected with the Portuguese authorities, who, it was reliably rumoured, had suddenly decided to enforce the regulations governing all mariners in their waters. Nobody would be allowed to handle a boat unless he possessed the appropriate qualification; for offshore sailing a Coastal Mariner's Certificate was required. This could only be obtained by examinations (in Portuguese) held in Beira or Lourenco Marques twice a year. I fretted continually over this problem, for all our laborious plans could be frustrated at the last minute by the action of a petty official. The trouble was that no precise information was available, and the Portuguese authorities never replied to any letters. I decided to travel down to Beira soon after Christmas and interview the port captain himself.

Our last Christmas in Salisbury was a quiet, indeed rather sombre, affair. For me the essence of Christmas Day is a warm and sticky atmosphere with rain thundering on an iron roof, and I wondered whether I could ever accustom myself to the bleakness of a white Christmas. That year the rains poured down in earnest. The children were subdued by the realisation that we were actually leaving Salisbury. Presents were small, for we could carry little on the boat, and their bicycles had just been sold, which caused much distress. Bruce wrote a letter to Eric which summed up his feelings.

> "Dyer granpa, mi bisikl is solt and Kivn and Mark run ivrywer withot me and I got a nyu nif and cut a mango and thin I cut mi fingr and thir is blud ivrywer."

A week after Christmas I motored down to Beira and spoke to the port captain, a charming and urbane gentleman, who expressed faint surprise on the subject of examinations, and smiled enigmatically when asked in what circumstances certificates of seamanship were needed. In one breath he told us not to worry, and in the next pointed out that he had absolute authority to prevent any craft leaving port if, in his opinion, all was not in order. I gathered from this courteous discussion that he could do anything he felt like, but did not feel like doing anything at the moment.

I went on my way partly eased in mind. While in Beira I registered *Walkabout* in my name, and went to see the shipping agents about the sextant. They knew nothing about it, and warned me that the Portuguese customs would probably seize it.

When I returned to Salisbury I found that the press had learned of our plans and wanted an interview. So far we had avoided all publicity, but of late it had become necessary to tell more and more people of our plans, and inevitably the news had reached the *Rhodesia Herald*. I managed to stall an interview until the day before we left, so as to ensure that the feature was not published until we were across the border. We did not expect any official action at this late stage, but there was no point in taking any chances.

The last fortnight passed in a whirl of frantic but dreary activity. I stopped working a week before we left, and was able for the first time to devote all my attentions to our preparations. The rain still poured down every day, and there were reports of cyclones in the Mozambique Channel. Liz and I had had a surfeit of this refugee existence in a transit camp, and we longed to be on our way.

One bright note was the splendid farewell party held at a friend's house, for, as Gerald said, "The only good reason for setting out on a voyage is so that you can give a terrific farewell party and get totally smashed."

We did just that.

The day before we left, Saturday, January 22nd, I telephoned the agents in Beira about the sextant.

"Sorry, it hasn't arrived yet," said the girl at the other end.

"Oh Lord! What are we going to do now? We have to leave Salisbury tomorrow and I can't even write to you from B.D."

"Maybe, Senhor Saunders, you can . . . One moment, please, the messenger has just arrived from the post office. No, bring it here, Carlos, I want to see the label. Ai Jesus! Senhor Saunders, your parcel has just arrived from England!"

"Thank God for that!" I was weak with relief. "Now as for getting the parcel to me," I went on, "it is just as arranged when I was in Beira. First thing next week you send it to the airport and put it on the fish-plane. They will take it to the hotel at Inhassoro and I'll collect it there. We should be in Inhassoro about Tuesday next week."

"Very well. Goodbye." She rang off.

The rest of the day was spent packing, and Brendan Conway, celestial navigator extraordinary, came to help. As we had sold our car I had borrowed a van from a friend, and had hired a Land-Rover and trailer. My father and our broker friend, Mike Hill, who had taken a keen interest in the voyage, were coming down with us for a short holiday and would drive the vehicles back again.

At every stage of the preparations we had pruned ruthlessly—hundreds of books had been reduced to a dozen, clothes were minimal, the children's toys were down to a couple apiece, all personal luxuries had been shed. Only under the Amusements List did we allow ourselves a few non-essentials—a cassette tape-recorder with a dozen classical music tapes, all a parting gift from Mike Hill; a minute chess set; Scrabble and several board games for the children; a clarinet and recorders; a tin of water paints and rags for collage. School books were also included in the Amusements List, much to the children's disgust. None the less, when all the gear was laid out next to the vehicles it amounted to an appalling pile. This was partly due to the fact that three months' food supply had been laid in, for we could not be certain how long we should have to stay in B.D. while we fitted out. We had to carry down every plank, every screw, every bolt, every type of glue required. When all this was crammed into the vehicles there was just enough room for the children to stretch out on top of the pile.

Early on Sunday morning a group of close friends gathered in the drizzle to bid us goodbye.

"Goodbye," shouted Bruce, jumping on to the bonnet and giggling. "Goodbye goodbye you big fat flea, I'll see you on the Christmas tree."

Rachel sucked her fingers moodily, then climbed into the car and huddled down on the seat out of the rain.

"Goodbye, Saunders," said Chris and Ann Wortham unsteadily. "We wish you weren't going—it's never too late to change your mind."

"It is too late. Goodbye," we said, equally unsteadily.

Kevin and Mark were having a friendly punch-up with the Brown children.

"A bash and a bang till we see you again," chanted Mark as he grappled. Kevin turned traitor and pushed him from behind into the muddy flowerbed.

We drove away, Liz swallowing and staring straight ahead. In an odd way I felt cheated. I had played a going-on-a-voyage game subconsciously expecting to be thwarted. But, astonishingly, all the difficulties had been overcome. The game was for real. Now we were leaving Salisbury with little more than the proverbial shirts on our backs. At my side was a slim plastic briefcase with all our documents and £700 in cash.

III

ONCE AGAIN WE travelled the road to B.D. It had become an old friend. But this time it was wet. The warm rain beat down incessantly and gradually penetrated the cars. The clothing and bedding became damper and damper and the comfortable dust was replaced by mud.

Because of the children, we could not travel without rest. Rachel was called by nature every thirty minutes when happily occupied kneading plasticine with mud, and more frequently when bored. Mark and Bruce lolled around playing or squabbling, and Kevin, for the most part, lay on the bedding, his knees drawn up, reading. We stopped for lunch with a farmer friend near Umtali—where blood had been shed in riots the previous day—and crossed into Mozambique that afternoon.

It gave both Liz and me an unexpected surge of feeling to cross the border for the last time; part sadness for the delightful home left behind, part excitement at the prospect of adventure, and part fear of the unknown ahead. I kept a good grip on the plastic briefcase which contained all our money. Kevin and Mark were old enough to grasp the significance of the moment.

"I don't want to leave Rhodesia," began Mark plaintively. "All my friends are there and I'll probably never see them again."

"I don't want to go either," said Kevin. "I want to go back to school."

"That's because you're always coming first in class. Daddy, when are we coming back to Rhodesia?"

"I'm not sure. Maybe never."

A disconcerting wail of disappointment greeted this statement.

"It will be better when we get to B.D., won't it, Daddy?" said Kevin suddenly, assuming the responsible role of the first born. "I mean swimming, fishing and sailing *Puffabout*, and all that."

"Of course it will," I replied with relief. "While I'm fitting out *Walkabout* you lot will have the time of your lives. Just think of all the exciting things you can do on a desert island while all your friends are sitting at their desks."

In the late evening we made camp in a deserted construction site by the roadside. A thatched roof supported on poles but with no walls served as a shelter from the rain. Mike Hill was a city man, accustomed to the comforts of a civilised life. He had had little experience of bush technique and roughing it along the road, but he is one of those people who are interested in everything about them and will cheerfully try their hand at any job. Now he applied himself to the evening meal, and showed his prowess in this direction. A good cook is worth ten men, and Mike was landed with the job for the rest of his time with us.

Next morning we pressed on through the rain, and reached Inhassoro that evening. We pitched our tents next to the hotel. The skies cleared and the children could spread out freely again. Kevin and Mark circled cautiously around a pair of tame monkeys that had the run of the hotel. The monkeys eyed Mark malignantly, and then terrified him with a swift attack. Monkeys are treacherous creatures, and whenever we returned to the hotel this pair would attack Mark.

Quite naturally my sextant was not at the hotel. I warned them to expect it soon, and went down to the shop and the garage to look for a carpenter. I knew that an African carpenter worked in the vicinity, and hoped to employ him to help fit out the boat. Quite naturally he too was not to be found. He had apparently returned to his village for a ceremonial booze-up, and was expected back in Inhassoro that very night. Everyone assured me that he would be at our camp at dawn. This was too much to hope for, but I spread word around anyway, knowing that it would reach him. There were no proper roads and no regular market traffic between the scattered bush dwellings, but sooner or later the rumour would seep through to him, and somehow he would make contact.

Early next morning, at low tide, Mike and I set off to the end of the spit in the Land-Rover with Kevin and Mark in the back and *Puffabout* lashed to the roof. The plan was to launch *Puff*-

about in the lagoon, and while Mike returned to Inhassoro for the rest of the expedition, I would sail the little boat over to B.D. and fetch *Walkabout*. All our stores could then be loaded directly aboard.

It was a crushingly hot day, and by the time we reached the end of the spit we could no longer touch any metal part. When the stores came to be unloaded we found that all the cardboard boxes had distintegrated in the rain on the journey down. Fortunately the labels had been removed from the tins and the tins themselves marked with paint. While Mike raced the tide back to Inhassoro, the boys and I carried the stores above the high tide mark and stacked them in a semblance of order. Kevin and Mark worked like Trojans, glancing longingly from time to time at their little boat. At last, slippery with sweat, we carried *Puffabout* over to the lagoon and launched her with proper ceremony, using a glass of orange juice. Kevin and Mark went sailing while I lay gratefully in the tepid water of the lagoon, in the shade of an overhanging casuarina tree. The heat mounted remorselessly. It was too hot to swim in the open water.

An hour later I sailed over to B.D. leaving Kevin and Mark with strict instructions to keep out of the sun. The hop over to the island was only 5 miles but it took a long time, for the wind was faint. I rowed most of the way, trying to keep the sun off me with a towel and some rags.

My spirits lifted as I approached *Walkabout*, rolling gently at her moorings. But remembering the mound of stores left behind on the spit I could not shake the feeling that she had shrunk a little.

I climbed aboard and sluiced water over the burning decks, then went ashore and, with the help of Lampião and Manueri, ferried aboard the batteries from the Owner's store and motored back to the spit. When Kevin and Mark scrambled aboard they were thunderstruck.

"Is this really *Walkabout*?" asked Mark.

"Yes, of course it is," I said testily. "Well, what do you think of her?"

"I thought she'd be bigger," said Kevin.

"I thought she'd be a proper little ship," said Mark.

"Well, she is."

"There's only one cabin," said Kevin, rooting around below.

"Daddy, it smells," said Mark.

"Oh, come and help get the stores aboard," I said irritably.

A few minutes later the rest of the party drove up from Inhassoro, my father spreadeagled on top of the plywood on the roof of the Land-Rover to hold the sheets down. Apparently he had been up there since Inhassoro. He came aboard with Mike Hill and they made dutiful comments about *Walkabout*'s elegance before expressing doubts about her size.

"I suppose you have worked out how you're going to fit everyone aboard?" said Mike.

This was getting too much. "If we don't set to work," I burst out, "it will be dark before we get over to B.D."

Dinghy load by dinghy load the stores and the gear were ferried over to the boat. First we filled the cabin entirely, then the cockpit, then the cabin top and finally the decks. *Walkabout* settled deeper into the water with each load. When everything had finally been piled on the ship and everyone had settled on top of that, she was more than a foot down on her marks. And we hadn't even loaded fresh water or fuel!

I knew then that I had made a crashing mistake. The boat was too small. What a time to make the discovery, I thought, out here in this fiery deserted lagoon with no possibility of changing our minds. We had truly burned our bridges behind us. Depressed beyond words, drained by the heat and, I suppose, by hunger—I had not eaten for nearly twenty-four hours—I slumped on a tent bag ready to weep. The children, too, were fretful. Kevin and Mark were burned an angry red by the sun, and Rachel could only loll around whimpering.

Liz assessed the situation at a glance. She went rummaging in the mountains of gear and emerged with food and drink. With great speed she prepared a snack meal and distributed it to everyone aboard. She refused to be intimidated by the loading problem, pointing out that the boat was not fitted out yet, and that with Lampião and Manueri there were four extra adults aboard and all sorts of extraneous gear such as tents and spare wood which would later be unloaded.

Thus refuelled with food and sensible advice, we all cheered up. The children scrambled around tugging ropes and fiddling with the engine controls. I told them to cut that out. Can we climb the masts now? No, you can't. Bags me the main. Bags me the mizzen. Daddy, they've got a mast each and I have nothing. Nobody is climbing masts this afternoon. Things were back to normal. We raised the anchor with some enthusiasm and motored back to B.D.

The sun was low over the western swamps by the time we reached the cove. We hurriedly moored the boat and ferried the essential camping gear ashore. There was no time to mess around with tents before dark. I chose a camp site on the corner of the cove closest to *Walkabout*; it was a sandy patch of land just behind the low rocky shore, cleared of bush but protected from the sun by half a dozen casuarina trees. Twenty yards inland lay a well used by bands of roving fishermen; surprisingly it gave water fresh enough to drink, although the bottom was below the high tide mark. It was a good camp site, overlooking the lagoon, though exposed to weather from the west. But no prevailing winds blew from the west in this region so that did not worry us.

The tropical night quickly followed the sunset, and swarms of silent mosquitoes drifted out of the scrub and began to feed. Ankles were tastiest, with shins a close second, but the hungriest thought nothing of tackling kneebone or even scalp. The only safe place was in bed with a sheet over one's head. The children were popped into their sheet bags and fell asleep at once. We followed soon after, each easing into a comfortable hollow among the roots of the casuarinas. The last thing I remember is Mike muttering that he had known softer beds in his time.

The next day was a busy one. The first priority was to make efficient camp, for we expected to live there for several weeks. Two living-tents were erected and a stone hearth was built for cooking. Boards were laid for a table and stumps for chairs. Other boards were suspended one under the other in the main tent and under a tree for shelves, so that the ants could not get at the open food. A canvas water-bag with a tap was hung from a branch in the faint hope that the drinking water at least would not get too warm.

A tin trunk specially constructed with shelves and compartments held the pots, the crockery and a variety of other implements. A toilet hole was dug in a thicket some distance off, and near the well, in another thicket, a shower room was carved. It was paved with stones to keep the feet free from sand, and was provided with a bucket and a mug for showering, while notches were cut in the branches for the orderly storage of toothbrushes and toilet gear.

On board Mike and I packed the tinned foods into the lockers. With careful stowage most went in and my fears abated somewhat. The rest of the stores—still more than half—were wrapped in heavy-duty polythene bags and placed under a shelter made from branches and a tarpaulin.

In planning a camp the whole object is to maximise comfort, and the enemies of comfort under those conditions are sun, sand, rain and disorder. Altogether, our camp was a reasonably efficient one, and in normal circumstances would have been perfectly adequate. We little guessed how abnormal the circumstances were to become.

That day was hotter, if anything, than the previous one. It was the hottest time of the year, but even so the temperature was unusually high, and by lunch-time it required a conscious effort of will to keep working. The worst sufferers were Kevin and Mark. They had spent a good deal of the previous day swimming, without shirts or hats, and had been badly sunburnt. Their faces were blistered and swollen. Mark's face was so swollen that he could scarcely see, which was just as well, for his eyes had also been scorched by the glare. The best treatment seemed to be tea compresses. All day they lay in the shade, whimpering fretfully, their faces covered with cloths soaked in very strong tea. It was the most serious case of sunburn I have seen.

Bruce, on the other hand, was as happy as a sandboy. He is eternally fascinated by the world around him, and especially the natural world. He set off among the rocks and tidal pools with Rachel trotting dutifully behind, and by evening I was cursing the collection of marine bric-à-brac lying underfoot around the camp: shells, unusual stones, hermit crabs, tiny bizarre pipe-fish swimming disconsolately around soup bowls, a starfish already beginning to curl and stink in the sun. He had also discovered a creature which I can only describe as a sort of horror comic Martian. It looked like a flying saucer about 1½″ in diameter. Above and ahead of the body were antennae, while below were leg/fin-like limbs which propelled it slowly through its habitat, the region of flat sand covered with a skim of water at low tide. It also possessed a ferocious sting, as Bruce discovered. All absorbing entertainment, but the worst of it was that he brought his spoils back for Liz to cook for supper.

"As if I haven't enough work to do without cooking Martians," she said crossly.

The next few days the camp settled down to a routine. Every day my father went fishing. He had borrowed a boat from Thai Lee, a lonely Chinese fisherman who lived with his entourage of Africans ten miles up the lagoon towards Inhassoro. His catches, which were unfortunately far from regular, were none the less welcome, for there was no other fresh food to be had. Liz spent most of the time washing, baking bread and generally camp-keeping. In the morning she gave the children their lessons: in the afternoon they were free to do as they pleased. Kevin and Mark spent most of their free time sailing *Puffabout*, or, when the heat abated a little in the late afternoon, swimming. Everyone was very careful of the sun now, and hats and pyjamas were regulation wear for all sunlight activities. Thin cotton pyjamas are ideal for this purpose because they are loose and cool yet cover you completely.

Mike mucked in with a will. When he was not cooking or doings things for Liz he was helping me on the boat. The first job I tackled was the engine, which needed thorough servicing and some minor attention. There was no way, for example, of stopping it without leaping down into the cabin, removing the engine cover and manipulating the injector mechanism. A cockpit control was fitted. The next job, which Lampião helped me with, was the rigging. The standard rigging on *Walkabout* is not fixed to the masts and bowsprit by metal tangs but loops right over the spars. This old-fashioned method of rigging is immensely secure, but involves a great deal of work. Each shroud had to be removed and a new steel rope spliced to suit. With the boat forever rolling at her moorings this was not an easy task. To protect the new rope from corrosion I parcelled the lower 6 feet with the heavy-duty bitumen tape used for underground electric cables, then sized and varnished it. The upper part of the rope was dressed with boiled linseed oil. The main mast shrouds, however, were covered with black polythene tubing which was sealed at the bottom and filled with linseed oil, using a horse syringe. The tubing also acted as a good anti-chafe device. All this took time but was worth it, for I never had the slightest trouble with standing rigging.

The 1,000-odd feet of running rigging, on the other hand, proved to be a false economy in the long run. When, however, it had been installed, and when all the shackles, blocks and thimbles had been inspected and if necessary replaced, *Walkabout* was at last a sailing boat again, and in good running order.

On the fifth day after our arrival the weather broke. Thunder clouds with inky bases mounted heavenwards, and the atmosphere became as thick as custard. That evening the rain poured into the camp, accompanied by a violent display of crashing lightning and gusting wind.

We all retreated into the main tent and tried to barricade ourselves against wind and water. In vain. The bedding and clothes soon became soaked. Fending off the wind, Liz and Mike cooked a stew over the unhappy primus stove, while the rest of us helped by trying to keep our feet out of the kitchen. All except Rachel, who scrambled around looking for a dry spot, shrilling in protest as her brothers swatted her in passing. After the meal we reclined in the damp, sipping hot coffee, and listened to a Schubert string quartet on the cassette recorder that Mike had given us.

Thunder cracked overhead, and the behaviour of the weather since our arrival at once seemed more logical. The intense heat, the thunderstorm and now the wind blowing hard from the west all spoke of a tropical revolving storm in the vicinity. Not too close, because the weather was not extreme enough, but probably somewhere in the Mozambique Channel. The frequency of cyclones (called hurricanes in the North Atlantic) in the area is quite high, higher in fact than in the West Indies. Most of them, however, remain further north and west, beyond Madagascar. The average frequency in the Mozambique Channel itself is reckoned to be about one in every two years. That we should choose the wrong year, I thought gloomily, seemed inevitable.

That night the wind twice boxed the compass and the rain sheeted down. For the next few days the weather continued to be unsettled. Either it was fiercely sunny and hot or it was wet and windy and hot. There was always something to grumble about.

At the end of the week Mike had to return to Salisbury. We were sorry to see him go, for he was ever a positive companion who added vitality to any situation. I believe that he was sorry to leave too, despite the heat, the wet and the mosquitoes. We ferried him over to the spit and dug the hired Land-Rover free from the sand piled up around its wheels. After a quick hand-clasp Mike was on his way. I watched the car dwindle out of sight. The penultimate link with Rhodesia was broken, and I felt slightly relieved by this, for it was not until the last link was severed that the voyage could be said to have properly begun.

Less than a week after Mike left, my father decided to follow suit, urged as strongly by the mosquitoes as by pressing business in Rhodesia. Every island mosquito now knew of the camp, and after dark the entire mosquito population flew in for dinner. Sheets and light clothing no longer deterred them, and they bored directly through the fabric. It was necessary to light mosquito coils and sleep under nets. Naturally, we all took Daraprim to ward off malaria, but this had no effect on the creatures themselves.

My father's departure gave us a good excuse to take *Walkabout* down to Inhassoro and I hoped to return with the sextant and the carpenter. But first, at spring tides, *Walkabout* had to be beached for more antifouling. The procedure was to run her into the cove at high tide and anchor her. Then, with four heavy mangrove props each lashed to a chain plate, one waited for the tide to ebb. The tidal range was very large—nearly 26ft—so by half-tide she was high and dry.

On this occasion things went wrong. Nearly half a ton of foodstuffs had been stowed in the port lockers, and as the tide ebbed, the ship began to heel heavily to port, driving the props and their footpads askew into the sand. We frantically shifted the tins over to starboard, and I hauled all the anchor chain on to the starboard deck. Mercifully she settled at an angle of about 10 degrees and went no further. She was antifouled with a soft copper paint, and two skin fittings for the proposed new galley were installed through the hull. The next day I installed the life-raft on deck just abaft the main mast, and then cleared the ship of the incredible quantity of timber and debris that had accumulated over ten days' work.

We sailed down to Inhassoro in a holiday mood. The

weather was delightful and my forebodings of a cyclone lifted; but there was little wind and we motored most of the way. The boys fished, taking turns with the fishing rod. Kevin and Mark became bored after a while, but Bruce persisted and finally caught a 10lb. barracuda, fighting it with fierce determination. As soon as it had been landed Kevin and Mark, smarting under the injustice of baby brother catching a fish, were clamouring to be at the rod again. It did them no good; there were no more fish that day. Rachel, we noted with concern, was prone to seasickness. She cried a little at first, then put herself to bed and slept it off, waking as fresh as a daisy. This became her standard method of dealing with seasickness.

As soon as we reached Inhassoro the tender was unshipped and I went ashore in search of a sextant and a carpenter, leaving the children swimming around the boat and swarming up the anchor chain to dive off the bowsprit. Rachel could not swim and splashed around in an inner tube with the valve vulcanised on the outside.

The sextant was not at the hotel. The pilot of the fish-plane told me, however, that he had heard there was some delay because of customs, but that the matter would soon be cleared up and the sextant would be in Inhassoro within a few days.

I had as little success with the carpenter. To my chagrin I discovered that he had set off to B.D. that very morning, cycling up the beach to the end of the spit. We must have crossed on the way somewhere. I hoped that he would have recognised the boat, and would return to Inhassoro. After all, everyone claimed that he was a highly skilled and experienced shipwright, and there was no other vessel even remotely like *Walkabout* for a hundred miles or more. If he did come back, I said, and we had left, he was to return at once to the end of the spit, light a smoky signal fire there and wait for us to collect him.

I returned to *Walkabout*, somewhat dispirited, to sup on Bruce's fish. That night the foul weather returned, bringing heavy rains and strong onshore winds.

The anchorage at Inhassoro is totally exposed to the open sea. The beach faces due east and the sea floor, covered in thick seaweed, slopes very gradually out to sea. There are shoals about a mile off-shore which afford some measure of protection at low tide but none at high water. Virtually all the winds have an easterly component, and when they blow strongly the anchorage is extremely uncomfortable. All night we rolled and pitched at anchor, while the rain seeped through the joints in the sun-shrunk decks. My father was staying at the hotel, but even so the cabin, only partly fitted out, was cramped. The children were tucked into odd corners with pillows and blankets, Liz slept in the main bunk and I lay on the floor.

In the early hours of the morning there was a crash just over my head. Something thudded on to the floor near my ear and a roaring, gushing sound filled the cabin. I reacted with commendable speed and decision.

"She's sinking," I yelled, and, grabbing a pillow, threw myself on the new seacocks for the galley. It was obvious that the seacocks had snapped off and the inrush of water had to be staunched immediately. With all my strength I pressed the pillow on to the hull. It was only at this point that I actually began to wake up, and noticed that the pillow remained bone-dry.

Liz was awake by now and shouting, "Mike, what's happened? Where are you?"

She stumbled around in the darkness looking for a light. The roaring subsided. Suddenly an awful suspicion seized me. I groped around on the floor, and everywhere my fingers sank into a soft powder.

"Please don't switch on the light," I begged. "I couldn't bear it. The fire extinguisher has gone off. We'll sort it out in the morning."

I placed the pillow at the other end of the floor, turned round and went to sleep again. The children had never awakened.

Next morning my worst fears were confirmed. The dry powder extinguisher had broken out of the cupboard and detonated itself by my head. The mess was indescribable. Blue powder had been jetted into every corner and on to every surface. The powder is unwettable, so it resists mopping up, and because of its static properties it resists sweeping. For months afterwards we were finding pockets of the wretched stuff. I am convinced that it makes more mess than the fire it extinguishes. Nowadays I use gas (B.C.F.) extinguishers; one by the galley, one by the engine and one in the cockpit.

After clearing up the worst of the mess we rowed ashore in the rain for a farewell breakfast with my father. Six of us in *Crawlabout* called for a high degree of discipline and agility when surfing in the breakers, but we had learned by now not to rely on that alone to keep dry, and always tied up our shore-going clothes tightly in polythene bags. But the boys, and Kevin in particular, enjoyed the excitement of beaching and were becoming skilled in the art.

When we reached the hotel (after making a wide detour round the chained monkeys, who eyed Mark malignantly) we found a number of gloomy faces. There were only three guests, including my father, and all were marooned. Apparently this latest bout of bad weather was caused by another cyclone in the Channel, and heavy rains inland had rendered the road to Beira impassable. One man had tried to get through the previous day, but had broken his gearbox and suspension and had been loaded on a truck. This in turn had bogged down and had been rescued by a bulldozer. It was rumoured that the bulldozer was now also stuck.

The second guest and my father decided to attempt the road in convoy, and took enough provisions with them, in my opinion, to last till the end of the rainy season. In the event they did get through, but only just, and they were the last vehicles to do so for many weeks. In the rude weather that followed whole sections of the road were washed away, together with the bulldozers and scrapers working on them.

Meanwhile it was time for us to return to *Walkabout*. We had to get under way quickly to catch the high tide. Moreover, one of the monkeys had just bitten Mark, who was screaming his head off. Definitely time to leave. We said goodbye, and my father shook his head sadly and said he would try and send down some insect repellent. He stood on the beach and waved until we had sailed out of sight.

We did not get very far. After an hour the wind backed to the north and increased in strength. I was still nervous of the boat, and, unsure of the sails and the strength of the spars, I relied too much on the engine. It is a strong engine, a 31 h.p. diesel, but it could not force the boat through these choppy head seas. After a couple of hours the rain and wind rose yet further, and I realised that we were not going to reach B.D.

that night. I decided to put back, and when I told Liz relief flooded her face. She was feeling sick and so were the children, except for Kevin. Rachel and Bruce had got to sleep, curled up tight on the bunks, but Mark was still miserable.

For the second night we rolled and heaved at anchor off Inhassoro, listening to the interminable rain drumming on the decks. But the next day a new world was born. The sky was clear and the water sparkled. We laughed, consumed several hundredweight of breakfast, and dried the wet things. Bruce got out his fishing tackle and we sailed northwards to B.D. again. The wind was still fresh, but it had veered round to the south-east and was blowing strongly on our quarter. For the first time we sailed the ship as ships should sail, for the first time I heard *Walkabout*'s song—a roaring organ note rising and falling as she surged over the waves with a bone in her mouth. I called Liz and the children to come and listen. We lay on the foredeck looking down on the tumbling bow-wave. No one was sick now; everyone enjoyed this sailing. Except for Bruce. He was angry because his fish lure was skipping over the water in our wake. I was flying the main, the mizzen and a big jib. I adjusted the sheets, and *Walkabout* sang just a little louder. Now I could really sail—at least, I could with the wind behind me. It usually took us six hours to cover the thirty miles to B.D., but that day we whistled up in three-and-a-half. The treacherous gap into the lagoon was rough and the currents tugged at the keel, but I steered safely between the white water to port and to starboard, and soon we were laying at the familiar moorings.

Next day we moved back to the camp and then sailed up the lagoon in search of the carpenter. Lampião stated categorically that he was on the spit, though how he knew I cannot say. Lampião was wrong. The spit was deserted. On we sailed, right up the lagoon, and went ashore at the house of Thai Lee, the Chinese fisherman. He was a lonely old man, for it was said that his family refused to live in that remote place and had decamped to the city of Beira. He told me in pidgin Portuguese that the carpenter had indeed been there, had waited for a couple of days and had then returned to Inhassoro that morning!

I had had enough. I could not, I told Liz angrily, continue

to chase alleged carpenters up and down the coast of Mozambique forever. A third of the fitting-out had been done already, and I would just have to complete the rest on my own. We sailed back to B.D. in ill-humour.

The following week is unpleasant to recall. As a result of the second cyclone—I was told later that it was in fact the fifth in the channel that year—which hovered somewhere between Africa and Madagascar, the weather became abominable. For seven days it rained and the wind blew strongly from between south and west, reaching gale force for some period nearly every day. Both the camp and the moorings were completely exposed to winds with a westerly component, and it is difficult to say which was less comfortable.

The tents had been secured with extra lashings to trees, roots and even boulders. But they flapped and tugged all day, and of course it was not possible to keep anything dry. Being wet all day was not too bad, but trying to sleep in a wet bed—or rather, on ground mattresses, for we had no beds—was most disagreeable. We cooked and ate in the main tent where Liz and I slept, while the children used the smaller tent as their bedroom. They just fitted, laid head to heel in the form of a solid square, and after a short period of squabbling every evening about territorial rights they fell asleep and slept soundly through the night. It would take more than a wee cyclone to break the habit.

Each morning for two or three hours Liz persisted with lessons for the boys. They usually had to work under a plastic sheet, but Liz felt strongly that it should be school as usual, come what may. Mark was by far the most conscientious, and took his instructions seriously. Kevin was idle and had to be coerced continually, or else he would slide off into his tent and read; but it was Bruce who had to be virtually shackled to the tent. He was an incurable truant. He would edge away from the camp after breakfast, insisting, if observed, that he just wanted to feed his pet hermit crab or fetch some water. The next time you looked, he had vanished into the rain. He would stay away for hours, sometimes for most of the day. Then he would return and, ignoring Kevin's and Mark's jeers of "Liar, liar", would relate fantastic tales of being besieged by crabs or being trapped by the tides. That he believed his own tales is certain, for he always screamed at the injustice of it when the inevitable punishment fell heavily on his bottom. Next day he would again be out hunting squid or bullying Lampião for bait.

Rachel was too young for lessons, but she enjoyed her colouring books and helping Liz, and was perfectly happy pottering in a humming sort of way around the camp. She did not really take much notice of the foul weather. But she was only happy provided she was certain that due attention was being paid to her activities. She was very determined about this, and would employ every technique, from a coy charm to strident naughtiness, to secure it. One certain method was to plunge into the sea. She had no fear of the water at all, and loved swimming, even though she could not. The sight of Rachel marching into the breakers without her tube was enough to make Liz drop everything and come running.

"Let her swallow a few mouthfuls," I said. "It's the best way to learn." But I failed to make an impression.

The children all had to help with the work of the camp, and this they disliked intensely, for they were used to servants for every little chore. We did, in fact, have a camp servant for a short while. Emanuel, who had drifted into my father's employ as a fisherman, came to us when my father left. He greatly improved the quality of camp life. At other camps previously we had always managed to hire help; otherwise you had to spend the entire day collecting firewood, washing, gutting fish and so on, and had no time left for any other activity. This was very much the case at B.D. But Emanuel did not last long. He developed what seemed to be acute 'flu, and none of the analgesics in the medicine chest had the least effect. He told me that B.D. was inhabited by evil spirits and implied that he had been bewitched. As soon as the weather improved he went home.

Work aboard *Walkabout* proceeded slowly, sometimes painfully. Every morning at dawn I would row out to the boat, return to the camp for a late breakfast and then stay aboard till dark. The journey from shore to ship was only a couple of hundred yards, but it took anything from half-an-hour to an hour if the wind and tide were both against me. When I reached the boat I would flop on to the deck in a state of exhaustion. After a while I would stumble down below and start the day's work.

Working in a boat is never easy. It is cramped and there are no straight lines, no right-angles. In any fitting-out operation on a boat due recognition must always be given to Sod's Law. Put simply, this states that in any operation, large or small, there will be not less than one snag. In a row of screws to be driven in, for example, at least one will strip its thread. If a locker can be moved quickly and easily, then the electric wiring will have to be altered. One day, for example, I decided to siphon diesel from a can into the fuel tank. The filler cap was jammed, and when I put a big spanner on it the whole fitting came loose, for the deck had rotted at that point. There is only one way of dealing with rot, and that is to cut it out. I cut out the affected area and then found that the filler pipe had also rotted. Delving deeper, I discovered that the discharge valve was damaged. By the time that had been repaired, the filler pipe replaced and the section of deck removed, it was dark. The diesel would have to be siphoned in the next day.

Walkabout's motion in periods of bad weather made things more difficult. She pitched, and when the wind and tide were opposed she rolled like a pig, so that everything ended up on the cabin sole and I was thrown from one side to another. I had no power tools, so I often had to use both hands, and then the only way to work was to lash myself to the ship like some tempest-driven mariner. I felt ridiculous, and was glad there was no one aboard to watch.

The first job was to make a tool stowage system. Underneath the companion way, accessible from cockpit and cabin, wooden rails were fitted, and canvas bags hung on rigid battens were slung between the rails. It was rather like an office filing system, with each type of tool in a separate file. Then the heads (toilet) were installed in a discreet site next to the main mast, and a bulkhead was put in between that and the proposed new galley. There was insufficient room to isolate the toilet completely with a door, so we made do with a curtain. I fitted a plumbing system for the galley, with salt water pumped to one sink tap and fresh water from a head tank running to a second tap, spring-loaded to avoid wastage. Half a bunk, a seat and the starboard cupboard were ripped out to make space for the galley. A pipe berth was fitted for'ard for Kevin, and I made a tiny bunk on a locker lid near the engine for Rachel. The chart table was mounted over the port quarter berth in a position for easy use, and next to it the radio was boxed in and shelves were built for navigation books.

One day, when the weather had at last begun to break, a small plane came from the north and flew very low over the camp. Everyone rushed out in excitement to watch.

"It's the fish-plane," I shouted suddenly. "He's trying to tell us something. Don't take your eyes off him."

Sure enough, he banked steeply into a circle and came roaring down the shore line again, below the tops of the casuarina trees. As he passed the camp Mark's quick eyes caught sight of a little package falling from the plane. It fell into the surf and the kids went wild with excitement. They leapt over the rocks and plunged into the sea. When they emerged Kevin was clutching a plastic bag with the neck tied tight. The plane circled again to make sure we had picked up the package, then waggled his wings in salute and flew off to Inhassoro. Air mail par excellence.

The bag contained a letter from my father and a dozen aerosol containers of insect repellent; a letter from Mike Hill with enough heat fatigue tablets for a desert army; a letter from friends; and the feature article published in the *Rhodesia Herald* after our departure. We had by this time acquired a castaway mentality, and the mail made quite an emotional impact. Everything was read aloud at least three times, but still seemed remote. Our isolation was most pointedly underlined, however, by the small food hamper sent by friends, which contained coffee and tinned stuffs, of which we had hundreds of pounds left. They had no idea that what was badly needed was fresh food. Only oranges, eggs and onions were left, and these were by now rationed.

The last letter in the bag was a note from the agent in Beira to say that the customs had seized the sextant and refused to release it without payment of duty amounting to about £40; alternatively, to avoid duty, I could claim the sextant in person. Liz and I talked endlessly round the problem. Ideally we should sail *Walkabout* to Beira, because I was still deeply worried about obtaining clearance from Portuguese waters from the authorities. But there were a number of shoals en route and the swamps provided no visible navigational marks; I was not prepared to risk it without a sextant. We decided in the end to sail to Inhassoro when the weather improved. There I would thumb a lift on the fish-plane, which would cost about £20. I cursed all officialdom and resolved that henceforth my politics were to be those of simple anarchy. No politicians, no officials, no regulations.

The next day dawned bright and sunny, and the gentlest of easterly breezes stroked the casuarina needles. How we worshipped the sun, how we revelled in dry sheets, how blissfully we wriggled our toes in warm, powdery sand! We declared a national B.D. holiday forthwith.

I went sailing with Kevin and Mark in *Puffabout*, to instruct them in the art, but I got the uneasy feeling that Kevin at any rate was becoming more skilled than I. So I joined Bruce and Rachel at low tide in looking for marine specimens. In the afternoon the whole family trooped over to the seaward shore of the island, a quarter of a mile away, to swim "in the proper sea with proper waves", as Mark put it. The sea left over from the gales was certainly impressive, and Liz watched anxiously as the heavy surf tumbled the children up the beach. She should rather have watched me, for a wave bent me backwards and then cast me ashore to nurse a bad back for several days.

The fine weather brought a band of itinerant fishermen to B.D. About fifteen men and boys rowed into the cove in an open boat one morning, laid wire mesh on stakes across the mouth of the cove and waited for the tide to ebb. At low water they simply picked the trapped fish up off the sand. The method is known as kavoko fishing, and was familiar to me. The other method which they used baffled us completely. A fisherman would wade through shallow water holding a hoop made of light iron rod. When he saw a fish lying near the surface he would throw the hoop over it and the creature would float to the surface, presumably stunned by the unorthodoxy of the attack.

Bruce ascended to his seventh heaven. He spent every moment with the fishermen, and usually returned with fish for supper. All the trees in the camp were hung with fish heads, octopus tentacles and other bait, much of it decomposing. After a couple of days he was not content with the passive role of trotting after the fishermen. He weaned the younger boys away from the tribe and formed a gang, doing heaven knows what. Liz and I were too busy to find out, and decided that it would be safer not to.

As a geography project Kevin and Mark were given the task of surveying the island. They had to walk right round the shores and, taking rough bearings, draw a map. The position of ridges, the type of vegetation and the siting of the buildings had to be drawn. The result was naturally amateurish, but it gave me a fair mental picture of B.D. and was to come in useful later on.

At last B.D. became what we had always imagined it would be—a tropical island paradise. The only drawback was that the weather again became hot, and the mosquitoes, voracious after their long fast, silently closed in at dusk for their nightly feast of essence of Saunders. But, after all, no person can be truly content without a legitimate grumble, and we were all well content.

A few days later the former Owner of *Walkabout* arrived. He flew down from Beira in his private plane, landed at Inhassoro and drove up to the end of the spit. Meanwhile, Lampião boarded the big motor yacht, *Janet Susan*, and motored across to meet him. An hour later the yacht returned with the Owner at the helm.

He listened to the tale of the sextant and other difficulties with sympathy as surprising as it was uncharacteristic. To obtain clearance from Portuguese waters he suggested that we should go to Inhambane, 200 miles to the south, in preference to Beira, and when I told him that I had no chart he lent us his to copy. As for the sextant, he said that he would be passing through Beira on his way home and would do all he could to help; he felt that the time had come when a little present to the right person might be the only way to start things moving again. He also offered to buy *Puffabout* when we left, and send the money on to South Africa. This was a satisfactory solution to an awkward problem, for *Puffabout* could not be fitted aboard *Walkabout* and was not sturdy enough to replace *Crawlabout* as the yacht's tender. I promised Mark that, to compensate for the loss of his new boat, I would convert *Crawlabout* to a sailing dinghy with the proceeds of the sale.

A couple of days later the Owner sailed to Inhassoro for the day, and returned with the news that the authorities were now insisting that I should pay for a customs official to fly to Inhassoro with the sextant. I rowed furiously into the lagoon, and when I was out of earshot yelled abuse in the approximate direction of the Beira Customs House, 130 miles away. I felt a little better.

But this was not the end of the story. The Owner departed towards the end of the week, and in some place concluded some negotiation with some person. Where, what and who with I am not too clear to this day, but the result was more than satisfactory: on payment of some £15 the sextant would be delivered to Inhassoro, the date to be advised by the fish-plane during the following week. All this was contained in a message dropped by the Owner from his plane on his way north again.

That same afternoon I was working in the cabin when I heard a faint hallooing from the shore. This was puzzling, because Liz always summoned me with a foghorn. I poked my head out of the hatch and spied a tattered little figure leaping around on the sands and waving wildly. A stiff westerly wind had begun to blow again, so not a word could I distinguish. But the strange figure was obviously calling me, and obviously, too, the matter was urgent. Liz and the children have met with a serious accident, I thought suddenly, and jumping into the tender rowed home like an Oxford blue.

The figure continued to leap and flail, and as I neared the net I could hear him screaming above the wind "Buya (come)! Buya! Buya!"

I rowed the boat full tilt into the sand and ran to the kavoko net. "What's the matter?" I shouted.

The figure thrust its fists heavenwards and kicked its heels up after them, clearing the sand, like some great spidery frog, by a full 3 feet.

In a high-pitched voice, torn for some mystifying reason with rage, it screamed, "I am the carpenter!"

IV

"I AM THE carpenter!" he repeated, delivering the message in a voice intended to carry across the lagoon.

I stared at him dumbfounded, for I had quite come to believe in the carpenter as a creature of Mozambique mythology. On the other side of the wire netting the stringy little figure continued to dance on the sands and began to chatter with rage.

"The Master sends me a message, 'Come, I need you!' As soon as I get the message, I come. I was working on other things, but I leave them and come. When I get to Inhassoro, the master has gone and left me. Still I hear him calling, 'Come, I need you!' So I ride to the end of the sands on my bicycle and wait. All day I wait and all night I wait without food. But the Master does not fetch me. It is raining and I start to shiver, so I go to the old Chinese and wait. But the Master does not fetch me. I go back to Inhassoro. There I hear the Master calling again, 'Come, I need you!' I am tired, my bicycle tyres have holes, but I come. All the way up the beach to the land of B.D. Then . . ."

I interrupted him, for I had by now collected my wits and felt it was time to put a stop to this outrageous version of the events of the past month.

"You have come," I said calmly, "but you have come too late. All the work is done. There is nothing for you to do."

He took this information like a shock dose of sedative. The dancing ceased at once and the dancer froze in a slight crouch, head a little to one side and right ear thrust forward as though it could not believe what it had just heard.

"Aiee!" exclaimed the carpenter in a low, mournful voice, and his shoulders slumped. The attitude was in such sharp contrast to his previous gymnastics that I relented.

"Perhaps there is a little left to do. Let us go to the boat and talk."

"The Master says, 'Come, I need you', and I come," he cried happily, starting a little jig for joy. He suddenly leapt high off the ground with a muted shriek. I should clearly, I reflected, have to get used to these violent expressions of emotion. But in fact the poor carpenter had trodden upon a Martian, and his little shriek was not one of joy but one of pain. He muttered and rubbed his foot, and neither of us gave the sting a further thought. But it was to have unpleasant consequences later.

Daniel—for that was his name—was shown what had to be done, and talked with me in the cabin. We agreed on £1 a day and double time on Saturdays and Sundays. This was very nearly twice as much as his normal rate, but I was desperate for help to speed things up, and he would be working, I knew, in harsh conditions. He smiled vigorously, and taking his little box of rusty tools, went ashore for the rest of the day to organise his own camp in the ruin of the new hotel that seemed to afford hospitality to any wandering African lighting upon the island.

But before he went he gave me disturbing news. Yet another bad cyclone was in the vicinity. It had struck the coast near Inhambane a few days before, and had caused severe damage. Then it had spun off into the Channel, and was reported to be heading north again. The authorities up and down the coast had issued disaster warnings, and all small craft had been dragged above the high tide mark. To my mind this sounded a grave business, for unlike the North Atlantic, where the Americans keep a close watch on hurricanes from their early youth to their death with ships and even with spotter aircraft, the Portuguese weather forecasting is of the most rudimentary kind, and they seem to have only the vaguest notion of the whereabouts of a cyclone over the sea.

The rest of the afternoon was spent in preparing *Walkabout* against heavy weather. There was little I could do. Everything that could not be taken down below was lashed securely on deck, and everything below was made fast. There were no safety lines, because Liz had removed the steel stanchions for chipping and painting. I wondered whether to lay out anchors, but with tidal currents running each way at about 5 knots I felt that anchors would only tangle with the permanent moorings. These comprised a massive block of concrete, to which was attached a ½″ chain followed by a 1¼″ diameter nylon rope, which was in turn attached to the boat's anchor warp—$\frac{3}{8}$″ chain, doubled. The samson post was as stout as any I have seen on a small yacht, but I braced it aft to the quarter bits with further lashings, and also lashed the tiller. Feeling a little happier I rowed ashore in a gusting wind to tell Liz the news.

We were awakened next morning by the canvas of the tent snapping angrily in the wind. The sky was low and black, and later it began to rain fitfully. All day Daniel and I worked hard on the boat. I gave him a simple shelf to build, and soon discovered that he was no shipwright. He claimed to be a cabinet maker, but his wares must have been made for an undiscerning clientèle. Nevertheless, every saw-cut he made contributed to progress, and I drew heart from his presence alone.

In the afternoon, when the tide turned against the wind and *Walkabout* began to roll, he started to perspire and his work became painfully slow. "Master," he mumbled at last, "my head goes round and round." He was seasick. To his credit, though, he refused to give up working.

Some time during that night the rain started in earnest. It roared down in tropical abandon and Liz, always better than I at waking up, stumbled about securing flaps in both tents and then crawled sleepily and damply back into bed, hoping the shower would soon pass. But the next morning it had abated not at all and everyone huddled out of the wet, groaning, "Not again, not again!" To add to their misery the children had been woken by several waves breaking into their tent, which was closer to the shore than ours and less protected. I explained about the possibility of a cyclone. They became very excited, now they knew that the deluge beyond the flaps was not rain of the ordinary tiresome sort but Cyclone Rain, but Mark asked thoughtfully, "If the cyclone comes and the camp is blown away, are we all going to get on *Walkabout*?"

This was a thought that had been concerning me.

"Probably not, but again it depends on where the wind is coming from and how strong it is. A cyclone in the southern hemisphere revolves in a clockwise direction, so if the eye passes to the north of us then the winds will be easterly and the island will protect *Walkabout* from the seas, though not from the wind. If the winds are westerly or southerly, though—as they are now—then I shouldn't think we stand a chance in these narrow waters, full of shoals. Anyway, we might not be able to get out to *Walkabout*," I ended hoarsely. One had to shout above the noise of the rain outside.

I marvelled at its intensity. There seemed to be a greater volume of water in the atmosphere than of air. The light canvas of the tent acted no longer as a barrier to the water but rather as a fine filter, excluding 99 per cent of the rain, but sheer pressure of water forced a fraction to pass through the fabric. Later I estimated the average rainfall as roughly 20″ a day, because *Crawlabout*, lying in the open, would be brim-full every morning and every evening.

There was no point in hanging around the camp, so Daniel and I rowed off to work as usual. With a second person in the tender rowing was twice as hard, and it took me three-quarters of an hour to reach *Walkabout*, Daniel perched tensely in the stern, bailing continuously. He was a hopeless seaman; he could not row to save his life, and getting him from the tender on to a plunging *Walkabout* was a pantomime. Moreover, he could not swim, and had to be strapped up in a life-jacket, a garment as alien to him as a dinner suit. But he did not lack courage, and seldom complained about his bizarre working conditions.

We stayed aboard the whole day, for I could not face another round trip. When we reached camp that evening the tide was high, and the bigger waves were again breaking into the children's tent. More ominously, a trickle of sea-water encircled our tent, which was pitched on a slight mound, and was seeping towards the well, which lay in a slight depression. Liz had organised the children to dig trenches and earth barricades to prevent the sea from reaching our fresh water supply, and this had been successful. I remembered then that spring tides were on Friday, the next day. Not only spring tides but the springs before Equinoctial springs, which are the highest tides of the year.

During the night the wind rose to gale force. Neither Liz nor I slept much. The cracking of canvas was horrible to listen to, and we both fully expected the whole straining, jerking structure of the tent to be snatched away suddenly. The children never once woke.

Friday came at last. There was no suggestion of dawn breaking. The darkness ebbed away reluctantly, and even more reluctantly a dark grey light seeped over the earth. Before we could see anything we knew that the tide was rising, from the crash of the waves on the rocky shore. This time the sea did not mess around lobbing the odd wave through the children's tent. Wave after wave swept through, and everything was evacuated to the main tent. The sea also filled the well. A little later the first wave struck the main tent, and then several more. We were eating breakfast at the time, and I jumped to my feet in a rage.

"This is too much! Can't we even eat breakfast in peace?"

This set everyone else off, and the whole family became furious at the interruption to the meal, which was somehow held to be sacrosanct. The anger seemed to have a salutary effect, for the tide turned shortly after and no more seas joined us at breakfast.

At the appointed time Daniel, wearing an old plastic fertiliser bag, presented himself for work as usual. But I looked at the angry sea and decided against making an exhausting and possibly futile attempt to reach *Walkabout.* Instead we rigged up a crude shelter and he worked most of the day on *Crawlabout* doing minor repairs and fitting a new fender rope.

The incredible rain continued. It seemed as though the Indian Ocean itself had been sucked into the heavens and was now falling back into place again. We no longer attempted to keep dry, accepting the rain as part of a new, denser habitat, where life went on but more laboriously. The rain was as warm as tea, and a dozen times a day I thanked heaven for this, for otherwise the situation would have been serious. It was still necessary to shelter from the wind, using the tent or oilskins to avoid loss of body heat, but we never felt chill.

From time to time a slight lull in the rain would reveal *Walkabout,* rearing at her moorings like an enraged horse. Occasionally a wave larger than the rest would make her pitch so violently that I could see the entire keel almost to the rudder. I tried not to think of her.

At low tide I bailed the well with a bucket until the water sweetened enough to drink. Then the children helped me to dig proper trenches and barricades, not only to protect the

You cannot convince anyone who is seasick that death is not imminent

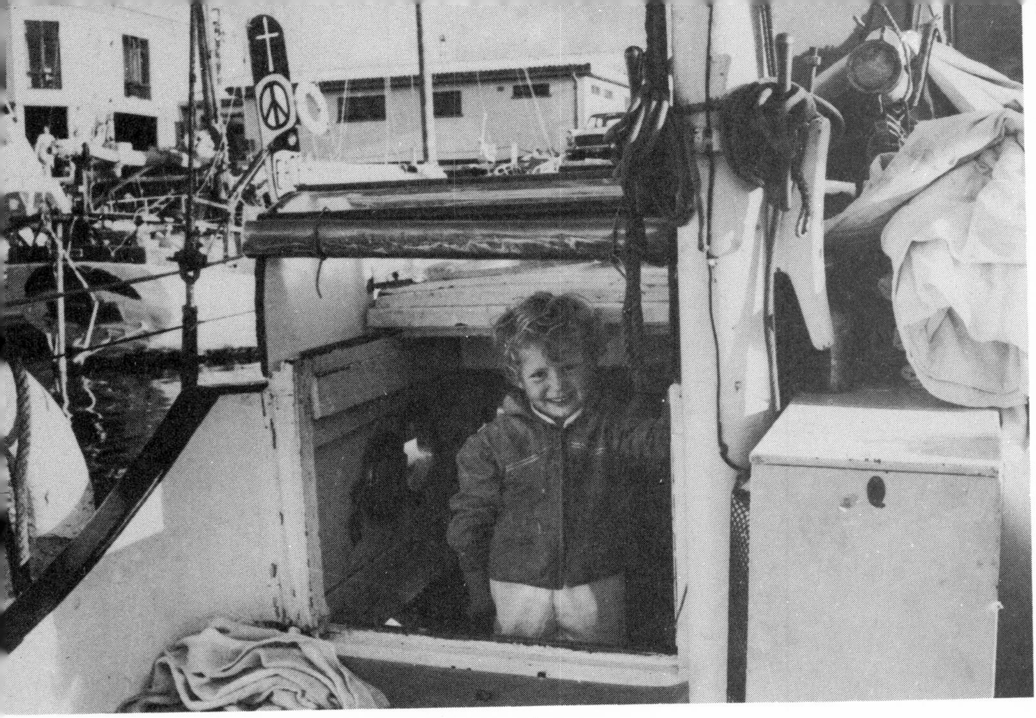

Rachel welcomes the Cape Town spring with a smile. The peace emblem in the background is *Siestar*'s self-steering vane

The Walkabouts attack the most important task of the day

well, but round the tents also. They were still excited about a cyclone, but were beginning to feel that it lacked proper dramatic impact; Cyclone Rain seemed as wet as any other, and nothing much else seemed to be happening.

In the afternoon we watched the tide rise and with it the wind. I sent the boys to find out what was happening at the hotel; they returned with the joyous news that the sea had reached the back door, flooding the whole area behind the building. By now the sea had again come through the children's tent, and was attacking the main tent and the well. I decided the time had come for a serious reconnaissance.

Liz and I struck out through the scrub paths towards the hotel, where we found the band of fishermen huddled motionless under blankets on the veranda. They were silent, staring vacantly at the floor between their knees or at a patch of wall opposite. I spoke to them, telling them that their kavoko nets, which had been left near our camp, would be washed away unless they were tied to a tree. None answered or even looked at me. They seemed to be gripped by a paralysing fatalism.

Just beyond the hotel was a cove, similar to ours but larger and cutting more deeply into the island, so that at its deepest point less than 200 yards separated it from the open sea. As we reached the edge of the cove an awesome sight confronted us. Huge breakers were rolling in from the open sea across what had once been the isthmus, and into the cove. Very little land was left; only two mounds were still held together by the roots of a grove of casuarinas. As we watched a huge eddy formed around each of the obstructing mounds and began to eat them away. Then two breakers, larger than their fellows, rolled in and finished off the job. The great trees toppled into the sea and the mounds vanished under the boiling water. The island had been cut in two.

The sea in the gap swirled and tumbled, brown and dirty-white with the land it had just consumed. In the water tumbled the debris, grass, bushes and trees.

Liz and I watched this spectacle of natural destruction completely awestruck. Occasionally we muttered, "Good God!", but there were no words adequate to the occasion. Watching the slowly turning trees, I began to worry at the peril they presented to *Walkabout*. If she were struck by one of them, she would surely sink, and then our means of escape to the mainland would be cut off. The motor yacht, *Janet Susan*, was, I knew, of lighter construction than *Walkabout*, and she too might be stove in. For the first time I realised that if the eye of the storm reached us our greatest danger might not be from the wind at all but from the sea. While I could probably reach *Walkabout* on my own, I was certain that I could not ferry the family over, for the dinghies would founder.

I told Liz that we must search for a suitable shelter on higher ground before dark, and we hurried back in the fading light. I knew from the survey of the island carried out by Kevin and Mark that the highest point was a low ridge, probably no more than 15 feet above sea level, running like a backbone down the centre. In the middle of the ridge was a cottage belonging to a Rhodesian doctor, a solid masonry house. Here we should certainly be safe. We were greatly reassured, but when we got back to camp we received a shock. In the hour or so of our absence the sea had risen more than a foot above the floor of the children's tent and several inches above the floor of the main tent. There was no sign of the well. It was somewhere in the centre of a lake, nearly 2 feet deep, that extended several hundred yards inland.

We decided to abandon camp immediately. Kevin and Mark were loaded with bedding and Bruce and Rachel were given the primus stove and a kettle of water. They disappeared into the fading daylight, but after a few minutes the two older boys returned.

"We can't reach the house," said Kevin. "The water is too deep."

Liz and I looked at each other in alarm. "I'd better see for myself," I said.

Kevin was right. In the short time since we had been there the sea had poured in from a different quarter across the area between the camp and the ridge. The water seemed to be nearly 6 feet deep, and eddies spun in the current which raced through. It looked too ugly to attempt with the children.

I sloshed back to the camp and delivered the news to Liz. "So it looks," I concluded, "as though we stay put. It's just about high tide now, so things shouldn't get worse. If they do we shall have to take to the trees." I felt very tired.

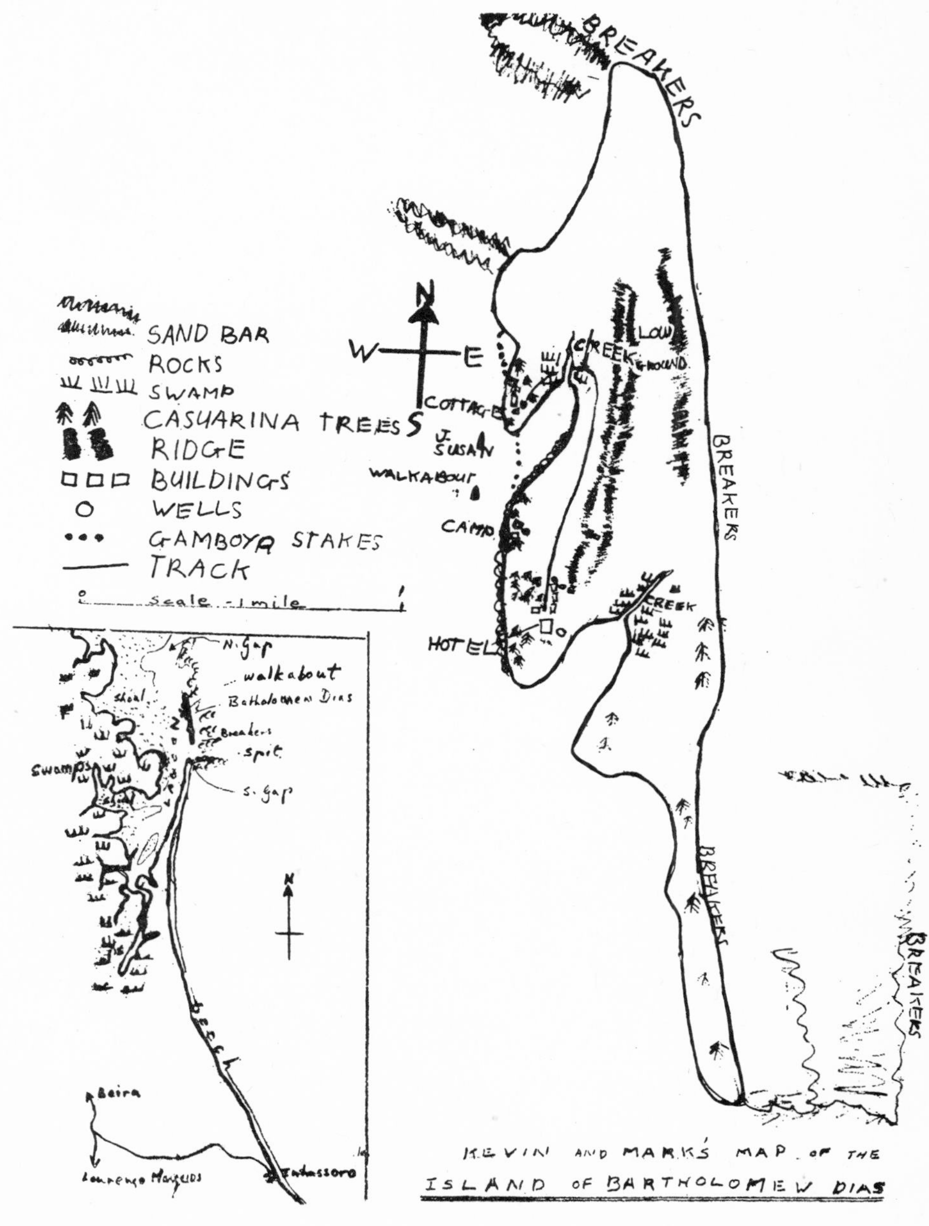

KEVIN AND MARK'S MAP OF THE ISLAND OF BARTHOLOMEW DIAS

"Where are Bruce and Rachel?" asked Liz suddenly.

Nobody knew. We began calling them. Soon there came an answering call and Bruce waded into view, slashing at bush tops with a stick.

"Where's Rachel?" asked Liz.

"I don't know," he said vaguely. "I thought she came here."

"Where did you leave her? Think hard." There was a hint of desperation in Liz's voice. But he could not remember.

We waded around in the twilight, calling her. No answer. I paired Kevin and Mark and sent them looking in one direction, Liz and Bruce in another, and I took the third. The search took on the reality of a nightmare. When we gathered again, Rachel had still not been found. Liz and I had one thought, and each knew that the other had had the same thought.

"The well . . . ?" said Liz in a small voice.

I nodded. Wading towards where I reckoned the well to be, I began fishing for the hole with my foot. A terrible dread seized me that my foot would touch what could only be a body.

Just then Mark shouted, "I can hear her."

We all froze. Faint snatches of song could be heard. Then there was silence. No one moved. A few moments later a shrill, somewhat tuneless voice lifted in song from behind a nearby thicket.

"I'll sing you one-o,
Green grow the Russian toes,
One is one and all alone
And ever more shall be so."

Rachel materialised out of the near-darkness, wading in water over her waist. "Hello, everybody!" she said cheerfully.

Liz snatched her up and hugged her. "Where have you been?"

"Oh, I just went for a little walk. I was looking for Bruce."

"What could be more natural on a pleasant Friday evening?" I muttered, more to myself than to anybody.

As though the Return of Rachel was a carefully staged climax, the tide turned. When we reached the main tent the sea had already retreated beyond the flaps. Friday night was, I think, much as Thursday night had been, but with one difference—Liz and I slept. Fitfully, perhaps, but I remember thinking—if a cyclone takes the tent away we'll know soon enough.

Saturday morning filtered dismally in to find us wide awake and waiting for the tide. The rain and wind had not abated, but on the other hand they were no worse, and there seemed to be a reasonable chance that the flooding too would be no worse than the previous evening. The first thing I looked for was *Walkabout*, dreading to see an empty mooring. But she was still there, snapping at her chain as she plunged in the seas. After a scratch breakfast I trudged off in search of water from one of the other wells. The hotel well was flooded, so I decided to try the Owner's cottage, to the north. All the way I waded through scummy brown sea-water. It seemed as though most of the island was flooded, and this disturbed and puzzled me, for I could not understand where the water was coming from. The fierce rain obscured the landscape, but the sea-water appeared to be flowing towards our cove instead of coming from it. The scene was reminiscent of news photographs of disaster areas. Bushes and grass, torn out of the earth, floated in the filthy water with their roots exposed, drowned rats and insects and a few birds floated by, while those still living clung, motionless, to some plant.

The Owner's cottage had escaped significant damage, and to my relief the water in the well, though somewhat contaminated, was usable. Before returning to camp I decided to do a bit of reconnaissance. As the water seemed to be flowing from the direction we had taken, ages ago, when the family had gone for a swim in the "proper breakers" on the seaward side, I followed this path. It led me over the ridge near the doctor's house. Here the water had broken through a low part of the ridge and was flowing swiftly from the open sea towards our cove. This explained why we had been cut off from the doctor's house the previous evening, and I was alarmed to see how the island was being cut through in a second place. Large chunks had been eroded and were now floating around our cove. I hesitated to carry on, for the water on the seaward side of the ridge was swirling fiercely, and hardly any bush tops were to be seen; then, yielding to an inner call to adventure as compelling as a bugle note in battle, and probably as foolish, I plunged into the flood.

It was only about 300 yards, but the going was difficult, for the current was too swift to swim and the water too deep to wade properly. I kept on stumbling over submerged scrub or falling into unseen hollows. Nearer the open sea a nasty herd of little white horses galloped across the water, and underneath them a bigger swell became noticeable. There was also a curious tremor that I could not place.

About 50 yards from the shore I swam across a hollow and climbed on to a rise. Standing in water to the knees I gazed seawards, and for the first time since the cyclone began I was afraid; not to be compared with its softer sisters, awe and anxiety, undiluted fear, like iced water, flowed through my veins. Monstrous breakers, totally out of keeping with the wind, which had only touched gale force from time to time, assaulted the shore. Their tops high above me, they roared majestically in from the sea in stately procession. As each one struck the shore the island shuddered, and a vast tonnage of water surged over the little cliffs. Each surge turned brown with eroded earth as it swept into the island.

For the first time, too, I grasped that if the cyclone passed directly overhead, the island might be washed away entirely. I had seen it cut in two the previous evening, and now it was happening here, and probably further north too. I remembered that B.D. had been turned into an island by a cyclone cutting it off from the mainland, and worst of all I remembered that it was entirely composed of sandstone. When weathered this looks reassuringly like solid rock, but it is weak and friable. The children were always demonstrating their strength by breaking up large rocks.

Much afraid, I returned to the camp as fast as I could and struggled over to *Walkabout* to study the *Mariner's Handbook* and the *Africa Pilot** and to think. The former has this to say of tropical revolving storms:

> Winds of Force 7 are likely up to 200 miles from the centre of the storm and winds of gale force 8 up to 100 miles from the centre. . . . Hurricane force winds (12 and over) are

* *The Mariner's Handbook*, N.P. 110, and the *Africa Pilot*, Vol. III, N.P. 3. (Both published by the Hydrographer of the Royal Navy.)

likely within 75 miles of the storm centre and gusts exceeding 175 knots have been reported.

It seemed, then, as though the centre (or eye) of the storm lay 100 miles or more to the north-north-east, for the wind had been blowing from the south-east. On the other hand, the barometer, as well as the dense rain, indicated that the storm centre was closer, for the *Mariner's Handbook* goes on to advise:

> If the corrected (barometer) reading is 5 millibars or more below normal it is time to consider avoiding action, for there is little doubt that there is a tropical storm in the vicinity.

The barometer needle lay more than 60 millibars below its normal position! That, more than anything, terrified me. The barometer has never been calibrated, so I do not know what the absolute reading was, but it was lower than I had ever seen it before, or indeed since. I wondered whether the eye was much closer than the wind strength indicated, and the storm was perhaps distorted in some way—not the symmetrical swirl of revolving winds shown in the *Mariner's Handbook* but a lop-sided affair—and that still seems to me a reasonable hypothesis. Or maybe the storm was simply a feeble one. But that hope was dispelled when I thought of the gigantic breakers on the other side. I thought also of the rise in the level of the sea. The *Africa Pilot* pointed out that a storm off a long coastline can pile water up against that coastline to a depth of 8 feet greater than normal. I reckoned that the sea had risen about 5 feet above the highest tide mark. That seemed to me quite severe enough. And if the eye was to the north-north-east it was probably heading south and would come much closer.

Thoroughly pulverised now, I began to plan an escape operation, for it was certain that the bedrock of the island could not survive a full cyclone "with gusts exceeding 175 knots", or anything like that. There were roughly twenty-five people on B.D., including ourselves and the fishermen, but not one person, apart from me, who could handle *Walkabout* or *Janet Susan*, for Lampião was on mainland leave. There were other difficulties, not the least of which was the absence of any safe place of refuge; but spurred on by the barometer needle I evolved a plan which stood a fighting chance.

It was never put into effect. Over the next day and a half the rain lifted and the wind veered to the south-west. The camp and the well were flooded for the last time on Saturday evening, and less than a week later the well began to produce potable water again. The wind remained in the south-west for five days, blowing constantly at or near gale force. It tried our patience to the limit. On one occasion, after trying unsuccessfully to saw a sheet of ply on deck for the third consecutive day, I stood up and screamed at the wind until I was tired; I felt much better. That evening Liz confessed doing the same thing after a wildly flapping blanket she had been trying to dry dragged her into a thicket. The children were irritable and quarrelsome, and there was sand in our beds and sand in our food.

Getting to *Walkabout* became a dreaded daily marathon, and once there Daniel and I would remain aboard till sunset to avoid an extra trip. Daniel was an engaging workmate. He told me of his time in the South African goldmines, which he liked because of the good money that could be earned and because of the fine food they fed him on.

"Meat and beans," he told me. "Good meat and wonderful beans that make you strong and fat, not like Portuguese beans. Ah, how wonderfully fat I was in those days. Now you can see all my bones." And he would gaze gloomily at the sardines and baked beans we ate for our lunch.

Often he would get the mutters and instruct himself in every tiniest detail of the work he was doing. "Now, Daniel, take this wood and cut it. Pick up your saw and cut it just so, straight, but be careful of your knee and don't twist the saw like that. Call yourself a carpenter!"

Sometimes he would fly into a sudden rage and start berating in a low, furious voice. "You, you . . . saw! Cut your carpenter, would you? Cut your own carpenter who keeps you warm in a little box! Cut your carpenter who sharpens you every day! Take that!" And he would snatch up a hammer and give the offending tool a sharp blow.

He was very good at fitting little pieces of wood together, but had not the vaguest notion of straight lines, levels or designing for strength, and needed constant supervision. But slowly the cabin took on a more serviceable and seamanlike appearance. Much thought was given to the galley, because even then we guessed at the central role which food was to play. The work-tops, shelves, and locker spaces were generous, and the sink even more so; deep enough to take a bucket and large enough to hold a meal's crockery safe in a seaway, it is a most seaworthy sink. Lacking suitable materials to make it, I laid strips of cotton sheet over a wooden base and saturated them with polyurethane paint to provide a tough, waterproof surface which lasted surprisingly well. Paraffin was piped from a converted diesel tank to the stove, so that we shouldn't have to pour from containers at sea, and this completed a practical and seamanlike galley. Liz was delighted with it and with the shelves and little stowage devices, and longed to move into our new home. Not long now, I assured her. But I reckoned without Daniel.

On the last day of the high wind, when it was already apparent that it would be the last day and I looked forward to slaughtering the rest of the fitting-out in fine weather, Daniel said that he wanted to go home to talk to the ancestral spirits about his leg. Ever since the Martian had stung him that first day he had had trouble with it. At first it had pained only a little, then it had swollen, and finally he had been unable to sleep and was even running a slight temperature. It had become a morning ritual before he would start work to relate how he had passed the previous night; how he had not slept once, and how he had writhed all night in pain, alternately weeping and calling on the spirits of his fathers for help. I had tried various remedies from the medicine chest, but the wound was no more than a pin-hole, too small to allow any medicine to pass, and nothing helped. Daniel concluded from this that an evil spirit had taken up residence in his leg, and the benevolent spirits of his ancestors were needed to exorcise the evil one. I knew that it was useless trying to dissuade him and, much annoyed, took him over to the spit.

It was fascinating to see what changes the cyclone had wrought. At least one place along the spit had been partially broken through, and from the lie of the breakers out to sea it was clear that the shoals through the gap between B.D. and the spit had been totally shifted and rearranged. It had always been a nasty passage, bedevilled with racing currents, and it worried me that I no longer knew how it worked. Nearer B.D. it could be seen that sifting sands had partially mended the break into the first cove, and at low tide a thin strip of sand linked the two halves of the island.

Once on shore with his bicycle, Daniel pedalled south with suspiciously even-legged vigour, promising to be at the same spot three days hence. To my surprise he kept his word and returned, not only with a mended leg but with his wife, a tall, fine-boned girl with Arabic features, as handsome as he was ugly. Wrapped in bright clothes she sat elegantly on the cross-bar of the dreadful machine, disdaining to notice its tyres stuffed with grass and its rusty spokes replaced with fishing line.

"She must work for me," he told me angrily, gesturing to both wife and bicycle. "She must cook plenty of beans and fish to make me strong. Then I can work hard and finish your boat quickly."

After the cyclone had passed we entered the final and in many ways the harshest phase of our stay on B.D. It again became very hot and oppressive, and with the heat came the mosquitoes. We had hoped that the insect population would have been decimated by the floods, but they were more numerous and voracious than ever. From late afternoon to early morning we were on the defence, swatting, spraying or just cowering under the shelter of nets and sheets.

Then there were the infections. These came mainly from scratched bites or cuts which were collected daily on the rocky shore and about the camp. These little wounds would no longer heal, partly because they constantly got wet. In many parts of the world sea-water is an antiseptic agent, but in places like Mozambique, where the water is warm and saturated with marine organisms, the reverse is true. Our lives revolved around the sea and were governed by the tides, and we could no more avoid getting wet than we could stop walking. So the wounds remained infected. Every morning and every evening, to a chorus of groans, I held surgery and doctored each member of the family in order of ascending age. But when Bruce and Liz were afflicted by a nasty crop of boils which would not respond to treatment, I realised that we were probably beginning to suffer from mild scurvy. The last of the fresh food had been eaten at the time of the floods, and although we took vitamin tablets with every meal and ate tinned citrus fruit, these do not seem equivalent to the real thing.

One depressing morning the fish-plane roared over the camp and dropped a message in a plastic bag weighted with a piece of coral. It simply stated that the sextant was waiting to be collected at Inhassoro. There were no qualifications. We could hardly believe it! That the sextant was only 30 miles away seemed as unlikely as an iceberg in the lagoon. Another week's work and *Walkabout* would be finished, but we decided to drop everything and snatch the sextant. We sailed before light the next day, picking our way through the new channels in the gap by eye in the first rays of an orange dawn.

When we reached Inhassoro I found that the mythical sextant was for real. But even then it did not fall into my hands easily. The hotel secretary insisted that the local official had sole authority, and the local official explained that he could do nothing because the hotel secretary held the instrument under lock and key. The two parties were separated by a mile of thick, burning sand track, and both were munching steadily through heavy lunches. But at last the precious instrument was aboard. We had a quick gloat, then struck anchor and motor-sailed straight back to B.D. The only disappointment was that we had been unable to obtain any fresh food in the village, not even an onion or a potato.

The last week at B.D. Liz and I worked furiously to finish the refit, with Liz mending sails and stitching up stowage nets. Now that the voyage itself was imminent I became anxious, and insisted that the boat must be as seaworthy as we could make her, even if it meant a few extra days' work. Kevin and Mark were shanghaied to help, Kevin to trace the Owner's chart of Inhambane and Mark to work on board. Bruce and Rachel developed colds.

One night Liz woke up to see a light flickering in the children's tent and thick smoke drifting out. She scrambled outside, shouting at me to wake up. With Kevin's help we dragged the younger children into the open air, where they stood coughing and bewildered. I found Rachel's bedclothes were burning; a large section of her sleeping bag had been burned around her head, but she had not been touched at all.

Her guardian angel, we agreed, was never off duty. The fumes we traced to a burning box of plastic Lego bricks which Kevin had had the presence of mind to hurl outside. The fire had evidently been started by the mosquito coil. This was housed in a fireproof container, but somehow Rachel, or perhaps Mark, had kicked it over into the box of bricks. We wondered what other treats B.D. had in store for us.

When the carpenter's wife became ill it came as no surprise. Daniel treated me to an angry tirade against "the land of B.D.", as he called it. It was evil, he declared, and evil spirits lived there.

"They suck all the strength from the food. You can see for yourself. Everybody in this land eats plenty but nobody ever gets fat."

We agreed, and could not wait to get away. There came a day at last when *Walkabout* was ready. When preparing a boat for a voyage it is sometimes difficult to know when to stop work, and only experience will tell what is desirable and what is vital. Those short on experience but not on money tend to concentrate on useless gadgetry, so that in mid-passage it is found that the refrigerator works a treat but there are no spare shackles aboard. I had heard of several such cases, and had been deeply impressed and rather frightened by the story of Donald Crowhurst,* who, driven by circumstances which in retrospect were not insurmountable, set out on his fatal circumnavigation in a state of chaos; for example, the boat was full of unimportant electronic gear but lacked a suction pipe for the bilge pump. From the early planning stages I had endeavoured to avoid the non-essential, and to resist moving the boat before she was ready. It had been tempting, particularly in the last fortnight, to move to Inhassoro or Beira or even make a dash for Durban. But for several hundred miles there were virtually no protected anchorages for a boat with a 6ft draught, and I was acutely aware of my own ignorance of the high seas. I should have to rely on *Walkabout* a great deal, and the voyage to Durban was not only a kind of test but could also be dangerous.

After sorting out first priorities such as sails, rigging and engine, I had concentrated on fitting out the boat for practical

* *The Strange Voyage of Donald Crowhurst*, by Nicholas Tomalin and Ron Hall (Hodder and Stoughton).

living; every item, every person and every activity had its place, and if beauty hindered, beauty be damned. Refining a boat should (and did) go on for ever, but the foundations were laid at B.D.

It took Liz and me three days to clean the boat and stow everything while Kevin and Mark ferried gear from the camp to the dinghy. It was amazing how much could be stowed if every cubic inch of available space was used. Everyone had his own tiny shelf and his own personal clothes net, and everything had its specially constructed stowage place.

The children became terribly excited about moving aboard. Kevin crawled into his dark berth, and with a secretive smile dreamed his own private dreams. He had matured in the last weeks, and when Liz or I was frayed with fatigue he would come unbidden to help. Mark had the quarter berth and complained loudly about Rachel's berth on a locker lid next to him. Rachel defended her rights with unladylike fury. Bruce's berth had been chopped in half to make room for the galley, and when he stretched he was longer than it was by several inches. Liz remarked that the voyage would have to be a short one. The main bunk, for skipper and mate, had been fitted with a length of sailcoth on a steel pipe which rolled out over the cabin floor and hung on chains to form a double berth for port use; we assumed that as one of us would always be on watch at sea the single bunk would suffice. In heavy weather the same cloth could be fixed vertically to form a bunkboard. Clever stuff—but it worked somehow, and when we took turns to breathe we fitted in quite comfortably.

It was time to strike camp and to dispose of everything deemed to be rubbish. This was everything, in my opinion, that had no foreseeable use or no stowage hole. Bruce, on the other hand, deemed everything useful, and shrieked with indignation as his marine collection was decimated. That, however, was only a front for smuggling most of it aboard later. Weeks later I was still hurling revolting objects over the side. A good deal of our stuff brooked no argument, for many stores had been damaged during the flooding and things like clothes rotted afterwards. But what amazed us was the damage done by ants. They had eaten away the bottom of the tents and had consumed tent bags, sail bags, blankets and, most astonishing of all, plastic bags. They had bored through the heavy polythene to get at the food inside, and then found the plastic so delectable that they had for the most part left the food to moulder and gobbled up the bags instead.

At last we were all snug aboard, and for the first time in weeks dry, sandless and mosquito-free. The last few jobs were done: the self-steering was set up, the compass swung, using a distant casuarina as a reference mark, and the heavy nylon mooring warp taken aboard while an anchor was dropped in its stead. The warp had lain in those waters for several years accumulating marine life. When it came out it was literally a live thing 3″ or 4″ in diameter and 100 feet long. I staked it out on deck to adapt to a new way of life.

On Sunday, March 12th, we were ready to leave the "evil land of B.D." The camping gear—or what was left of it—was ferried over and lashed on deck to be unloaded at Inhassoro. Finally the carpenter and his wife were taken aboard, together with an extraordinary number of belongings—three large bundles, a bicycle, a suitcase, a box of tools, a quantity of firewood and about a hundredweight of dried, smelly fish. We looked like an old tramp schooner, and none too seaworthy a one at that. An unusually fresh south-easter was blowing, and I hesitated. But the children were jeering at the island.

"Goodbye, you rotten old island."

"I hope we never see you again."

"I hope another cyclone washes you away."

Daniel was talking angrily to his wife and shaking his fist at the beach.

"Come on, Mike!" said Liz. "Let's go. I can't bear this place a moment longer."

Neither could I. I started the engine and went forward to raise the anchor. But B.D. had one more treat in store.

V

THE RUSTY CHAIN was hauled slowly over the stemhead until it stood vertically under the bow and then it would go no further, haul as we might. The anchor was fast. I clapped the chain on the windlass and we heaved, but all this did was to pull the bows down towards the anchor. I then slackened off some chain, belayed it, and motored the boat at full speed in various directions, hoping to jerk the anchor out. It would not budge. It was plain that 50 feet below the keel the anchor had fouled the concrete mooring block, and the only way to free it was to go down in person. The earliest opportunity would be at low water springs a week hence, and to wait that long was unthinkable. I drew my hacksaw, and with a heavy heart cut the chain.

The loss of the anchor had two consequences. First, it left us with only one anchor, and that made us unseaworthy, for every boat should have at least one spare. Secondly, it made us very late, and, had the whole affair not been the last straw in a saga of B.D. plagues, I should have waited till the following day. But I was exasperated and certain we could still catch the tide, so at 2 p.m. we sailed for the gap.

A fresh south-easter was blowing and the gap looked ugly. Broken water extended a mile out to sea and the new channel was no longer visible. But there was no turning back; the ebbing current bore us swiftly seawards. I close-hauled the sails, and with the engine running held an easterly course remembered from the previous trip.

The passage was rough. I found that steering a course was not good enough. One had to judge the channel by the size of the breakers, and of course by the echo-sounder. Twice the needle dipped to panic level. We took a lot of water on board, mainly white water, for the wind was only blowing about Force 6. But already it was evident that we were in for a thoroughly miserable trip. The carpenter's wife hunched grey-faced into a corner, and her husband for once found nothing to say. Bruce and Rachel had crawled into their bunks, while the rest of us sat stiffly in the cockpit.

By 3 p.m. we were well clear of the shoals, and I changed tack and headed south to Inhassoro. I hoped to make sufficient progress before dark to pick up the lights of the village, and in normal circumstances, with the sails sheeted in hard and the engine running, this would have been feasible. But circumstances were not normal, and they became less so as the afternoon wore on. The wind gradually increased in strength and the seas steepened, so that the decks were constantly awash. The ship would no longer hold a southerly course; hard on the wind and with the engine running, we were slowly being forced westwards towards the shore about 2 miles away.

A little before sunset the tack of the headsail suddenly slid down the bowsprit towards the stemhead and the sail began to flog violently. The headsail is hanked on the foredeck and the tack is then hauled out to the end of the bowsprit on a steel ring that girdles the bowsprit. It was the outhaul rope attached to the ring that had broken. I told Liz to take the tiller while I went forward to mend it. She gripped me tightly by the arm and pleaded in a rapid, low tone.

"Don't go forward. You'll be washed overboard. I know you will. Just look at the bowsprit. Please don't go." She was crying.

"I have to go. That sail will tear itself to pieces. Don't worry about me. I'll be tied on with a safety harness."

She did not believe me and shook her head again. I handed the tiller over and went slowly forward with a spare rope. To replace the old rope I had to crawl to the end of the bowsprit and reeve the new outhaul through a sheave set in the wood. The bowsprit was continually rearing skywards and then plunging below the water with a great slap. Sometimes I should be suspended 12 feet over the trough of a wave, and then after a sickening downward plunge I would be holding my breath under water. I have never enjoyed working at the end of the bowsprit, but that first occasion was grim. As I clung to the spar like a monkey to a pole, I remembered the nickname British sailors used to give the bowsprit: Old Widowmaker they called him.

The job was not a difficult one, but it took some time. After it was finished I set the headsail again, although the wind was really too strong. When I returned to the cockpit I found Liz in a state of near-shock. She was sitting very rigidly by the tiller and could not trust herself to speak. She was also feeling terribly seasick. The carpenter's wife was, if anything, in a worse state. She had covered her head with a shawl and clung motionless to the boat, having apparently abandoned all hope of living. Daniel sat shivering, his face grey. Of all the people aboard the children were the least affected, because they were not frightened. I had made a point of emphasising how strong and how safe *Walkabout* was. Moreover, she had a heavy lead keel, I told them, and even if she capsized, even if she rolled right over, she would always come up again. The propaganda was effective, and the children were never frightened. They were all in their bunks now, and although they were wet, and Mark in particular was feeling sick, they needed no attention.

At dusk the headsail went wild. First it sheared the chain plate that anchored the sheet fairlead, and then it ripped out its clew. Leaving the tiller to Liz, I struggled forward again and dropped all sail. We were less than a mile offshore, and unless I changed tack we should be forced slowly on to the beach during the night. I decided to motor direct to Inhassoro instead.

One's first night at sea is, I am sure, always a hurdle, an experience that looms as terrifyingly in the imagination as a shape under the bed in the dark. Happy is the skipper who passes his first night at sea bathed in placid moonlight and set about with lighthouses which tell him exactly where he is. I pity the skipper who passes his first night in a gale as much as I pitied myself that night. When it became too dark to see the end of the bowsprit I switched on the compass light, thereby admitting that night had fallen. The red glow under the tiller was no comfort; it merely emphasised the darkness around. I strained my eyes looking for Inhassoro through salt-smeared spectacles, but it was Liz, hunched in silent misery in a corner of the cockpit, who spotted faint lights ahead. We pressed onwards at full throttle, somewhat cheered. Then the lights faded and disappeared. The conviction gradually grew on me that we were being pressed backwards, and I edged more and more to the east and away from the shore. This only made things worse, because we were now heading directly into the seas. Virtually every wave was boarding us, and without a press of canvas to steady her the boat was rolling horribly. I shone a torch over the side but could discern nothing clearly, and the log, a great brass antique, was not turning. The depths along that part of the coast are an even 5 fathoms for miles out to sea, so the echo-sounder gave no indication of position either.

The suspicion that we were making sternway became a certainty, and at 9 p.m. I decided to anchor. Leaving the engine ticking over I made my way forward and with Daniel's help eased the anchor over the bows. As soon as it touched the bottom the chain rattled out at vicious speed. Although the bitter end was secured with a length of rope, I had foolishly not made the chain fast before dropping the anchor. Now it raced out with a force that Daniel and I could not match. It felt as though a submarine was towing us out to sea. Suddenly a great rage seized me that the sea, which had taken one anchor, was trying to get the other one so that it could beat us to pulp on the beach. Lying on the deck with my feet braced against the toe-rail I resolved not to let go until my arms were pulled off. "Tie the end, tie the end," I screamed at Daniel. He obeyed, and the crisis, which was of my own making, was over. There was nothing we could do now except pray that the anchor would hold.

I returned to the cockpit, passing our ludicrous deck cargo of dried fish, bicycle and camping gear. Liz, who was still a bundle of seasick misery, was persuaded to go below and lie down. She had tried once already, and had been driven out by the heat and the smell of the engine, aggravated because the hatches had been shut tight. The cabin was hot and salty wet. Three containers had broken loose and a mixture of rice, mustard, tomato sauce and broken glass lay underfoot. The noise below sounded worse than on deck. The thud of the waves on the hull, the shuddering crash as the boat snatched at her chain, convinced Liz that the bows were being torn out. She lay for most of the night rigid with fear, longing for land.

In the cockpit Daniel and his wife huddled together, waiting for death with the stoicism of their race. For the first few hours I too waited for the crunch of the keel on the sea-bed, fancying I could see shore breakers in the dark. After a time I realised that the anchor must be holding, and went below to heat up some soup. In the early hours the wind abated noticeably, and I tried to convince Liz that the danger had passed. But, tense and seasick, she could not believe me. She asked whether it would always be like this, because she couldn't take much more of it. "I'm sorry," she kept on saying, "I'm sorry I'm such a coward." I said that it wouldn't be always like this; tonight was exceptional; but I did not feel sure in my own mind, and she was not convinced. My principal feeling after the fear had worn off was one of guilt for getting my family into this horrid mess. I felt very tired and went to sleep on the floor, setting the alarm every half-hour.

The next morning dawned cool and grey above a choppy sea, but it was welcomed like the first day of spring in Siberia. We practically worshipped the light. The conviction that we had made sternway during the night proved correct. We lay only a few hundred yards from the beach, some 4 miles further from Inhassoro than we had been when darkness fell. Disaster had shaved by unseen. After a quick breakfast, which brought a little colour to everyone's cheeks, the engine was started and Daniel and I hauled in the chain. We had great difficulty breaking the anchor out, and when it came up I received another shock. The heavy steel shank had been twisted into a complete loop as though it were a hairpin, one of the flukes was bent, and the chain-links over the bows had stretched. The forces on the anchor must have been tremendous; surely Rachel's guardian angel held it fast during the night.

As we motored to Inhassoro I had plenty of time to mull over my seamanship and learn from the mistakes made over the last twenty-four hours. Obviously we should not have left so late, but one cannot always choose sailing conditions. If one is caught as we were, what then? The most striking fact to emerge was that an engine on a sailing boat is usually helpless against heavy seas. In three hours the boat had been forced back 4 miles under full throttle. Sails are more powerful, I decided, provided the boat is strong. And *Walkabout* evidently was strong; she had come through unscathed despite, rather than because of, her skipper. Next time, I resolved, I would set proper canvas to match the wind and beat out into deep water. Ground tackle too must be heavy, I concluded. Tiddly anchors on bits of nylon string are all very well in idyllic coves, but *in extremis* you want a brute of an anchor at the end of a sodding big chain.

There remained the biggest problem of all—seasickness. The children had not been affected too badly; Rachel and Bruce had slept, Kevin had merely felt queasy, and only Mark had really suffered. They were now loudly proclaiming their dislike of bad weather sailing, but bounced around the cockpit merrily enough. Liz, on the other hand, had been demoralised as much by seasickness as by fright. Tablets suppressed the nausea to some extent, but produced a soporific side-effect which, she said, was as bad as the nausea. What could one do?

"It's time to call in the experts," I suggested. "Ask Dr Paul B. Sheldon to step into the cockpit and testify."

The good sailor-doctor was brought up from his berth in the medicine chest and Liz read from his book *First Aid Afloat*.*

"Seasickness is classified under 'Medical Conditions—Usually Minor'. Mike, I've lost faith in the witness already."

"Proceed, please."

" 'The victim of seasickness does not behave as he does just to make your life difficult. He is, for the time being, not well. In fact his physiology may be so disturbed that he is in a state almost of shock, with a blood pressure so low that he may be actually unable to stand alone.' He then classifies the victims as 'the mildly afflicted', 'the distinctly greener looking individual' and 'the prostrated victim'. For each he offers homely advice like 'those of uncertain stomachs should stay out of the galley in rough weather' and 'keep yourself upwind from tobacco smokers' for the first type. The second type should lie down in the open air, and for 'the prostrated victim who is helpless almost from the start, nothing is as effective as getting him into a bunk and keeping him there'."

"Is that all?"

"More or less. No, here is the best advice of all. Are you listening? 'He [the sufferer] should not be tormented by hardier souls sounding off on the subject of *mal de mer*.' "

* *First Aid Afloat*, by Paul B. Sheldon (Yachting Publishing Corp.).

"Obviously a prejudiced witness. Call the next. Mr Eric C. Hiscock, Voyager Extraordinary."

Eric Hiscock's book *Cruising under Sail*, supplemented by *Voyaging under Sail*,* contains in explicit and economical prose virtually everything that a cruising man needs to know. It is bible and handbook on nearly every cruising yacht, and I have relied on it to advise me on everything from splicing 7-strand wire rope to how to provide toilet arrangements for a ship's cat.

Liz brought out *Cruising under Sail*.

"This witness classifies seasickness under 'Creature Comforts'. He states, 'Most people suffer in some degree from seasickness; a few unfortunates become completely incapacitated but the majority get their sea legs after a day or two at sea. . . . I do not believe that there is any cure apart from going to sea and staying there, but preventive pills have a remarkable effect in warding off sickness for a time.' He then also gives homely hints suggesting that stomach acidity caused by fats, alcohol and red meats is a major cause. He ends, 'You will almost certainly feel better once you have been sick, but avoid nauseating others; do it neatly and with as little fuss as possible over the lee side, and get someone to hold your heels, for a man overboard is much worse than a man seasick. If someone is laid up in his bunk with seasickness give him a supply of stout brown paper bags; they are tidier than a basin and are less likely to upset whoever has to dispose of them!' " Liz sniggered. "I've caught you out."

"What do you mean?"

"You forgot brown paper bags on your lists."

"The ants ate them. Inadmissible observation, anyway. There being no further evidence, I declare the hearing ended. It is clear that even expert witnesses are completely at sea. There is only one certain cure—cited, incidentally, by neither witness—and that is solid land underfoot."

By that time we had reached Inhassoro, and immediately another problem presented itself. We had no anchor. I managed to straighten out the big Danforth slightly and, as the seas and wind had died down altogether, dumped it hopefully over the side together with all the chain. Daniel, his wife, his bicycle,

* *Cruising under Sail* and *Voyaging under Sail*, by Eric C. Hiscock (Oxford University Press).

his wretched fish and the rest of his gear were ferried ashore. One should not assume one is a competent seaman until one has handled an 8ft dinghy with an African mammy and a bicycle aboard. She looked at the beach with hungry eyes, and when she reached it her reserve dropped for a moment and she turned to Daniel.

"I am never going on a boat again, do you understand? Never!"

For the second time Daniel had nothing to say.

Leaving the boys to play on the beach, and Liz aboard to keep an eye on the boat, I walked with Daniel and his wife into the village to settle accounts and say goodbye to this man who had been a prima donna, a clown, a wood-butcher, but who had above all stuck by us to help in our all difficulties, and whom I felt to be a comrade. But once money was mentioned he changed into a different person. His expression became secretive and cunning; he was consumed with avarice and cheated outrageously. Sickened by betrayal, I paid all he asked. I suppose he regarded it as compensation for the hardship he had endured.

All this took time which ought to have been spent finding an anchor. Anxious about the boat, I returned to the beach to check. *Walkabout* had vanished! For a moment I panicked. Then I spied a tiny dot lying offshore half a mile up the beach. I hared towards it. The dot was *Walkabout*, and when I climbed over the side from a borrowed dinghy I found Liz, metaphorically speaking, halfway up the mast. Soon after I had disappeared, she told me, a light breeze had sprung up, and *Walkabout* had slowly dragged her anchor along the shoreline. Liz blew the foghorn and shouted for help, then started thinking of wild schemes like throwing the tin trunk overboard on the end of a rope. Still *Walkabout* maintained her determined course back to B.D. Finally, when Liz had more or less resolved to throw herself overboard and swim for help, the anchor had snagged and the boat had stopped. Why didn't you start the engine? I asked. She said that she couldn't turn the key, and anyway didn't really understand the controls.

Another lesson learnt the hard way, I thought—must teach Liz to drive the boat. And Rachel? She had been perfectly happy colouring in, Liz assured me. If the boat went to the bottom Rachel would no doubt go with it, still colouring in.

I went ashore to buy an anchor from one of the small fishing boats. But in a place where one cannot buy an egg it is naïve to shop for anchors. Not one of the boats had a spare anchor. Eventually the skipper of the charter boat attached to the hotel kindly lent me one for the night. He regarded my plight with the sort of gloomy relish that the professional reserves for the bumbling amateur. I returned to the boat after dark with the borrowed anchor and the boys to find Liz climbing the mast again. *Walkabout* had started to drag once more.

Next day we sailed in search of an anchor. Somebody at Inhassoro had radioed a friend on Paradise Island and returned with the report that there was a good heavy anchor there. So to the island we sailed. Paradise Island (also known as Ilha de Santa Carolina) lies about 10 miles from Inhassoro in the middle of the large Bay of Bazaruto. The island itself is a place of little grace and interest, but Bazaruto Bay is a lovely stretch of water. It is formed by a chain of islands that runs parallel to the coast and encloses an area some 40 miles long and 15 miles wide. The waters are clear blue, and the floor is of white sand with occasional patches of coral. It is ideal for sailing and fishing; but it should not be attempted by craft with a draught of more than 4 feet unless sailed by someone with a good knowledge of tides and depths, for it is chequered with shoals.

The sail to Paradise Island provided one of those delicious contrasts that are the lot of the cruising man. A day and a half before we had been struggling in the darkness thinking of wreckages and life-rafts. Now we lipped over the dancing wavelets in a light breeze. Liz led the children in song and Kevin played his recorder. I experimented with the self-steering gear, which to my astonishment and delight actually steered the boat. We decided to dub him Muncher because of his unsociable habit of chewing dinghies that strayed under the stern.

We dropped our sick anchor in the centre of a large sand-patch some distance offshore. I had no detailed chart and was taking no chances. As we were unshipping *Crawlabout* a little Sunfish sailing dinghy skimmed across the water and a cheery voice called, "Need any help?"

"Can you give me a lift ashore?"

"Sure! Jump aboard."

When I was aboard my water taxi the skipper, who operated a fleet of little boats for hire, began to talk about the cyclone.

"We were protected here by Bazaruto, but even so it was pretty bad. That great motor launch you see there spent two days dodging around the island to keep in the lee. We heard a rumour that some nut with his family was caught up at B.D. That's you, I suppose?" He shook his head. "I never do business during January and February. The weather goes to pot. In fact, I won't allow my boats on the water at all during those months, and I send the family away to Rhodesia."

He was most helpful, tracked down the anchor (whose owner had gone to Inhassoro) and took me back to *Walkabout*. There I found Liz and the children involved in some sort of untidy struggle on the foredeck. I looked at Liz's brick-red face.

"You're halfway up the mast again, aren't you? Tell me the worst."

"It's anchor trouble again. While you've been gadding about on shore-leave your bloody anchor has been dragging the bloody boat right under the water."

What had happened, she told me, was that the wind had freshened—as it usually does in the afternoon in those parts—and the tide had turned against the wind. *Walkabout*, who can never decide whether to lie to wind or current in these circumstances, began sailing hither and thither, dragging her bent anchor behind her. Eventually the hook had seemed to catch on a coral and then, for some strange reason, the chain tautened and began to drag the bows under. Liz, assisted by Kevin and Mark, had sensibly let out some more chain. But a little later the bows again began to snub and they had let out yet more chain. When I arrived only a few feet of chain were left and they had, as it were, reached the end of their tether.

"You ought to see how strong it is. It just about jerked Mummy overboard," said Mark, accusingly.

"I know how strong it is," I said ruefully. "What I cannot understand is what is happening. There's only one way to find out. I'd better go down and look."

Donning a pair of goggles, I dived down. The water, about 40 feet deep, was perfectly clear. And there, round and round a great coral head, wound the anchor chain. *Walkabout*, in her indecisive mood, was sailing round the coral, with each circuit shortening the chain. She was literally sailing herself under. The obvious thing to do was to start the engine and, sailing the boat round the other way, unwind the chain. The only snag was that three people were needed—one to take up or slacken chain (a heavy job, clearly for me), one to handle the boat (again a job for me), and one with a pair of goggles to direct operations under water (who else but me?). This was ridiculous. *Walkabout* had a crew of six able bodies. I assembled them on the foredeck and addressed them as follows:

"Liz, I explained yesterday how to work the engine and tiller, so you work the boat. No 'buts'. It's a piece of cake. Kevin and Mark, you are more than little boys now, you are seamen. Take that chain and pull it in or out as I tell you. Use all your strength, but remember—always take a turn round the samson post first. Bruce, you help Kevin and Mark by holding the tail of the chain behind the samson post and keeping it tight. Rachel, you take this colouring book, go into the cabin, and don't come up until you're told to."

Having thus instilled into the crew a sense of Duty and Purpose, I started the engine, clapped on a pair of goggles and went over the side. Hanging on to the chainplate with one hand, my head was just level with the water, so I could tilt it downwards to see and upwards to speak.

"Forward and hard to port," I commanded the waterline in front of my nose.

Nothing happened. I raised my voice to a shout.

"Forward and hard to port."

Nothing happened.

"Forward and hard to port," I bellowed.

The boat lunged forward suddenly, hard to starboard. Arm stretched and toes streaming behind me, it was all I could do to hang on.

"Stop!" I screamed.

Nothing happened.

"Stop! Stop! Stop!" I screamed.

Nothing happened.

Far away on the foredeck Kevin and Mark began to shriek. Suddenly the boat stopped. Then went full astern.

"Stop!" I gurgled weakly. I was beginning to fill up with

sea-water and could not think of any new commands. Kevin and Mark began to shriek once more. The boat stopped. I clambered hurriedly out of the water before it could start again.

"What the devil is going on up here?"

"What do you mean?" said Liz indignantly. "I'm doing my best but I can't hear a word you're saying. You must speak clearly, not mutter under the water."

"Daddy, are the bows meant to be pulled under? Or are we supposed to do something? Because we can't, it's too strong," called Kevin.

"And," continued Liz, accusingly, "the controls don't work properly. The boat keeps rushing forwards when I want it to go backwards and the other way round."

I fought back a rising scream. And then a story flashed through my mind. Vasco da Gama, when he sailed on his first voyage of discovery, had a convict crew of such ignorance that they could not tell port from starboard. He hung a string of onions on one side of the boat and a string of garlic on the other. Thereafter the helmsmen were commanded to steer "to onions" or "to garlic".

"Bruce," I said firmly, "stand here in the cockpit by the tiller. When I shout 'lifebelt' you push the tiller right over to the lifebelt, and when I shout 'hand' you push it right over towards my hand. Got that?"

He nodded with great assurance.

Liz was demoted to the foredeck to take charge of the chain. Now began a comedy of Keystone Cops genre—slowly at first, then faster and faster, like frantic puppets. I put the engine in gear for a few moments, then shouted "lifebelt" and "chain out" and jumped over the side to find out how the chain lay. Just right. Now we had to go forward, but the other way, to unwind. I scrambled aboard and put the engine in "forward" for a few moments, and, shouting "hand" and "chain in", leapt overboard. Problem: chain had snagged on a coral ledge. Out again, astern, shout "lifebelt" and "chain out", plunge over the side. Chain free. Out, forward, "lifebelt", "chain in", overboard. Progress. Out, forward, "lifebelt", "chain in". In. Bad. Out. Astern. "Hand." "Chain out." In.

All at once the coral, disgusted with these silly antics, retired from the fray. The great niggerhead, as high as a two-storey house, toppled majestically towards the sea-bed like a slow-motion film. Broken at the base by the chain! Out and on to the foredeck, where I hauled the anchor aboard like a man possessed. We were free! We all stood panting and saying "Whew!" or words to that effect.

Suddenly Bruce pointed over my shoulder. "Look at those people on the boat. They're laughing at us, the big fat slobberites," he said furiously.

We had not really noticed them before. Half a dozen tanned figures lounging, drinks in hand, on the sundeck of a motor launch were enjoying the show. They laughed and pointed. We were all furious. Liz was livid.

"It's an absolute scream," she said, and held out a bloody hand.

"My God! What have you done?" I looked at her hand. The middle finger had been crushed between chain and stemhead. It looked nasty and gave her much pain for several days. I drew her towards the cabin to dress the wound. We met Rachel in the hatchway. She was waving a crayon and a book.

"Can I come out now? I finished colouring in and, Mummy, can we have tea now?"

For Rachel, embarking on a cruising career was clearly not the traumatic experience that it was for the rest of us.

Sailing back to Inhassoro with a brisk following wind, consuming orange juice and biscuits in the cockpit, we discussed our first day of cruising, wondering whether every day would bring similar excitements. Liz didn't think that she could take more than one crisis a week, say, and I felt that if our experiences so far counted for anything I should collect a coronary much sooner than if chained to an office stool.

Suddenly Liz asked, "What about the anchor? Was our trip worthwhile at least?"

"Er . . . I'm afraid not. The anchor is a genuine Danforth but it's too small. Only 30lb. It will do for the next few nights, but after our recent experiences I want the heaviest anchor I can lift. And none of these fancy designs like Danforths. I want an old-fashioned fisherman type. It will cost the earth, but I'm afraid we are going to have to order a 60-pounder from Beira and get it flown down in the fish-plane."

We had to wait for a week for that anchor, during which

time the weather was placid and there were no crises at all. The first thing we did was scour the village for fresh food. The sores were becoming quite a serious problem, especially with Bruce and Liz, and I now held surgery three times a day; at every surgery each member of the family needed at least one sore dressing. We were reluctant to administer antibiotics, knowing that the real solution was fresh food and dry wounds free from flies. Now that we were living aboard the last requirement could be partly fulfilled, but fresh food proved disappointing. Onions and potatoes could be had and a few green beans, which turned out to be bad, and one red letter day, eight very small eggs were carried tenderly aboard and broken into a pan under the anxious scrutiny of twelve greedy eyes.

Even fish was not too plentiful, although there was quite an important local fishing industry. In years past Inhassoro was known for its rich fishing grounds. For several miles along the beach beds of thick seaweed, shelving gently into deeper water, provided feeding and breeding grounds to support a large fish population. The local fishermen, using simple hand-nets and lines, could get all they needed. Then someone introduced the seine net, which was laid in a semi-circle away from the shore and hauled on to the beach. The catches were much larger and attracted outside interest. The next step was taken by a recluse Englishman who lived nearby. He invented a winch which enabled the nets to be hauled in much more rapidly. The catches were enormous and a canning factory was erected. But it could not last. Huge nets dragged thoughtlessly over the breeding grounds twice a day reduced the catch, in a few years, from a ton or more per haul to less than 100lb., and the average size of fish from about 8lb. to 1lb. And the poorer the catches became, the harder the fishermen worked the grounds, thereby further depleting the small fish population.

When we were there the canning factory was derelict. This sad story of fished-out waters was to be repeated at virtually every port we visited. Those who talk glibly of the vast untapped resources of the sea would be shocked to see how finite these resources are and how quickly they are being depleted.

The food at the hotel was also poor, but they kindly let us use the cold shower, which was blissful, and Liz was able to wash our clothes, which she said was also blissful; you didn't have to haul water from a well, it just ran out of a tap! Sometimes she and I would sit on the veranda for a coffee and a chat. Everyone said how worried they had been about us during the cyclone, but no one, I noticed, had made any effort to find out what had happened, either during or after. They preferred to issue grave warnings. The charter skipper, a bluff red-faced South African who drank like a fish, took gloomy pleasure in firing warnings, staccato.

"Seasickness can kill. Kill, like cholera." Or, "Twelve hundred feet of running rigging, you say. Who's going to help you handle it? That little boy?" And when I talked of the blue sea he held up a hand. "The sea is not blue; it's black. Black and bottomless."

Jolly company. In self-defence we decided that the whole village was slightly potty. What else could one expect with a few down-at-heel Portuguese, a handful of Rhodesian expatriates scratching a living from the meagre tourist trade and a tiny population of impoverished Africans? The only creature about with a sense of vigour and purpose was the large monkey. He nursed two burning ambitions: one was to bite Mark and the other was to get at the beer in the bar.

One day, when we were all sitting on the veranda, he broke free from his chain and came leaping over the wall, causing instant pandemonium. He landed on the table, scattering glasses and bottles. Then he seized Mark by the arm and gave him a savage bite. Mark screamed and everyone lunged, yelling, at the monkey. He sprang into the rafters and then, chattering with rage and excitement, landed on the bar counter, sweeping the glassware on to the floor. The barman fled with a yell. The monkey grasped a bottle of beer, and breaking the neck off drank thirstily.

"Grab him by the tail! They can't climb up their own tails," shouted someone. No one seemed inclined to follow this excellent advice, least of all the adviser. The monkey finished a second bottle of beer and closed his eyes in ecstasy. He opened them to see a stealthy hand approaching his tail. Furiously he bounded into the dining-room to indulge in an orgy of drunken destruction. From table top to table top he leapt, breaking open the tomato sauce, scattering the oil, smashing the vinegar. Each bottle he tasted. Then he took a swig of mustard. He didn't like that. Making curious huffing noises he raced back to the bar for a cooling draught of beer. And that was his undoing. The manager, a bolder soul than most, grasped him by the tail and carried him, shrieking piteously, back to his perch and chain.

Thereafter we avoided the veranda and spent most of our time settling in to our new home. And after five months of vagrancy it really felt like a home. True, it was very cramped, but at least there was a place for everything and a bed for everyone that the wind and sand could not reach. For the children we uncovered a special treasure, a box of new books that we had intended keeping for sea. They included various adventures of those Gallic heroes, Asterix and Tin Tin, which everyone could enjoy whether they could read or not. We listened to our tapes and played chess; Kevin and Mark became fanatics. Bruce attempted to bring further treasures aboard but I threw them off at once, together with a lot of other stuff like ant-nibbled blankets that were clearly redundant. This pruning of material possessions was becoming a religion. On the other hand, I was worried about money. The carpenter, the anchor and the time wasted had eaten into our resources, and I privately wondered whether we should be able to reach England that year.

One day the anchor arrived and the next morning, March 20th, we hoisted sail and started on a voyage that was to cover some 14,000 miles. The first port of call was to be Inhambane, about 180 miles to the south. It could not have been a less dramatic start. There was no one to wave goodbye, no storms or heavy seas, nothing of interest at all, in fact. The wind was so mild that it took most of the day to pick our way through the shoals of Bazaruto Bay. For the day's arithmetic lesson I taught Kevin and Mark some simple coastal navigation; how to read a chart, how to take compass bearings. In the late afternoon we passed Bazaruto lighthouse, and for the first time found ourselves in the open ocean.

Notwithstanding our skipper friend's black warning, it *was* blue. The intense translucent blue of deep tropical waters, so incredible that it cannot be imagined and once seen can never be forgotten. A swell as huge and placid as the downs lifted our little ship so gently that it could not be felt at all. Over the swell rode the smaller waves, which quietly rocked the boat.

I laid a course to clear the land with its attendant dangers and get out into the Mozambique current, which, I hoped, would lend a helping hand in our journey south. Then the whole family stripped off in the cockpit and had a shower, on three pints of fresh water; not a cat's lick but a proper shower sequence—wet, soap and rinse. This feat was achieved by means of a garden spray with a pressure container and an adjustable nozzle. A great step forward for mankind, it was unanimously agreed.

Now it is night, one o'clock in the morning, to be exact. The children are all fast asleep and Liz is meant to be too, but I expect she is awake. When I go below in an hour's time I shouldn't think I'll be able to close my eyes at all, let alone sleep. Right now I'm wedged comfortably in a corner of the cockpit. Above and slightly behind me, hissing loudly, is the Tilley lamp lashed to the mizzen mast to warn ships that *Walkabout* is in the Channel. By its bright light I am reading—Joshua Slocum's *Sailing Alone Around the World*,* of course, what else? He always read like this while his ship, *Spray*, sailed herself. He is probably responsible for luring more people to sea than anyone else, the mischievous old sailor. *Walkabout* is sailing herself too, close-hauled into a light wind; every time I look at the compass it is steady on course. Bless you, Muncher. We could not do without you. I can take some credit as well, can't I? I tell you, I really know how to sail at last. Very conscious that everything must be done in proper seamanlike fashion: ship's log, food and stores log, water log, fuel log, engine log and chronometer log—everything recorded, everything lashed tight. Perhaps it will wear off in due course and I'll become blasé, and that would be the most dangerous time, so I must watch myself. Because we are always alone at sea, and can never rely on anyone else. It is rather odd to think that there is not another soul for miles around. Odd, but pleasurable too. It is so peaceful, so . . . Solitude. That is the word. One can savour the solitude like old brandy, and like good brandy it relaxes one from the core outwards. The weather helps, too—being able to sit here in nothing but shorts and shirt, neither cool nor warm.

* *Sailing Alone Around the World*, by Joshua Slocum (Rupert Hart-Davis).

Two o'clock already! Time to call Liz. Just a turn round the foredeck to check for ships. They frighten me. Slocum was lost like that. Careful to clip on the safety harness. An iron rule for the lone night watch-keeper, no matter what the weather.

Liz was awake. And glad to go on deck because she was feeling a little queasy. Naturally, I could not sleep. One seldom can for the first night or two, and then one can never get enough. At 4 a.m. Liz called Kevin. It had been decided that Kevin and Mark would take the 2-hour dawn watch alternately, but for the time being they were in training, and stood watch with Liz or myself. They had to learn how to watch out for ships and judge whether we were on a collision course; every five minutes they had to take a compass bearing on the ship and enter it in the deck log. If in doubt they were to call me.

Next morning we lost the wind and spent most of the day with the sails slatting. It was a horrible sound, and the wear on the gear was much worse than when the boat was sailing normally. A new problem. Obviously I did not know how to sail at all. The children were given lessons as usual in the morning and in the afternoon were banished to the cockpit with safety harnesses, there to keep very quiet. Or as quiet as it is possible for small human beings to be. Liz and I tried unsuccessfully to sleep. Without the wind it was too hot, and both of us were running slight fevers from infections. That night we were very tired but still could not sleep, because now there was too much wind. We tore along for half the night and then dropped the main for fear of passing Inhambane, and without the sail we rolled badly.

At dawn we had our first close encounter with a ship. It frightened me out of my sleepy wits. I was on watch with Mark, who caught sight of a tanker on the horizon. We were sailing west towards land, and the ship was heading south. Mark duly took a bearing on it. It did not need a second bearing, though, to tell us that we were on a collision course, for the ship was sailing at great speed. I called Liz to bring the flares, and altered course to achieve the fastest point of sailing and get out of the way. By that time it was only a few hundred yards off. It was incredible how quickly a smudge on the horizon had become a menacing great tanker. I started the engine, and

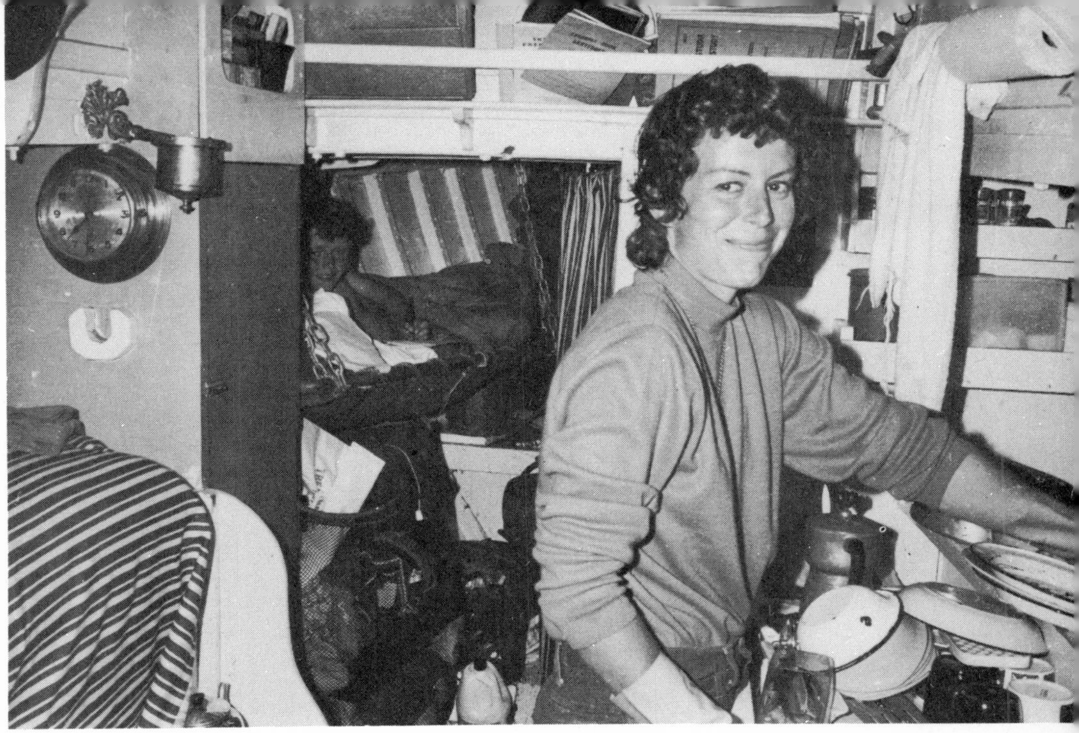

Liz grins triumphantly after a successful dinner

There was enough space below if we took it in turns to breathe. Bruce, Mark and Rachel settle down for the night, Rachel in her bunk on the engine cover

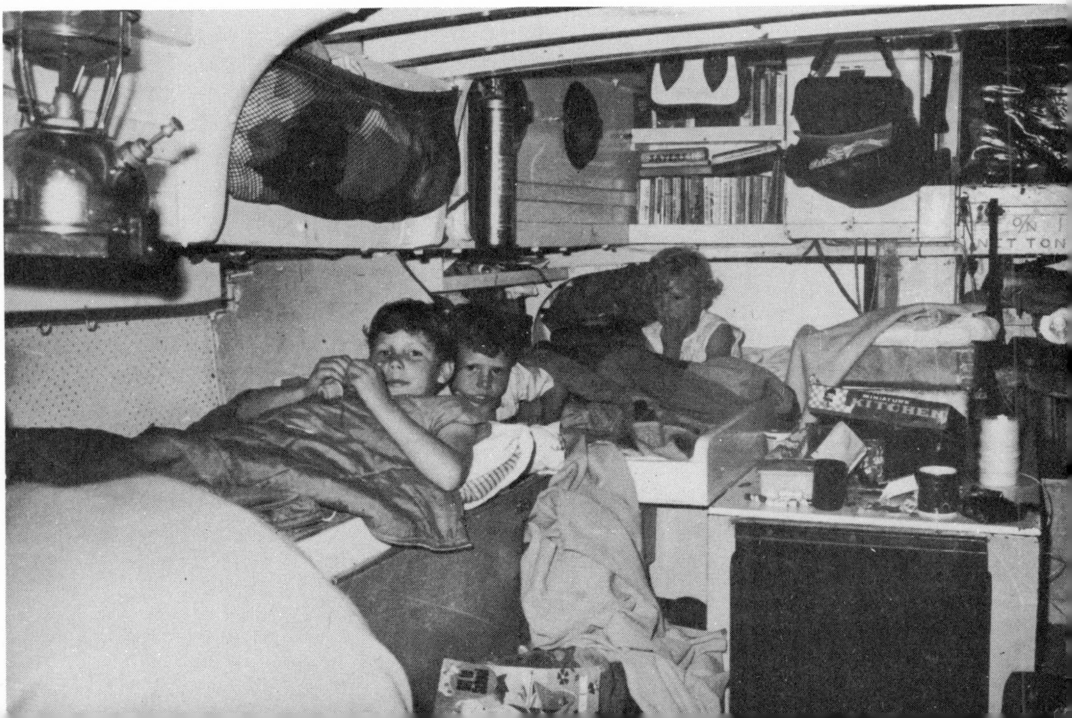

In port *Walkabout* tended to become a floating slum

Trade-wind sailing; genoa set as spinnaker boomed out to starboard, mizzen staysail to port

at *Walkabout*'s highest speed we scurried across its bows. The tanker passed a couple of hundred feet astern of us but it seemed no more than ten. Later we learned that this was by no means a dangerous encounter, but it left us all shaken.

"We could hear every beat of its engines," I recorded incredulously in the log, and Bruce declared (untruthfully) that he had seen the captain in his cap on the bridge.

A little later Liz spotted the sad, rusty little buoy that marks the outer edge of the bar at Inhambane. Inhambane lies 14 miles up a tidal estuary; the channel is tortuous and the bar has a bad reputation. *Walkabout*'s former Owner had advised us to batten down all hatches and cross the bar with the engine opened to full throttle. But there was a fair wind and we wanted to sail in style, not motor everywhere. Since that miserable night near B.D. everybody had taken an intense dislike to the engine with its noise and smell. We crossed the bar—which was rough, as we had been warned—and continued to navigate the river under sail, meticulously following the directions in *Africa Pilot* and on the chart that Kevin had traced. Line up buoy No. 3 with the beacon on the hill until two beacons on the hill behind are one above the other, then turn left on course 191° until the third beacon lines up with buoy No. 5, until . . . It was like a parlour game and I left it to Liz, who played it better than I did.

It worked beautifully until we found ourselves in the upper reaches of the estuary. Here one had to follow a course that kept in line two great concrete pillars, built on sandbanks in the river. This we did with naval precision, but we began to get the feeling that all was not well when the echo-sounder showed a depth of 15 feet, then 10 feet and then 7 feet. The feeling was reinforced when an African fisherman climbed out of his little boat and ambled through the water not 20 yards ahead of the bows.

"I don't care what the *Pilot* says," I declared. "We are not going there."

We tacked, and cautiously picked our way by sight and soundings for the remaining few miles, and finally dropped anchor in front of the town of Inhambane, terribly pleased with ourselves at having made our first port, and under sail at that.

When the officials came aboard to clear us I told them about the concrete pillars luring us on to the shoals. The assistant port captain laughed merrily and nudged his companion in the ribs.

"Another one caught, eh! The last one went aground, ho! ho! Those marks mean nothing, my friend. They are redundant, out of date. The sandbanks have shifted."

"You mean all the marks? The pillars, the beacons . . . ?"

"All of them," he replied gaily. "All out of date. For years now they mean nothing at all."

"Oh," I said faintly.

"But did you see whether my buoy lights are working?" he asked anxiously. "I haven't been out to the bar for months and hardly any boats come here any more. I hope the lights are working, because only the buoys mark the channel."

"None of them are working, my friend," I said with great relish.

They nodded resignedly, as if this was what they had expected all along, and left us.

The old town looked fascinating, and the bustle on the waterfront and the fresh food beckoned. But only one thing mattered—sleep. We sent the children ashore in the dinghy to seek that luxury from another world—an ice-cream. The four of them put on clean clothes and donned their best straw hats; Kevin and Mark took an oar each and in high spirits they rowed away. The boat became quiet and lay so still at her anchor that she might have been a church. And we fell fast asleep.

VI

IT SEEMED THAT I had hardly shut my eyes when *Crawlabout* bumped against the side and a babble of treble voices, followed by a clatter on deck, told us that the tribe were back. We cowered under the sheets, hoping the invaders would be overcome by respectful silence at the sight of their parents apparently sunk in a sleep of exhaustion. Not a bit of it. A broadside of shrill, angry voices blasted us without so much as a warning shot. They were upset, it appeared, by a number of things; they couldn't find any ice-cream, and anyway they didn't want to cross the road because the cars frightened them and they had forgotten how to, and on the way back Bruce had insisted on spearing an imaginary fish with a stick and upset the trim and wouldn't listen to Mark, who had told him again and again, and so naturally Rachel's hat had fallen into the water and of course it was Mark who had to get it out for her while Bruce obstinately continued to stab the water even when Kevin was thumping him, and who was in charge of the dinghy anyway?

And who indeed, I wanted to know? Who, for example, had made the painter fast? And Kevin said he'd handed it to Mark and Mark said Bruce was making trouble again and I wanted to know if the painter was fast and never mind about Bruce and never mind at all, I'll see for myself and . . . it's gone! There it is, floating away on the tide. Really, Liz, don't be ridiculous, there is no time to find my swimming costume, underpants will do. Except that they are not designed to resist a racing dive from the stern. But it's the dinghy that's important, and if the underpants have sunk under this dirty water it's too bad, and I don't care if we are the only boat here and the whole town is watching from the jetty this afternoon; an escape attempt by *Crawlabout* has been foiled, no thanks to you crummy lot of unable seamen. Heads hang and there is—at last and just for a moment—exquisite silence.

But that, effectively, put an end to sleep for the afternoon, and so we all went ashore to explore. We found Inhambane to be a delightful little town. It is old—dating back, I believe, to the first landing made by Vasco da Gama in what is now Mozambique—and much of the architecture has an Arabic flavour underlying the Portuguese structures. So too do the narrow streets. As an old connoisseur of back streets I sniffed the mixture of spicy aromas that oozed from under doors as eagerly as a cat on the prowl. The desire of us all for fresh food amounted to a craving, and that evening we gorged on eggs fried in butter, tomatoes, cole slaw, cucumber, carrots, all washed down with red wine and followed by oranges, bananas, pawpaw and delicate pastries, which the Portuguese are very good at. The strong coffee brewed from freshly-ground beans was heaven on earth.

For the rest of our stay we concentrated on finding and consuming fresh food. Every day we would visit the municipal market, where the African women settled down in the shade of the mango trees with their wares spread around them and passed the day, chewing betel nut and shrilling to their neighbours. Plenty of good cheap food flowed into the market from the countryside, which, unlike the land further north, supported a fair-sized population on its rich, red soil watered by frequent streams. It was prettier than Inhassoro, too; low wooded hills rolled right down to the sea, while great groves of coconut palms flooded the valleys. A land of milk and honey, one might say, except that the milk was missing—much to the children's disappointment. Cows and coconuts, I have noticed, do not mix well. I do not know why.

If fresh food was a delicacy, the abundance of sweet water was a luxury. One evening the whole family clattered into the best hotel in Inhambane and I called for the manager. A pleasant, plump man bustled in with a professional smile of welcome on his face. As his eyes took in the bleached clothing, the worn sandals and the frayed sponge bags dangling from our wrists, his smile became a little fixed.

"Can I help you?"

"Er . . . we should like a bath. Would that be possible?" I said, conscious all at once that perhaps Liz was right in asserting that our best clothing was fit only for the best dustbin.

"A room with a bath? Certainly that can be arranged."

"No, er, no room. Just the bath, please."

His face froze for just a moment, then to his credit the welcoming mask of mine host was donned again, and when I explained the circumstances he went out of his way to be helpful. A little later we were ushered into a neat tiled bathroom hung about with laundered towels. I turned the tap and we gazed, first in fascination and then in guilt, as the hot water gushed out. Gallons and gallons of it flooded into the bath; we felt positively licentious. The sense of sin mounted as the bath filled and at last I could bear it no longer. I turned it off. A quarter-full bath was quite wasteful enough! For a cruising yachtsman, flowing hot water is holy.

For Liz perhaps the greatest gift of all was the laundry, which lay in a courtyard off one of the narrow streets. Half of the courtyard was taken up by the large stone washtubs over which plump girls scrubbed and chattered, while round the perimeter of the yard lay the open ironing alcoves where they swung the heavy charcoal irons through the air to heat them. The owner of the business, a white-haired old African, presided over his prattling girls with grave dignity. Every other day he would send one of them with a basket of beautifully laundered clothes on her head to the end of the jetty, where Kevin or Mark would be waiting in the dinghy to exchange it for a bundle of dirty washing.

I spent hours at the pavement cafés nursing a cup of coffee and chatting with the locals. The first thing that strikes a visitor from Rhodesia or South Africa is that there is no colour bar. In the shops, on both sides of official counters and at work there is no sign that Africans are discriminated against, though they naturally form the bulk of the poorer population. In the gangs of youths who roam from café to café, showing off their latest clothes and shiny motor scooters, complexions range from the light-skinned, almost Aryan type of Portuguese to pure African, and every strain of dilution between can be seen.

This casual blending of the races is not confined to the younger generation; it is evident, though to a lesser extent, in their elders too. Only the Indians, clannish and secretive, remain aloof, while they exploit the country through their stranglehold on commerce.

The Portuguese government have for many years declared a policy of racial integration and harmony. But such a policy cannot be enforced by law, as the Americans and indeed the British have demonstrated. Only an intimate rapport between the races on a personal level can make the policy successful, and what is more personal and intimate than miscegenation? In every case of conquest a major fear of the vanquished is that the conquerors will steal their women. Yet this is one of the surest ways of overcoming the superior military strength of the conquerors. And while it is galling to have one's women stolen, it is far worse in the long run to have them spurned, for this means that they and all the conquered race with them are despised.

The evidence that many Portuguese do not despise the Africans could be seen walking in every street, and after Rhodesia the complete lack of racial tension was refreshing. That at least is the situation in the larger towns. In the bush, and especially in the north of the territory, it is quite another story. There the policy has failed to penetrate, or perhaps it was applied too late, and the Frelimo wage a bitter and damaging guerilla war against the authorities. Most people, including the Chief of the local P.I.D.E. (Policia International e de Defesa do Estado, the secret police), assured me that the Portuguese were winning. But a few more thoughtful individuals, the port captain among them, wondered why, if the Frelimo were losing, the Portuguese army was growing and the tax burden becoming even heavier. They felt it could only end with the loss of the Portuguese territories.

The port captain was not the ogre I had been led to expect when everyone had warned me that we should never get clearance from Portuguese waters. He was a charming man who spoke perfect English and dismissed the bogy of clearance with a casual signature. He told us that, with the building of the new tarred coastal road from Lourenco Marques, the importance of Inhambane as a port had steadily diminished, for it was no longer worth a ship's while to sail up the long, difficult estuary. Only fishing boats used the port now, and we were the second yacht to call in six months. He came aboard for drinks and was very nice about Muncher eating up his dinghy's foredeck, and afterwards even offered to have the big

Danforth repaired and the batteries charged in the official workshops. I gratefully accepted.

So it was that, when the gale struck suddenly the next evening, I was unable to start the engine. We had been lulled into the dangerous supposition that the estuary was always the placid anchorage we had known, instead of bearing in mind that any bit of sea anywhere in the world is totally unpredictable. The wind came whistling down the river, and within an incredibly short space of time waves were slopping on to the deck. The sun-awning over the cockpit ripped in two, and the mizzen mast began to hum like a tuning fork. The anchor could have held, perhaps, against the wind alone, but not against the tide as well, running strongly then with the wind. *Walkabout* once again humped the chain across her sturdy bows and dragged her anchor determinedly down river. There was no time to bend on sails, and the engine, as I have said, could not be started. So I dropped the second anchor, nicely straightened and with the shank heavily reinforced. If *Walkabout* slowed at all I could not detect it. The holding ground was evidently very poor. On we went, past the port workshops, past the convent, past the sports club and on towards the end of the town. We could see now where *Walkabout* was heading. A submerged sandbank, revealed by the waves breaking over it, lay directly in our path. There was no danger to life, but on the other hand *Walkabout* would be damaged, perhaps severely, and there was absolutely nothing we could do. I gnawed my knuckles and cursed all anchors, and then cursed myself for not having a third one to hand. Suddenly, to our enormous relief, *Walkabout* stopped. We were no more than 20 yards from the sandbank.

The gale died down during the night, and the following day I ferried the heavy batteries aboard—it took most of the afternoon, so far had she dragged—and decided to move back to our former anchorage straight away. Not perhaps a wise decision, for little of the afternoon remained. But the job would not, I assured Liz, take more than half an hour, and 20 yards from the stern the waves growled softly over the sandbank. So I started the engine, and leaving the tiller to Liz went forward to winch up the anchors, one of which was on the chain and the other on nylon warp. I tackled the chain first, and strangely heavy it seemed. So much so that I called Liz to leave the tiller to Kevin and come and help. We both heaved on the handle of the windlass and on the nylon warp until we had no breath left to curse the anchor and our bodies were covered in sweat.

At last *Walkabout* swung broadside to the current and began to drift downstream, indicating that both anchors had broken free. I ran aft and showed Kevin how to work the engine controls and keep her heading upstream without moving too fast, while we got the anchors aboard. He grasped the idea quickly and I left him to look after the boat while Liz, Mark and I raised the chain, inch by inch. Long before we saw the anchors we guessed they were entangled. But I was not prepared for the knitted ball of chain, rope and anchors that finally broke the surface; it weighed over 200 lb. It was too large to pass between the bowsprit and its shroud, so I started to unravel it, partly on and partly under the water, head down, hanging by the heels. Mark patiently held the torch and passed things, occasionally making sensible suggestions. Liz pulled sail halyards and lengths of rope which had been co-opted too help. It was a beastly job and it took a long time. By the time the last rope was coiled and the last anchor cleared the church bells could be heard faintly chiming nine o'clock. Kevin had been motoring to and fro for three hours, judging his position by the street lights. Hungry and cross we returned to our original anchorage, and with a silent prayer I dropped the hook. Praying over a sinking hook appealed to me just then.

In the cabin we indulged in what can only be described as a hate session on anchors. Even Rachel, who seldom knew and never cared what ocean we were in, was complaining of "horrid old anchors that make us late for supper". I certainly learn the hard way, I reflected. A second anchor should clearly never be dropped over the bows after the first one. It should be placed in the tender and carried away before dropping, just as Eric Hiscock recommends. Another point had also been driven home, namely, that for a cruising family the size of the yacht is limited not so much by the size of the sails as by the weight of the ground tackle they can handle. This means, for a man and wife crew with children too young to provide extra muscle power, an anchor in the region of 60lb.

Our time in Inhambane flew. I had planned a stop of four

days, but in fact we stayed ten. That, I reckon, is an average ratio of resolution to reality for a cruising yachtsman. The children whiled away pleasant days doing nothing very strenuous. Kevin and Mark rowed round in *Crawlabout*, and Bruce and Rachel fished from the boat or played along the shore. On a couple of occasions we gave way to popular demand and put them on the motor ferry that plies between Inhambane and Maxixe, on the opposite side of the estuary. To the children sailing boats were old hat and they thought the ferry very glamorous, particularly when the friendly skipper broke his normal run to bring them right over to *Walkabout*. Liz and I preferred the sailing dhows that still compete with the ferry. They are open boats about 30ft overall with twin masts and lateen rigs. They are not allowed to use the jetty, so the skipper and his crew carry their passengers aboard from the shore, the men astride their shoulders and women on a modest "chair" formed by two men gripping one another's arms in a square. These boats are crude and their sails are more patch than cloth, but they sail like the devil. I was so impressed by the lateen rig that I promised Mark that I would fit one to *Crawlabout*.

But there came a day when I said, "Thus far and no further". Bruce's rubbish was thrown overboard—a small collection, this time, for the poor lad was under the weather with his rash of boils—and we went alongside the jetty to take on good water, replacing the brackish, slightly putrid liquid from the well at B.D. It was there that we first encountered the International Brigade of Lookers. At every place in the world where a cruising yacht comes alongside, the Lookers will swiftly gather to stand and stare for hours and hours. Cruising yachts' folk must just get used to it, for the Lookers are not malicious or even intentionally discourteous. For them the yacht is a free show and the "yachties" are not altogether real, rather like circus performers. The Lookers at Inhambane were a gay lot, and presently a group of youngsters arrived with a guitar to serenade us. But when the time came for showers (which we always took in the cockpit, behind a sail screen) they drove us below to sponge the children down in the cabin. Nothing daunted, the Lookers peered down the hatch, and catching sight of Mark standing in a basin exclaimed, "Look! There's one that looks like a skinned rabbit." This was too much, and we erected anti-Looker screens forthwith.

Very early next morning, April Fool's Day, we motored out to sea again on the ebbing tide, bound for Durban. There was not enough wind to sail, but even so the bar was surprisingly rough and Liz straightaway reverted to her customary feeling of seasickness. The children recovered after we had crossed the bar. All day we tacked slowly into a light headwind, heading out to sea to pick up the favourable current.

On Easter Sunday, as we lay in a landless expanse of blue ocean, the Easter Bunny did not seem wholly credible, so we called in the services of an Easter Dolphin, who obligingly hid chocolate Easter eggs in the dinghy, under the sails and behind the life-raft. The children eagerly ferreted them out in the dawn watch and consumed the vile, sticky things before breakfast. We gathered that they were no longer troubled by seasickness.

For the greater part of the voyage to Durban the winds were infuriatingly light and variable and the seas lumpy. The motion of the boat was very irregular, and for the first time I was affected by it; not seasickness but indigestion, caused, I think, by bracing the stomach muscles against the next roll.

The children proved very adaptable, and we soon settled into a routine. They were on galley duty every other day, Kevin and Rachel one day and Mark and Bruce the next. Those on duty were required to do the washing up, clear the cabin and pump water into the head tank—280 strokes of the wing pump filled the 3 gallon head tank—and this was noted in the log. Those not on galley duty were kept busy with lessons.

The best part of the day was after supper, when Liz was washing up and the children were in their bunks; then I would read aloud to them a chapter or two from that delightful book *The Hobbit* by Professor Tolkien. Reading aloud to the family is an entertainment that has been overwhelmed for a couple of generations by television and other outside stimuli, but it is a pleasant pastime and one that we have kept up since.

The children's safety was something that worried us a good deal at first. The inflexible rule was that anybody leaving the cockpit had to wear a safety harness, regardless of the weather. A heavy steel rope was strung between the masts, and the children could clip on to this and slide along like a dog on a leash. Liz and I wore safety harnesses when the weather was rough or whenever we were alone on deck, particularly during night watches. Life-jackets, we decided, are a complete waste of time. They are too uncomfortable to enforce wearing, especially in the heat, and while a child drowned may be worse than a child afloat but lost, a child tied to a rope is better than either.

For us the main problem was sleep, for after the cooking, the navigation, the lessons, the general sailing of the boat and the watches there were not many hours of the day left. We found it impossible to remain awake for four hours of darkness at a stretch, and at Liz's suggestion we reduced it to two. Then, of course, there was not enough time during the off-watch to sleep.

On the fifth day the sky darkened and the wind freshened from the east. *Walkabout* roared along at great speed, and during the night I dropped the mainsail. The next day we sighted, for a short time, the distant crags of Zululand, and the weather continued to deteriorate. By the afternoon the wind, which had fortunately backed behind us to the north-east, was strong enough to leave white streaks of foam down the backs of the waves. The large jib had had the hanks torn out, and we were down to the smallest working jib and mizzen. It was obvious that we were in for our first serious gale at sea.

Hitherto, the gales we had experienced were what might be termed "yachtsmen's gales". They were winds that had reached Gale Force 8 (34–40 knots) for short periods rather than winds which had sustained this strength continuously and gusted into higher strengths from time to time. Moreover, they had all occurred within sight of land and within easy reach of it; and while this is certainly more dangerous in real terms, in psychological terms weathering one's first gale alone at sea is much more terrifying.

I was frightened, though I tried not to show it (which did not deceive Liz), and called on Eric Hiscock for advice. Liz read from the hatchway the opening remarks to Chapter 18, "Management in Heavy Weather".

> " 'Everyone who has read the small-boat classics'—here he cites some—'must surely be convinced that a decked yacht of good design, strongly built and soundly rigged, will

survive a severe gale no matter how small she may be, provided that she is in deep water . . . and is properly handled. It is therefore more often lack of confidence in themselves than in their yachts which causes many sailing men to worry. . . .' There you are, love, there is no need for us to worry. In fact, we are lucky. Listen! 'Fortunate indeed is the man who early in his sailing career encounters and successfully weathers a hard blow.' "

I privately agreed with that, but felt there was no need for unseemly haste; next week or even next month would do.

Liz continued reading from the sub-chapter "Procedures under Gale Conditions".

" ' . . . should therefore be regarded only as suggestions on which to base one's procedure.

" 'There are four ways of dealing with gales. The yacht may be hove-to under sail; she may lie ahull, i.e., be left to look after herself with no sail set; she may run before under reduced sail or bare poles, perhaps with drag ropes out astern; or she may lie to a sea anchor.' "

I listened carefully to Liz as she read to the end of the discussion on each of these four methods. Sea anchors were not deemed to be good practice in the majority of conditions and I recalled that most authorities nowadays agree on this point. For that reason we had no sea anchor, so this method was out. Which of the other three methods to use depends largely on whether you want to go (or can go) downwind, or whether you want to go (or have to go) upwind, or whether you don't care a damn and retire to your bunk with a bottle of whisky to leave the yacht to take care of herself. The last method is not as irresponsible as it sounds. But I wanted to go downwind. When running from a gale there is a lively controversy whether to slow the yacht up by trailing warps, or fly as much sail as the yacht will carry. Bernard Moitessier, in *Cape Horn, The Logical Route,** advocates the latter method, controlling the speed of the yacht by sliding down the face of the waves at an angle. He writes convincingly, claiming that he was inspired in

* *Cape Horn, The Logical Route*, by Bernard Moitessier (Adlard Coles).

his hour of need by the wonderful Argentinian yachtsman, the late Vito Dumas. I think this depends on the yacht herself and how she behaves under various conditions, but I favoured Moitessier's method and decided to try it.

By this time the wind was snatching off the tops of the waves. I dropped the mizzen, leaving only the small jib, and we slowed down to a controllable speed. Half an hour later we were again charging downwind like a runaway horse, so I changed down to the tiny storm jib, made of canvas as heavy as plywood, and sheeted the sail in hard. It was heavy work on the foredeck, and by the time I had finished night was falling. It was time to get the children down below.

All this time they had been in the dinghy, which was carried right way up on the cabin top. A wild elation had seized them, a sort of primitive response to the wildness of the elements. They shrieked when the wind howled and yelled at the wave tops that broke alongside. They hurled themselves at each other and noticed no pain. They were virtually out of control, and it took Liz some time to tame them and get them down below. Once in the cabin and out of the wind they calmed down quickly. Liz heated some tinned stew, fed everyone quickly and put them to bed. Then she closed down the heavy hatches, locked them tight and came into the cockpit.

In the cockpit I was nursing the tiller and two worries. The first was a navigational problem. To the west of us lay the notorious rock-bound coast of Zululand, where only a year before a yacht had been wrecked and two lives lost; to the south lay Durban, too close to run straight for and risk being swept past in the powerful Agulhas current. There were no lighthouses to show us the shore, and yet it was too risky to head out to sea for fear of again being swept past Durban. I decided to head in to the coast until the echo-sounder showed 15 fathoms, then head away for a couple of hours before turning back again, and in this way zigzag downwind. My second fear was of being run down by ships, for I could see, from the size of the waves against the night sky, that they were already large enough to conceal us completely in the troughs. We brought out the flares and the home-made spotlight, and, notwithstanding the poor batteries, switched on the navigation lights.

Throughout the night we stood hour watches only, for the

strain of holding the tiller as *Walkabout* careered down the waves was exhausting. It was Liz who discovered later in the night that *Walkabout* handled herself perfectly with hardly more than a steadying touch on the tiller. With the storm jib backed and the dodgers acting as mizzen sails she was beautifully balanced, and sailed herself with the wind on the quarter *à la* Moitessier. After a time I realised that *Walkabout,* as always, knew more about sailing than I did and was in no danger. Nevertheless, it was unnerving not to be able to see the seas but simply to hear the roaring crescendo of an approaching wave, until suddenly we were caught in the crest and hurled forward while the white water boiled up over the gunwales. The wind was blowing so hard that we could lean back with all our weight against a bulging dodger as though it were a stiff cushion. Throughout the blow *Walkabout* behaved like the great lady she is.

Once a crest smacked down on us from the dark. Gallons of water poured down into the cabin through a gap between the washboards and hatch cover, and I heard Rachel squealing with rage as her bunk was flooded. Liz must have dried her and put her to sleep in another bunk, for she soon became quiet. The same wave had dealt Muncher a hefty blow, and when I looked aft the wind vane was lying askew. Three out of the four bolts holding down the main bearings had been sheared off. I was afraid the last bolt would break, so, waiting for a relatively calm period, I crawled out on to Muncher with a rope in my teeth and secured the vane.

The wind reached a climax just before dawn, and when the darkness lifted I wished it had not. The seas were huge. *Walkabout* had ridden them so calmly during the night that I had had no idea of their true size. I am still hazy on this point. It seemed when we were lying lulled in a trough as though the advancing crest towered well over the top of the masts, but this may have been an illusion. Later on we were to get thrashed far more severely in other gales, but the height of the seas never matched those of our standard, "the Cape St Lucia gale".

The children came out, fresh after a good night's rest, though they all complained of wet bunks. They were frightened by the seas at first, but when they realised that the waves always raced under, not over, us we had a repeat performance of the previous evening's riot. In truth we all became a little riotous. It was impossible to resist the exhilaration of swooping along on a roaring crest, riding nature's grand roller coaster.

The wind abated rapidly in the morning, and a few hours later I was able to snatch a sun sight. I was distressed to discover that we were apparently being swept past Durban in the Agulhas current. Apart from the problem of beating back against the current we had no charts for the coast further south. I decided to motorsail to Durban, but the batteries had been flattened by the navigation lights and the engine would not even turn over. Once I tried, twice, and on the third attempt Rachel's guardian angel turned the crankshaft—a single turn—and that excellent B.M.C. engine sneezed and started. This was just as well, for within the hour the wind had died away completely and all that was left of the gale was a mild swell.

"Look out for Durban, everybody! The first person to see it gets an extra pint of milk."

Six pairs of eyes gazed eagerly into the haze for an hour, and then another, and then . . .

"I can see skyscrapers," cried Kevin.

"Nonsense," I said. "The *Pilot* says the Bluff is prominent."

But Kevin was right, and later we found that nearly always skyscrapers are the most remarkable feature of a city, whatever the *Pilot* may say. The *Africa Pilot* also says that pilotage is compulsory for all vessels entering Durban, so we hoisted the flags and stood off in the roads waiting for a pilot. After an hour the pilot vessel came out of the narrow harbour entrance, and to our relief made straight for us. We could not wait to get in to meet my sister, who lived in Durban, and to rest after our Adventurous Voyage and Mighty Struggle with the Storm. The pilot passed by without even acknowledging our presence, and carried on towards a big cargo ship. Obviously the pilots had no interest in small boats, we decided, and as it was getting late, we would go straight in. Durban is the busiest port in South Africa, but the harbour entrance is so narrow that only one large vessel can pass at a time, and a rigorous system of signals controls the traffic. We observed the signal system (which is detailed in the *Africa Pilot*) and, feeling rather pleased with ourselves, entered the harbour.

No sooner were we inside than a large police launch bore

down on us. I stopped and waited. The launch came alongside, smashing into *Walkabout*'s toe-rail and two middle stanchions, and a pilot jumped aboard.

"Did you get permission to enter?" he demanded angrily. And then, because we simply stared at him in bewilderment, he went on irritably, "Do you speak English?"

I said that I did and he directed me, not to the yacht basin, but to what appeared to be a derelict dredger moored in the middle of the harbour, and ordered us to tie up alongside.

"Customs, Immigration and Health will come and clear you in due course," he told us. "Until then you are not to leave your boat, or move it. I'll arrange a place for you in the yacht basin."

He climbed over to the launch and left us feeling rather crushed. Some time later the Customs launch appeared, and a small weasel-faced official with a thick Afrikaans accent boarded us. He handed me a sheaf of forms and on these I declared, and Liz declared, and every child declared, that he/she/we had nothing to declare; no liquor, no pets, no drugs, no jewels, no uncut diamonds, no firearms, no Indian saris (very particular about saris, are the South Africans). The official looked at all the forms unhappily. He seemed to have something on his mind.

"Have you any literature aboard?" he said at length.

"Literature?"

"Yes . . . you know . . . literature."

He made it sound like vulture droppings, and suddenly I realised what he was driving at. But I was not going to let him off the hook.

"You mean books? Certainly, we have various kinds, the children's school-books and . . ."

"No, no! Lit-er-rat-ture," he said desperately. He was visibly embarrassed, and glanced at Liz and the children. Then, as Liz turned away for a moment, he leaned forward and surreptitiously moved his hands in an hourglass shape of the female form. "Literature, you know . . .?" he said, man to man.

"Oh no!" I exclaimed in a shocked voice. "With young children aboard, really!"

"Of course, I understand. I have children of my own." He was actually blushing faintly as he hurriedly took his leave.

That was the only light note struck by heavy-handed South African officialdom in its dealings with us. After the Customs man left no one came to see us that evening, or that night, or indeed the following day.

The children became increasingly resentful, and I was anxious about the boat, for the main bilge pump had broken. A lot of water had been taken aboard during the blow, mainly through deck leaks, and the level in the bilges had risen to the cabin floor. Eventually we formed a chain and emptied the boat with buckets. Then, regardless of possible official censure, we launched the dinghy and I went ashore.

No berth had been arranged in the yacht basin, and in fact nobody knew anything of *Walkabout*. Once I found the manager of the company who leased the basin, however, he was most helpful. Getting the boat cleared required that I should visit several authorities in various parts of the city, and it was not until after midnight that the job was done. We were declared prohibited immigrants and restricted to the Port of Natal. I was told that this was the usual procedure with visiting yachtsmen.

Visiting yachtsmen, we found, were unwelcome in Durban, partly because there is little free space in the harbour and partly because Durban's hospitality had been abused in the past by yachtsmen who came for a month and stayed for a couple of years to earn money, for there is plenty of money in that booming town. The locals also claimed that visiting yachtsmen left bad debts behind, and it only takes one or two incidents like that to give the breed a bad name. We found the atmosphere disagreeable and the racial tension between blacks, whites and Indians noticeably unpleasant.

But that was later. Our first interest (after twelve hours' dreamless sleep) was, as usual, food. My sister was out of town so we took the children in tow and, as a great treat, went in search of an eating house, huddling fearfully at traffic lights like country mice on their first visit to the city.

After the meal I lit my pipe and wondered how to broach to Liz the subject uppermost in my mind. Durban, I knew, was a crisis point in the voyage. We had completed the test run, as it were, and had taken a thrashing. Liz had suffered more than any of us, and it would be perfectly reasonable for her to call the whole thing off. I fully expected her to do so. We were still within the ambit of family, friends and familiar terrain, and I could easily sell the boat and get a job.

"Well, that's that," I began abruptly. "Something to tell one's grandchildren about."

"What on earth are you talking about?" said Liz.

"The voyage. Exciting enough, but hardly practical, is it? I mean, the lack of space and the seasickness and the wet bunks and . . ." I floundered about.

"Are you trying to tell me you want to pack it in?"

"No, of course not. But I thought you would. What with the bad weather and your seasickness and . . . Well, don't you want to throw in the towel?"

"Mike, don't be ridiculous. I have no intention of throwing in the towel and wasting all that effort and hard-won experience. Mind you, it's just as well you didn't put the question a couple of days ago when we were being thrown around the channel. Then I would happily have exchanged *Walkabout* for a lift to the nearest bit of dry land. But now I'm actually on dry land I'm full of resolution again."

I was enormously relieved. The thought of creeping away with our collective tail between our legs had been nagging me for a week past.

The children were not so enthusiastic. For one thing, they all disliked the daily chores in the galley, and the constant need to keep the cabin tidy which the lack of space imposed on us. Each person had only one clothes net about 18″ long by 9″ high, and one shelf about 1′ long and 6″ high for personal effects. When Mark wanted to build a model plane he had to find a sheltered spot ashore, and when the plane was complete there was no safe place to stow it. Kevin had another complaint, namely, that his bunk was never dry because water leaked in around the main mast. I promised to put that to rights. Bruce never complained but held a decisive opinion none the less. When Liz asked him if he liked the boat he said flatly, "No!" Then he wrote to his grandfather, "Ay dont lik bots becos thay are tu smorl and th wavs ar tu big and ay get wet."

We wondered what experiences other yachts had had, but were disappointed to find that the atmosphere in Durban was so poor that people kept themselves to themselves. We spoke, however, to two other cruising yachts that had children aboard. One was a concrete ketch, *Bernice,* built in Australia and sailed over by an American couple with two young children, while a third had been born in Durban. *Bernice* was much roomier than *Walkabout*, but we gathered they still found it too small and were planning to sell up and return to the States to build a bigger boat.

The other boat was the cutter *Windsong*, of similar size and vintage to *Walkabout*. Aboard were a Hungarian/Norwegian couple who had sailed from New Guinea with a little boy of two and were working in Durban before carrying on to Europe. The skipper was delightfully casual about everything. The engine had stopped working two days out of New Guinea, he told me. When I enquired what watches they kept he replied that they kept none at all; they slept every night. How did his self-steering work, I wanted to know? "It doesn't," he said. "It was a Q.M.E. horizontal wind vane type, and halfway across the Indian Ocean I sawed it off and threw it overboard. Now I sheet the staysail to the tiller and that works much better. It keeps course to within 20 degrees whatever the wind strength."

We heard, however, that they had had a nasty experience when one day the little boy fell overboard. The husband went in after him, leaving his wife without the least idea of what to do. In a panic she rushed around releasing every rope in sight in an effort to stop the boat. Meanwhile he had grasped the fishing line and somehow entwined it around his little finger. She pulled on the line, and after a struggle managed to get him and the child aboard. But his little finger had been almost amputated.

While we had decided to carry on with the voyage, we were still worried about what we felt to be the most difficult part of it, namely, the next leg to Cape Town. Kevin and Mark could look after themselves, but Bruce and Rachel were still at an age when they required constant supervision, and we did not feel confident of coping if much heavy weather were encountered. It should be explained that this 800-mile passage has an unwholesome reputation. Gale winds are frequent and fierce, and one has to double Cape Agulhas (near the Cape of Good Hope, or Cape of Storms, as it used to be called), which is one of the three great capes of the world, jutting south towards the roaring forties. The coast is inhospitable and there are only three ports of refuge—East London, Port Elizabeth and Mossel Bay, with Knysna as a possible but difficult fourth. For more than half the distance the Agulhas current, one of the fastest ocean currents in the world, sweeps southwards at a rate of up to 5 knots, and when the wind is against the current dangerous seas are built up. Every year boats, sometimes ocean steamers, find themselves in difficulties. The shipping, moreover, is heavy, for since the closure of Suez, the oil from the Middle East to the West is carried round the old Cape route. Lastly, we should be sailing in winter when the seas are cold and the days are short.

The Old Salts at Durban—many of whom, I later discovered, sailed only over the wooden bar of the yacht club—were only too pleased to discuss these dangers with me. This coast is the most dangerous in the world, they assured me. I later discovered that every stretch of water is the most dangerous in the world, according to the natives of the area. And they are all right.

Anyway, the propaganda made its impact, and we decided that Bruce and Rachel should stay with my sister and then fly down to meet us. We would take one extra crew to help. The whole problem was solved in a curious way on the following day. By chance I met a man called Eric, who, it transpired, was an experienced trawlerman and yachtsman. He offered to crew as far as Cape Town. I was delighted to accept. Though it was only mid-morning I suggested that we should splice the main brace. He agreed at once and we returned to the boat, where I handed him a full bottle of cheap brandy. He was an interesting companion, and talked entertainingly of his careers in journalism and on the trawlers. We were impressed. By lunch-time half the bottle of brandy had gone and he was still talking. We fed him and listened on. By mid-afternoon the bottle was finished and his remarks were becoming a shade personal. I handed him a bottle of whisky, and he got his second wind. By nightfall three-quarters of the whisky had gone and he had sunk into self-pity and was tipping out the most appalling (and fascinating) hoard of hang-ups concerning his relationships with his father, his sister and his inner self. Anyone as unstable as that would be a liability at sea, regardless of his seamanship. When he became abusive we decided to get him off the boat even if it meant throwing a bottle of booze overboard as bait. By this time Eric was nearly, but unfortunately not quite, incoherent.

"Gimme dinghy," he roared. "You don't even know how to row. Want to shail to Cape Town and you can't row to jetty. Huh! Gimme oarsh, damn you."

As the lesser of two evils we handed them over and the boat lurched erratically towards the jetty 20 yards away. When we bumped against it Liz sprang ashore with keen perception of what was to come. Eric grasped the edge of the jetty and heaved himself up ineffectually. The dinghy shot sideways, and with a yelp Eric fell into the oily water. Liz and I shrieked with laughter at this summary justice. We stopped when Eric failed to appear. I began to remove my shoes, cursing the fellow for making me fish him out. He surfaced just then, however, and we hauled him out on to the jetty. The ducking had not had the slightest effect on him. I doubt whether he had even noticed it.

We gathered that he lived on a trawler somewhere, so we half-led, half-carried the ranting figure to the fish harbour a couple of miles off. He seemed to recognise the place when we got there, and made straight for a trawler. The tide was out, and the boat was at least 10 feet below the level of the wharf, but he lurched straight over the edge and fell on to the steel deck below. After a moment he picked himself up, apparently unhurt, and tripped into a hatch-way. We heard him bumping down the companion steps one by one, and a little later snores came floating out of the hull.

Henceforth, we resolved, we would stick together as a family, and never take crew. Since then we have encountered hardly one cruising yacht where relations between crew and skipper (or owner) are entirely amicable. Often the relationships are so bad that the entire cruise is threatened, and I remember one crew which arrived in port communicating with each other only through terse memoranda. The most serious dissension seems to be between members of a syndicate which owns a boat, for there is likely to be a wide divergence of interests and the "crew" cannot be thrown off. Oddly enough, crew problems are more likely to occur in port, where each wants to do his own thing, rather than at sea where common interest tends to bind them together. The best set-up is undoubtedly a family or a man with one or two girls as crew; girls are more easy-going than men and do not compete, subconsciously or otherwise, for the skippership. To that word of advice I would add another. If you do decide to take a crew, and you have not been to sea with him before, get him in his cups and see what spills out.

After this incident we settled down to work on the boat and

the children to their lessons. My brother-in-law, David, spent many hours of his valuable time working on *Walkabout* and supplying me with a bewildering variety of paints, glues and fillers from his paint laboratory. And while he was filling the lockers with strange epoxies and polyurethanes, my sister Jenny was filling us with food. Like every Jewish housewife she is firmly convinced that if you are not actually eating you are dying away like a little fire without fuel. How they both came to be as thin as pencils was a paradox I could never solve. If Jenny could not get us to her flat, she would appear on the jetty with casseroles of food wrapped in a blanket. She would shake her head over Bruce's boils and David would shake his over the primitive toilet arrangements, and would point out that the cost of flying was only a fraction of the cost of sailing. But they did more to help us than anyone else, and more than we had any right to expect.

We needed all the help we could get. The finishing touches to the fitting out had to be done. Carpets (carpets make the world of difference to the comfort of a cabin), bedspreads, curtains, paintwork, galley lighting and a dozen other things were completed. Then a hundred and one maintenance jobs demanded attention: every sail needed repairing: the sick batteries were replaced; the bilge pump was rebuilt; and, much to the children's delight, *Crawlabout* was overhauled and fitted with a lateen rig. To lighten the boat and pay for the batteries, I sold some of the internal lead ballast. The problem of cabin lights and engine-starting was solved when my father paid us a visit from Rhodesia and presented us with a neat little Honda battery generator; to avoid the danger of petrol reaching the bilges, fuel was stored outside in the dinghy and the generator run dry each time. A Smith's ship's clock with a tuning fork mechanism was also installed as a chronometer; it was not sold as a chronometer, but once adjusted it kept time to within ten seconds a month and ran for a year on a single dry cell battery. It proved to be an invaluable instrument, worth every penny of the £18 it cost. Maintenance, I was beginning to discover, constitutes the cruising yachtsman's eternal labour, and a permanent leak in the ship's purse. The only benefit one seems to derive from this endless expenditure of labour and cash is that the ship does not actually fall apart; it seldom looks any better.

The days passed and then the weeks. The bills came in and our money dwindled. At the end of a month's work we were still not quite finished, and less than £300 was left in the ship's purse. We realised that it would be impossible to reach England that year. We had not the funds to do it, and anyway we were too late to clear the West Indies by the beginning of the hurricane season in July. After B.D. we did not even want to be in the same ocean as a hurricane. This meant, we decided, that we had to stop and earn money somewhere in the southern hemisphere until the beginning of the following year.

This one simple decision broke a psychological barrier. Hitherto we had looked on the boat as a rather unconventional means of travelling from Rhodesia to England. Now we had suddenly decided to double or treble the period of the voyage and earn our living as we went. The boat had become a home and sailing a way of life. We had become walkabouts. We could go anywhere, we realised, and with this new-found freedom we debated, in a casual way, where in the southern hemisphere to sail to next. It had to be a large city where I could find work. Durban was unthinkable, Cape Town too cold and wet in winter, so we selected Rio de Janeiro. I had some knowledge of the language, we had just enough money to reach the place, and anyway I had always been fascinated by Brazil. We had never been to South America, and Brazil had an adventurous ring to its name.

One day we received a note from the secretary of the yacht club to the effect that, while he greatly admired the boys' ability to concentrate unsupervised on their lessons in the spare room, would I kindly prevent my daughter from "running amok amongst the members". We were distressed by this note, for we depended on the hospitality of the club for showers, and felt, with four children, more vulnerable than most. It transpired that Rachel had been entertaining in the lounge; she was just beginning to discover the power that a head of blonde curls, a pair of big brown eyes and impulsive gestures of affection had over adults—club secretaries excepted. But the incident highlighted the strange mixture of freedom and dependence enjoyed by walkabouts. They have the freedom of the oceans, but from time to time they are utterly dependent on shore folk for essentials like food, water and sheltered anchorages; they have few of the rights that rate-paying citizens take for granted. The only rights that are yours to insist on are those you pay for, and for that reason we came to prefer a moderate charge for facilities. In Durban the first month is free, and thereafter fees are charged on a sliding scale that rises to astronomical proportions.

We reacted to the secretary's note by placing the yacht club out of bounds, which was just as well, for Bruce, with Rachel in tow, had started collecting again. Even worse, he formed a gang of collectors from the ragged mob of Indian youngsters that hangs about the water-front. The gang went everywhere, and each day "treasures" consisting of such things as half rigging screws, old combs, bent shackles, coloured stones, fish-hooks and iron piping would be hidden aboard; each day I would search them out and dump them overboard. When the collectors were not collecting they were trawling home-made nets behind the dinghy, somewhere in the harbour, leaving the rest of the family marooned either ashore or on board. I put the dinghy out of bounds, but the only effect this had was to make Bruce disappear faster when he did get hold of it.

After five weeks of maintenance we decided that anything not done would stay that way. We laid in provisions, Kevin and Mark loaded *Walkabout* with water bags, and I obtained clearance for the boat and her crew, a procedure that involved five government departments (in a specific order) and enough wax seals, parchment and pink tape to float a solicitor's office. The day of departure was gusty and wet, but the meteorological office promised weather of an unremarkable but faintly favourable sort, and we left. This time we enjoyed an authentic farewell, with Jenny and David and a group of friends waving handkerchiefs from the water's edge and shouting good wishes. Mark hoisted the flags and we all waved bravely. I put the engine in gear. It was an embarrassing moment to discover that *Walkabout* was stuck on the mud by the fuel jetty. I pretended that this was perfectly normal and we shoved furiously until she came free. Then we repeated the brave waving and hurriedly motored away.

As soon as we cleared the harbour entrance *Walkabout* began to plunge in the heavy swell that was running. Within minutes Liz was seasick. I hoisted sail and we beat into a stiff headwind that became stronger and stronger by the hour. By the time the Bluff had dropped below the horizon it was blowing a near-gale and every soul on board was thinking, in one form or another, the same thing:

"I'll never go to sea again. I wish to God I was back in port."

VII

No sooner had the Bluff finally sunk out of sight than the wish was granted. The mast band that carried the belaying pins, which in turn held half a dozen halyards, sheared its bolts and the sails fell down. There is nothing that demoralises the superstitious sailor—and all sailors are superstitious—more than limping back into a port he has just left, but we had no alternative. Everyone was, in truth, greatly relieved, including myself, for the meteorological office had apparently changed its mind, and a warning that severe gales were soon expected in the area had been forecast shortly before the sails fell down. I started the engine and turned back. With the wind behind us the Bluff soon appeared over the bow, and a few hours later we were creeping down the familiar yacht basin.

I rang my sister and told her what had happened but not to worry, because the bodies which a few hours before I could have sworn were drawing their last breath were now gustily eating brown bread and oranges in the cabin. I should have saved my breath; Jenny appeared on the jetty half an hour later carrying a casserole wrapped in a blanket.

That night a severe gale from the south-west swept up the Natal coast into Mozambique, and while we lay snug in port and Jenny's stew lay snug in us, the unfortunate crews of five ships struggled in massive seas for survival. Three were commercial vessels, one of which was blown ashore near Lourenco Marques. The other two were yachts. The first was a British yacht with a couple and two children aboard, wrecked on the Zululand coast. They all managed to reach the shore and were brought into Durban the next day, destitute but alive. The second was the Durban yacht *Trimtwa*, whose mast broke off at the crosstrees. When she was towed in by the lifeboat and rafted alongside us, the skipper told me that they had made the mistake of starting the engine before the tangle of rigging from the broken mast had been cleared. A line fouled the propeller and they lay helpless until rescued. The five men aboard were all safe. Both disasters had occurred in the region of Cape St Lucia, where we had encountered our gale and where, a local fisherman told me, "the wind lives".

It took a day to repair the damaged mast band and a further day to obtain official clearance for the second time from the five government departments. Once again we bravely waved farewell to our faithful audience (noticeably smaller than the one which had attended our first departure) and motored out of the yacht basin. This time we got no further than the harbour entrance. A tug stopped us and the skipper advised us to turn back. The swell outside was so heavy, he said, that the pilot boats were in difficulties, and he hinted that the port authorities would not be responsible if we carried on. Sadly we returned to the yacht basin and I telephoned my sister.

"Oh! You're back, are you?" she said without surprise. "What happened this time? Yes, I see. No, you could hardly carry on when he said that. And you're going to try again tomorrow? Fine. Now I'll just pop down with some food . . ."

"Jenny, no!" I said firmly. "Have you no sense? Don't you realise that you'll never get rid of us if you continue to feed us?"

I am not superstitious, but there are times when one cannot help wondering.

Very early the following morning we crept quietly out of the harbour. We did not wave a brave farewell because there was nobody to wave to. There was not even a Looker to watch us. Outside the bar we picked up a stern breeze and headed south into what, in our thin-blooded, tropicalised state, we felt to be an antarctic winter. The breeze freshened and *Walkabout* began to roar along with a bone in her mouth. As the wind was behind us, Mark and I decided to try the new mizzen staysail, which was in fact an old torn genoa that had been repaired at Durban. We mounted the sail upside down with the head at the foot of the mainmast and the clew sheeted to the mizzen boom. Mark managed to haul the sail halfway up, but then the wind caught it and the sail billowed out, dragging him up the mast at the end of the halyard. As he squealed with alarm I grabbed his heels and pulled him down again. He treated halyards with great caution thereafter. The mizzen staysail proved to be a powerful sail but, in common with all flying sails (i.e. those not held along at least one edge by a spar or a stay), a difficult one to handle, and we handed it after a couple of hours. Later on in the Atlantic, when I had learned to handle it better, lashing the foot to the windward gunwale so that the sail stretched partly across the wind, the mizzen staysail became a great favourite when sailing off the wind, and could be relied on to give us an extra 20 miles or so a day.

That day we covered enough mileage to satisfy any cruising man. We did 22 miles in 2 hours and 180 miles in 20 hours, which, even allowing for a current of 2 or 3 knots, was very satisfying. But the self-steering was unable to cope with the strong following wind and one of us had to wrestle with the tiller all the time. The wind along the South African coast is said to blow strongly nearly all the time either up the coast or down it. It behaved true to form.

At exactly four o'clock in the morning, while Liz was on watch, the wind changed abruptly from a strong tail wind to a stiff head wind. Liz struggled to remain on course for some time, then lost her temper and veered on to a course that seemed at least to be comfortable. When I crawled out of my bunk to investigate the cause of the hideous language bouncing about the cockpit, I found we were heading directly back to Durban. I remonstrated (gently and reasonably, as is my wont) and Liz replied, with faultless logic but in horrible language, that anyone who was idiot enough to be plunging around in a small boat at four o'clock on a winter's morning with icy drizzle trickling down his neck could not be regarded as sane enough to express cogent views on the direction in which he wished to plunge.

None the less, I turned *Walkabout* around, and for two exhausting days we crashed into head seas. We crept painfully past East London, where the distant lights, glowing warmly on the horizon, spoke of dry warmth and stillness, and above all sleep. They beckoned so insistently that I understood suddenly why sailors in years past were lured on to rocks by false lights ashore. I averted my eyes and we held our southerly course, hoping for a change of wind that would take us to Port Elizabeth, a couple of hundred miles to the south. But the wind held on, and conditions aboard became unpleasant. It was difficult to eat, and even more difficult to cook and do the boat-keeping. I have a vivid mental photograph of one incident when a sudden plunge sent Liz flying across the cabin with a bucket of slops. Liz is in mid-cabin, arms outstretched; just ahead of her is the bucket, its open end tilted downwards, and ahead of the bucket, also in midflight, is a ragged great globule of slops. One second later, all three had landed in Mark's bunk. It is this sort of experience that convinces one—if one needs convincing—that a small yacht is indisputably the most uncomfortable mode of travel ever devised.

The children adapted remarkably well, and amused themselves with a further batch of books which Liz had been hoarding for just such an occasion. They were driven into the cockpit once a day for a breath of fresh air, but as they did not have proper oilskins they could not stay outside for long. I tried to ease the motion some of the time by retreating inside the 100 fathom line to where the powerful Agulhas current faded, but then a counter current carried us northwards. And as the arrangement for running the headsail to the end of the bowsprit was misbehaving, *Walkabout* beat poorly to windward and we made little progress.

We became more and more weary. In three days I had snatched only three or four hours' sleep, and while I felt competent, I realised from several minor incidents that my judgement was no longer to be trusted. I had reached that state of weariness where coherent thought dissolves into formless dreams and saliva dribbles uncontrolled out of the corners of the mouth. We decided to put into East London and to rest and dry out until the wind changed.

We arrived at the harbour entrance at dawn, and, wary of the authorities after the unpleasant episode in Durban, ran up the "G" flag (G means "I request a pilot") and waited until the pilot launch escorted us in. East London proved to be quite different from Durban. The formalities were identical to those enforced in every South African port, where a visiting yacht is required to obtain full clearance on entering and leaving, whether she is "going foreign" or not. But in East London we were welcomed and the authorities were helpful. When our engine embarrassingly failed on crossing the bar, the pilot launch towed us in and the launch engineer offered his services to put the engine to rights. As there was no yacht basin, *Walkabout* was rafted alongside the fishing trawlers, and the manager offered me the use of the company's workshop facilities, while the tug crews lent us their shower in the docks. Later the secretary of the local yacht club came aboard to greet us and offered to help in any way he could.

The facilities in East London were poor and the harbour area was sordid, but the friendliness of the people was heartwarming, and more than compensated for the unattractive surroundings. Later the children walked into the town, several miles from the docks, to buy provisions. It was a deliberate policy on our part not to wrap them in cotton wool. We encouraged them to act independently and look after themselves, while at the same time they had to pull their weight in the running of the boat. Mark helped me to repair the fuel trouble in the engine and mend some rigging, and both he and Kevin filled the water bags and loaded them aboard, a job they detested.

We should have liked to linger in East London, but winter drew closer every day, and the hurdle of Cape Agulhas loomed constantly in my mind. After two days in the port we pressed on to Port Elizabeth. There was no real necessity to stop there, but I had promised to take the children to visit the famous dolphins at the Oceanarium, so to P.E. we sailed. We enjoyed such a fine following breeze that we were able to lounge around the cockpit pretending that we were members of the martinis-on-deck set, while *Walkabout* sped steadily southwards under self-steering. In little more than a day we had covered the 180 miles and were tied alongside a derelict dredger in the harbour—this time from choice. The children walked into town to examine the toy shops—their first and favourite action on reaching a new port—and Liz and I went to sleep, invariably *our* first action on making port.

A week passed by in Port Elizabeth, and, as in East London, people were very friendly. The local yacht club kindly handed us the keys of the shower, and some friends took the children to their farm. One day we duly trooped off to see the dolphins and other fauna at the Oceanarium. The dolphins were put through a remarkable performance designed to demonstrate their intelligence, but it was in effect a circus act, and we were saddened by the way these clever animals, who in their natural environment range over vast distances, were confined to a small and dull pool. We had often seen dolphins playing under the bows of *Walkabout*, and we all believed that when they were with us we were in no danger.

The break in our journey was justified by bad weather, but when the forecast became propitious we could delay no longer and continued our voyage round the bottom corner of Africa, determined if at all possible to make our next port Cape Town, 400 miles away.

Near Port Elizabeth the underwater cliffs which hug the coast of South Africa, plunging rapidly into depths where light never reaches and the icy temperature never varies, flatten out into a continental shelf, called the Agulhas Bank, which extends a couple of hundred miles towards the Southern Ocean. The Agulhas Current, which races in a narrow stream along the face of the cliffs, fans out over the Agulhas Bank, becoming progressively weaker until it curls back into the Southern Indian Ocean, or drifts westwards and northwards into the South Atlantic. As one sails over the Agulhas Bank, then, the intense blue of the sea discolours to a dull green, the restless current fades, and the subtropical climate of the east coast gradually gives way to a succession of east-bound depressions which characterise the marine climate of the higher latitudes.

It rapidly became much colder, and a chill rain drizzled night and day. Inside the cabin we were able to ward off the winter with the primus stoves, but outside it was difficult to keep warm. Longjohns were dredged up from the bottom of nets and heavy oiled guernseys were worn, but we had no hats or gloves or waterproof footwear. The main hatch was covered with a sheet of polythene, and if he could the watchkeeper crouched on the steps under this sheet, emerging only to check the compass and search for ships. Kevin and Mark were standing their dawn watch alone now, and were becoming increasingly competent at adjusting sheets and keeping the ship on course.

One of their favourite duties was to throw bits of paper over the side and time how long they took to pass between the foremost and aftmost stays, and from that calculate our speed. The reason for this operation was that we had not been able to afford a log to measure the mileage, which therefore had to be estimated from the day's crop of paper readings. With experience one develops a sort of sixth sense, and my estimated positions were seldom more than a few miles away from the true positions, calculated by sextant. After a time I was even able to estimate our speed and the day's run simply from the noise the boat made through the water.

The voyage to Cape Town took an extraordinarily long time —nine days, which I am inclined to claim as a record. The reason was that we experienced hardly any wind; day after day it blew faintly or fitfully or not at all. It was exasperating, and we found it more nerve-racking than heavy weather, for the swell continued to roll us and the boat's gear would slam endlessly from side to side. If we dropped all sail, a light breeze would spring up to harass us until the canvas was spread, and then it would steal away again. Conditions like these cause far more damage and wear to the gear than strong winds and high seas.

The protracted voyage did, however, allow us to establish a routine, which one cannot do over a couple of days. Liz and I were always short of sleep, but we discovered that if all the cat naps were added together, Liz was getting about 6 hours a day, while I seemed to need about 6½. Sleep for the children was no problem, but we wondered whether boredom might be. However, they developed the ability to draw on their own imaginations for entertainment, and entered a world of make-believe which was in effect a romanticised version of their true existence. They always lived on a boat, but it was a high-speed gun-boat or a hovercraft ranging on secret missions.

On the evening of the sixth day Africa's southernmost lighthouse on Cape Agulhas loomed above the horizon, and a few hours later we doubled the tip of Africa in a fair breeze. The shipping lanes between the Atlantic and Indian Oceans handling all the oil from the Middle East converge around this point, and the traffic was intense. Traffic lanes and separation zones are laid down in the charts, but most ships took not the least notice, and we spent the whole night dodging tankers, passing nearly sixty vessels in all. On one occasion when Liz was on watch, a ship passed so close that the wash from the propeller pitched me out of my bunk clean across the cabin into the galley. I woke up in the sink wondering if the sky had

The squaresail billowing strongly in the trades

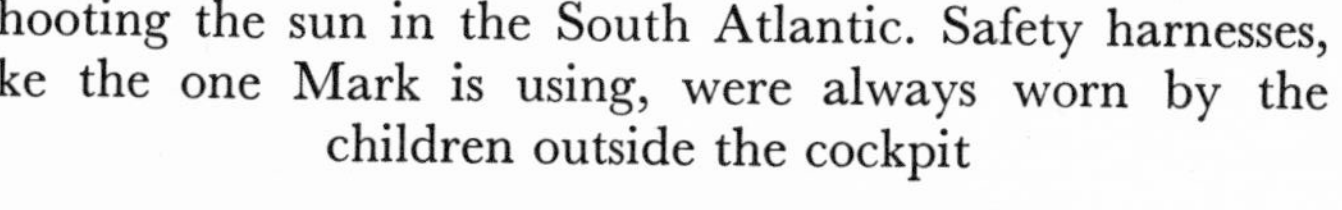

Shooting the sun in the South Atlantic. Safety harnesses, like the one Mark is using, were always worn by the children outside the cockpit

Bruce's first action of the day was to collect and gut the flying fish for breakfast. Note the plastic hatch cover behind Mark

fallen on our heads. The children slept on with no more than a protesting grunt or two, for Kevin was wedged against the main mast and the other three were thrown into the corners of their bunks.

The following day we were attacked by a brief but vicious gale. It was forecast not by the meteorologists but by Mark. Seeing Liz preparing to bake bread, he remarked, "Mummy, the last time you tried to bake bread at sea we had the gale off St Lucia. I bet you anything we get another one today."

"If you're so sure, Mark," I said, "you had better go outside and keep a lookout for it."

Grumbling, he climbed into his oilskins and disappeared through the hatch. Ten minutes later his voice came floating down into the cabin. "Daddy, the wind is getting stronger. I think the gale is starting."

"And I think you are a peanut. Now just belt up and let me sleep. I spent half the night in the sink."

But a few moments later he called down again. "Daddy, the gale has started. If you don't believe me come out and see for yourself."

The boat did seem to be heeling rather sharply, so I pulled a guernsey over my longjohns and went outside. The wind was certainly very fresh, so Mark and I went forward to change the headsail for a smaller one. The sail was only halfway down when a strong gust came shrieking down from the mountains and struck us, throwing the boat hard over. The running forestay, which was of stainless steel, an untrustworthy material, broke, and the sail went over the side. The boat immediately luffed up into the wind and hove to with sails flogging. By the time we had retrieved the headsail, which was only slightly damaged, everything was in a mess. Ropes were tangled, and worst of all my precious longjohns were soaked with salt water. The proper thing in such circumstances is to drop all sail and put everything in order, ignoring the boat, which will usually look after herself, and then hoist sail again correctly reefed. But there was something slightly ridiculous about a bread-baking gale, a sort of joke wind that would go away after it had had its bit of fun. I called Liz up on deck and we tried to reef down. Before we could shorten the mizzen sail it had blown out, and reefing the main was a long and exhausting job, for we had no roller reefing at the time. Then another headsail had to be rigged on the inner forestay, which was used so little that it was stowed against a shroud. When at last everything had been attended to, the wind rapidly abated to a fresh breeze as though waiting for this moment. We went down below in disgust.

As we stooped through the hatch into the cabin a horrible sight confronted us. The boat had obviously been leaking badly, and the water had risen over the cabin sole so that it sloshed about, an inch or so deep over the carpet. A good deal of the bread dough, the root cause of our misfortune, was floating in the water, while the rest was smeared over the seats and around the cabin. Worst of all, a large pot of strawberry jam had emptied itself over the seat, the floor and the engine hatch. There were even sticky pink smears over the chart table.

Now everyone has his own private horror, a particular thing that draws an involuntary shriek to the throat. For some it is spiders. Others cannot stand cockroaches or snakes or plaster garden gnomes. For me it is sticky things. The worst sort of nightmare has me trapped waist deep in a swamp of strawberry jam or ginger marmalade. To be confronted by the nightmare, weakened as I was by several hours' immersion in cold, salty underwear, was too much. I fled into the cockpit and remained there until everyone had given me cast iron assurances that the cabin was clear, clean and smooth as baby powder.

The leak gave us considerable trouble for the remainder of our journey to Cape Town. At first I feared that it was caused by toredo worm, but it proved to be a torn gland around the propeller shaft. If the engine was running we were obliged to pump the bilges every two hours throughout the day and night. The engine was giving a good deal of trouble, too, because of dirty fuel that had been sold in Durban; every hour or two it would stop and I would have to clean the filters and bleed the fuel system. We decided to use the engine at last, when the wind again died away completely and we had drifted 30 miles south of the Cape of Good Hope. There seemed little point in beating back from Antarctica.

But these difficulties were relegated to the standing of minor irritations in the face of the excitement of doubling the famous Cape. It loomed out of the drizzle in the first light of the ninth day. The entire family sat outside fascinated by the majestic mountains that populate the Cape Peninsula. An enormous swell rolled in from the Atlantic, but scarcely a ripple disturbed the smooth surface. I dipped the thermometer over the side, for there is an abrupt change in temperature round the Cape, where the cold waters of the Atlantic Ocean meet the remnants of the warm water from the Indian Ocean. The temperature was down to 56°F. Then we knew that we had reached the Atlantic. All day we remained outside watching each cliff and mountain unfold—each of the Twelve Apostles and finally, as we came into Table Bay in the evening, Table Mountain itself, with the lights of Cape Town city spread about its feet.

We stopped outside the harbour entrance and tried to attract the attention of several passing pilot launches, but as in Durban they ignored us, and at last we crept in cautiously. When we reached the yacht basin we nosed around blindly in the rain until a lamp flashed to show us the way. Several people were waiting on the floating catwalk, and as we came to rest a man wearing a floppy blue hat over a lean, intent face took our mooring warp. We later came to know him as Colin Syndecombe, a peripatetic cruising consultant, handyman extra ordinary, yachtsmen's friend, and like ourselves a true walkabout in spirit if not yet in fact. Having made the rope fast, he leaned forward and asked, "Is this THE *Walkabout*?"

"Yes, it is," said Liz happily.

"Then welcome to Cape Town," he replied, and led us to hot showers.

That first welcome was symbolic of the extraordinary kindness with which we were treated throughout our stay in Cape Town.

We intended to remain there for about two weeks, which, we felt, would be long enough to prepare for the Atlantic crossing to Rio de Janeiro. I sent the sails off for repair, ordered a new and stronger forestay, and arranged to get *Walkabout* out of the water on the fine slip that is operated by the Royal Cape Yacht Club. When the boat was hauled out we were dealt several nasty surprises. The rudder pintles were quite badly worn, but they were in bronze, and so massively constructed that I decided they would get us to England. At the suggestion of a new friend, Dave Smedley Williams, who had literally adopted us the day after our arrival, a pair of stout loops were secured to the trailing edge of the blade so that, in the event of the rudder stock or tiller breaking, tiller lines could be fastened to the rudder under water. The next shock was the propeller shaft. It and the stern bearing were also so badly worn that one could rattle it to and fro like a spoon in a cup. The cause was a poor installation that prevented proper water lubrication, and the cure was a new bearing and shaft, which would cost far more than we could afford. It was obvious that henceforth *Walkabout* would be strictly a sailing boat, and the use of the engine would be restricted to manœuvring in harbour. *Walkabout* was antifouled, and the waterline was raised some 9″ to accommodate her heavy load. One often finds the waterline on a cruising yacht being raised but I have never heard of one being lowered, and that is one of the reasons why multihulls (which are highly sensitive to weight) make poor boats for walkabouts. Before antifouling we scraped a marine village off the bottom of the lead keel, which for years had rested on the sand when the boat was beached for painting. There were dozens of large oysters in residence, and these were prised off and eaten.

The children relished Cape Town, and after a ritual tour of the toyshops, busied themselves about the yacht club. Rachel used her charm as a skilled cowboy uses his lariat to ensnare everybody, from the club messenger to the Commodore. I became known merely as "Rachel's father", a title I bore with due modesty. People would come to the boat and say, "Rachel has invited us for supper. I suppose that's okay by you, is it?" On one occasion an elderly gentleman accosted me on the porch.

"Excuse me. Are you Rachel's father?" he said.

"Why yes," I replied. "I do have that honour."

"The children do seem to work terribly hard. Not that I disapprove," he added hastily. "I mean, it's wonderful to have the whole family sailing. But it must be hard on the children."

"What has Rachel been telling you?" I asked suspiciously.

"She told me that 'at sea Mummy and Daddy sleep all day and we children are the galley slaves'."

To our surprise, the boys pestered us to send them to school. Once, in a moment of exasperation in Port Elizabeth, Liz had threatened to send them to school in Cape Town if they did not stop bickering. Now Kevin, in particular, demanded that she should keep her promise. We made enquiries, but found that it was the midwinter school holiday, and we had to shelve the idea.

We met several cruising yachts in Cape Town. One was the newly built yacht *Zanj*, a bulky, short-masted vessel, on her way from South-West Africa to the Seychelles. She was stolen a few months later by four French Foreign Legionaries based in the Comoro Islands. They knew nothing whatever about sailing and were later picked up by the Portuguese drifting off the northern coast of Mozambique near the port of Nacala. A most interesting voyager was Dr Meyer, who, in his yacht *Paloma*, was completing a solo circumnavigation, stopping only at Panama, Port Moresby and Cape Town. He was a retired engineer who had never been sailing before, and a most charming man who embarrassed me by asking for advice on sailing routes. What could I tell such an intrepid sailor that he did not know already? In a sense he was the German counterpart of Francis Chichester.

Perhaps the most fascinating voyager of all was Humphrey Bowker, who had temporarily abandoned his roving to settle near Cape Town. Many years previously he had set out from Rhodesia and had walked all the way to Khartoum, where, he says, he became tired and took to hitch-hiking and motor-scooting. He travelled around Europe searching for a suitable ship, and sighted her at last on the other side of a bay in Scotland. He swam over, boarded her and bought her immediately. Sailing down the Irish Sea in *Manora*, as the boat was called, he had the misfortune to be knocked out by the jib. He awoke to find himself in the net under the bowsprit with a mouthful of blood and loose teeth. He wired the teeth back with copper wire, and made such a sound job of it that they are still in good working order. Later he sailed to Rio de Janeiro, and after a year continued his voyage to Cape Town. Aboard was his new bride, Dilys. When they reached Cape Town, Humphrey and Dilys dragged *Manora* up the side of a mountain to their house, and there we found her, being gradually refitted by Humphrey. He knew *Walkabout* well—had sailed in her, in fact, as far as the Comoro Islands—and he told us intriguing stories of his voyages aboard our boat.

One day the whole family went to the Bowkers' for a solemn and symbolic ceremony of the Planting of the Avocado. It came about in this way. While in Durban Bruce had claimed the stone of an avocado pear, and his inventive mind had immediately conceived the idea of planting it. "Over my dead body!" I swore. "As if we haven't enough stowage problems without planting thundering great trees on the boat." But Bruce suspended the stone in a jar of water and hid it. After we had left Durban he produced the jar and it was placed in the galley. The sprout flourished, regardless of the way it was flung about the cabin. It drove me potty; at least three times a day the jar would sail out of the galley and spill water over the cabin. The plant would fall to the floor and Bruce would rush, wailing, to the rescue. One day the stone split in two and I declared that the plant had had it and must be flung overboard immediately. But Bruce clung to his avocado, or rather to half of it, and amazingly the plant not only survived but prospered. When we reached Cape Town I acknowledged defeat. The tree, I said, had been carried at great peril across the sea and nurtured by Bruce. It was a symbol of life, and must be planted by its guardian in a safe place in the new land. And so the tree was planted with proper ceremony in the Bowkers' garden, and there it stands to this day.

It was difficult to leave Cape Town, and we had just resolved to get away regardless before the end of June when our plans were abruptly wrecked, as the plans of mice and men so often are. On midwinter's day Bruce, playing on the soft green lawn in front of the yacht club, fell on his arm and broke it. The Smedley Williams rushed him and Liz to the famous Groote Schuur Hospital, where they found not a broken arm but a severe fracture of the wrist. It was a difficult break to set, and in fact two attempts were made. There was now no question of sailing until the wrist mended. On the other hand, funds were too low simply to wait until Bruce was fit again, so we decided to winter in Cape Town and postpone our departure to Rio for four or five months, by which time we hoped to have earned enough money to reach England.

I was lucky enough to find work within a week with a firm of consulting engineers, who manfully averted their eyes from my holed jeans and flapping plimsolls and kindly took me on. It was a curious sensation to be back in the rat race, working from eight to five in an office once more, and a fascinating experience to boot. For the first time I was a rat without ambition or pretension, able to stand aloof from the other rats and observe the compulsive and often self-defeating jostling for position in the unwritten hierarchy of office politics. That my stance was itself one of conceit did not escape me, but it was at least a conceit that did not consume working time and energy. And above all I was glad to have the work.

The boys got their wish and went to Rondebosch School. They all loved it and judged it to be a great adventure, not to be compared with the tiresome business of sailing halfway round the world on a boat. We were interested to see how they fared after six months away from school. Academically they all stood well amongst their fellows. As was to be expected with three such contrasting personalities, they each adapted in different ways. Kevin, being conventional and with a strong personality, adapted rapidly and easily to school life. He was ashamed, however, of living on a boat, and at first mentioned it to no one. Bruce had no such scruples. He burst confidently in on the class, and was soon the spearhead of various activities which were expressly outside the school curriculum. Mark found it more difficult to adapt than his brothers, perhaps because of his thinner skin, and he also kept the secret of his shipboard life from his schoolmates. When it did eventually become known that the boys actually lived on a yacht, they became objects of admiration and envy. That was the turning point in their acceptance of their new way of life. From then on they tended to regard themselves as adventurous young dogs rather than as little unfortunates dragged away from home and school, except perhaps for Kevin, who would occasionally hark back to rosier days in Rhodesia.

We settled down to a semi-normal life again. The boat became a sort of friendly floating slum, bulging with school-books and uniforms and boxes of apples, or sometimes a bizarre laundry with washing hanging from all the rigging. Life was not easy, especially when the winter north-westers drove rain in through the main hatch and snow on the mountains brought bitter weather. For one thing, the yacht club was sited in the docks, miles from the city centre, and there was no public transport. I borrowed the messenger's old bicycle for work and Liz had it for her shopping on Saturdays. For another thing, the wind carried all the filth from the railway yards behind the club into the yacht basin, and one would wake up in the morning with a black pillow and a mouthful of soot. Our health deteriorated, and we all suffered from attacks of flu and gastric infections; Bruce and Rachel contracted mumps, and my chronic bronchitis worsened.

For these privations, however, the hospitality and generosity of our Cape Town friends more than compensated. We were driven round the beautiful Cape peninsula, and on each of the children's birthdays a special treat was arranged. On Bruce's birthday we rode up in the cable car to picnic on Table Mountain. There we enjoyed the magnificent panorama of the Peninsula for at least three minutes before an icy eiderdown of thick mist, the so-called "tablecloth", rolled over us and blotted everything from view.

The only other cruising yacht wintering in Cape Town that year was *Leona III*. She was a heavily constructed 36ft Bermudan ketch, built in Rhodesia over a period of five painful years by George and Hetty Durant to replace their previous yacht, *Leona II*, which had been lost on the Mozambique coast near Bazaruto Island. When *Leona III* was three-quarters finished George retired and the couple quietly sold up their house and possessions in Rhodesia and shifted the boat overland to Durban where they lived in a caravan while they worked to complete their new retirement home. As so often happens with yachts, the months slipped by in an endless chain of tasks. When at last they sailed their resources had trickled away, and now, like us, they were working in Cape Town before carrying on to England.

October brought the spring, and a man's fancy turned to crossing the South Atlantic, for the winter north-westers were being gradually displaced by the fierce winds from the south-east that gave the Cape of Storms its notorious name. Two of the local boats were dismasted, both through failure of the stainless steel rigging. The favourable winds brought a fresh migration of walkabouts sailing west about the world. Most of the cruising folk knew *Walkabout*, at least by reputation, and would come for a chat aboard. Liz always kept a jug of aromatic Colombian coffee bubbling, and was delighted at the interest brought by the newcomers.

The yachts were as varied as the crews who sailed them. The most beautiful was *Santana*, a 48ft yawl built in America during the depression as a stylish racing craft, and once owned by Humphrey Bogart. She was being sailed round the world with various crew by her owners Charlie and Marty Peet. Tastefully appointed in rosewood, she was a handsome boat, and her owners cruised in a style to match. We thought that the most interesting boat was the 36ft yacht *Siestar*, which at first glance looked like a battered relic from bygone years, though she was in fact a fibreglass boat fitted out by her owner, Al Sies, in California about three years previously. Drums of fuel and water were lashed on deck, weathered wood carvings adorned her bows and hull, and a huge self-steering wind-vane painted with the anti-bomb symbol and the word "Peace" dominated her stern. Down below she was equally remarkable. Her cabin was fitted out like a Californian beach bungalow with stove and fridge (which did not work), wall-plugs (also defunct), and swing-doors from an old western saloon bar. Planks inscribed with hippie-flavoured verse hung about the walls, and on a great slab lying at the foot of the mast was engraved a declaration of her origin beginning, "This good ship built by Al Sies . . ."

Al Sies himself was worthy of his boat. He was a tall wiry man in middle age with deep-set glittering eyes and a shock of wild grey hair hanging about his shoulders. At any moment one expected him to climb a mountain and utter a prophecy. His teenage son accompanied him, and together they had sailed the Pacific and Indian Oceans and were on their way back to California. When I first saw the boat I thought she was a schooner—that is, with the mizzen mast higher than the main mast—but Al corrected me.

"Sure she's a schooner now," he said, "but a couple of weeks back she was a ketch. Until, that is, we hit that gale near Port Elizabeth and the top of the main mast broke off and, crack—instant schooner! It really began in New Zealand when one night we ran aground. My son and I got off all right, but the boat was rolled over in the surf. For three weeks she was battered and rolled in the breakers. The masts and everything on deck were smashed off. Finally this farmer came along and hitched his tractor on to the boat and dragged her out and up the beach. Amazingly the hull was perfectly sound. We propped her up and began to fix her, and when we came to the masts we went to the farmer to ask him for wood. 'Sure,' he said, 'just pick yourself a couple of trees and chop 'em down!' So now you know why the masts are kinda kinky and full of knots, and why the top of the main mast broke off."

"What are you going to do now?" I asked.

"Why, we'll just carry on. I can't afford to do anything else. We'll reef down the main and stay the mast a bit better and carry on as a schooner. Anyway, I've always kinda wanted a schooner," he added reflectively.

With great courage and tenacity he and his son did carry on, and we later received a message to say that they had arrived safely in Recife, Brazil.

We ourselves intensified our work to prepare *Walkabout* for the Atlantic crossing, for the yacht club needed our berth for the competitors in the Cape to Rio race. In my view, crossing an ocean is less hazardous than coastal sailing—provided, of course, that the boat is seaworthy and one is properly prepared. None the less, one's first ocean crossing is somewhat frightening to contemplate; it is a psychological rather than a physical barrier that must be surmounted, but no less formidable for that. One has to accept that one will be completely on one's own and far from any help whatever for weeks on end, so we looked first to safety measures if the yacht should go down. *Pioneer* had been sunk by a whale in the Cape to Rio race two years previously, and a letter from New Zealand pinned up on the club notice-board described how *Bo-Peep* had been lost in a similar way (we had not at that time heard of the saga of the Robertsons).* The life-raft provisions were thin, so we supplemented them with a survival pack, consisting of 6kg. of survival rations (biscuits and glucose), 2½ gallons of water (which, in a polythene container, floats in sea-water), fishing line and hooks, a plankton net, a knife and some cigarettes and matches. I felt that a solar still should also be included, but had no time to make one. The pack was attached to the life-raft with a lanyard so that one need not worry about it when abandoning ship.

* *Survive the Savage Sea*, by Dougal Robertson (Elek Books).

From the experiences of Robin Knox-Johnston on his non-stop circumnavigation,* I also conceived the idea of preparing two large canvas patches bordered on two sides with wooden battens with bronze nails already in position. If the boat sprang a plank one could dive below and nail the patch over the leak.

But it struck me forcibly that the very concept of a life-raft was basically wrong. An inflatable life-raft was conceived for use in frequented waters like the English Channel. Its purpose is to provide instant protection from drowning and exposure at the moment of disaster, and to remain on the scene, shielding the crew, until rescue is effected. But if one sinks in the South Atlantic this sort of craft is far from ideal. Because of its construction, which is usually circular, it cannot be propelled anywhere, and because of the need for lightness it is not very durable. What was needed, Humphrey Bowker and I agreed when discussing the matter, was a craft that could actually sail; tales abound of ocean crossings in tiny craft, and the chances of covering 1,000 miles in twenty days in trade wind regions and reaching land are very high. In Appendix III some ideas are given for a sailing life-boat which could be carried by boats of *Walkabout*'s size and larger.

Apart from safety a host of other preparations preoccupied us. We were severely limited by lack of space and money, so our lists were combed and refined to the last primus spare, the last light bulb and the last tube of toothpaste. Repairing the propeller shaft and the rudder was still beyond our means, and instead I turned my attention to sails. I rigged up an experimental squaresail from the piece of tarpaulin, and bought some lengths of wood for jib booms. The boat was slipped and scraped and painted in a 70 m.p.h. south-easter which snatched the paint off the brushes and threatened to blow *Walkabout* clean over, slip and all.

The last ten days in Cape Town passed in a frenzy of activity. Every single cubic inch of space aboard was investigated and ruthlessly filled. After all, stowing 1,000 lb. of food (which in Cape Town is cheap and very good) into a 33ft yacht, together with 120 gallons of water, tools, sails, spares, children's Christmas presents (concealed), Christmas decorations (also con-

* *A World of My Own*, by Robin Knox-Johnston (Cassell).

cealed), fuel, books, tapes, charts, a typewriter and a clarinet, requires not only skill but obstinacy.

Bruce helped enormously with a new idea which had struck him after I had thrown his ninety-second collection of treasures overboard. He decided to start a stamp collection. "Thank heavens stamps are so small," I said to Liz, and I urged Bruce to collect to his heart's content. It was fatal. He tackled his new hobby with such enthusiasm that nearly a thousand stamps had been taken aboard by the time we sailed. I feared we might founder before we reached Falmouth. Already *Walkabout*, like an iceberg, was nine-tenths under water, and an alarmingly small part of her smart new coat of paint showed above the water-line.

Finally, one midnight during a farewell party the last egg was greased and we were ready to sail. Friends brought kind gifts and Christmas presents for the children, but remembering the farce in Durban we declined to stage a departure. This was just as well, for the wind promptly vanished, and for three days we fretted in a breathless calm virtually unknown in Cape Town.

On November 13th a faint wind stirred from the south. We took our last fresh water shower, waved to Pam and Colin Syndecombe, first to welcome us, last to bid us farewell, and motored slowly into Table Bay.

VIII

Walkabout WAS SAILING again, and this felt most odd. For five months she had been used as a miniature flat, a floating slum, where the tiller was in the way of the cockpit seats, the boom took up space needed for sacks of potatoes and boxes of fruit, and the chart table served only to obstruct everybody in the cabin. Now she was transformed once again into a sailing machine with a bowsprit pointing purposefully out into the Atlantic and sails tautened to cup the wind. Behind us the distinctive outline of Table Mountain crouched over the city of Cape Town, while ahead of us, nearly 1,800 miles away, lay the tiny island of St Helena, and a couple of thousand beyond that the new world.

"Isn't it great to be sailing again?" I said enthusiastically.

"It's jolly cold," said Liz.

"I'm glad we're sailing again," said Mark. "I was getting tired of sitting in one port all that time and going to school every day. Also the bosun at the club would never let me build my boats and aeroplanes in the shed. It wasn't fair."

"Can we put out our new fishing line now?" asked Bruce. "I can see a sort of thing following us in the water. I think it must be a shark."

"You're lying again, Bruce, you can't see anything. He's always telling stories," complained Mark. "Daddy, can I stream the new log?"

"Okay. Careful you don't tangle the line and make sure the log is on zero." I turned to Rachel. "And what does little Rachel think about sailing again?"

She removed her fingers from her mouth and shook her head. "I don't like it, Daddy, because I'm sad that I've left all my best, best friends behind."

"You might see some of them in Rio. Some of them are going over for the race, you know."

Rachel brightened up at once.

All day we tacked out of Table Bay in light winds, and late in the afternoon we scraped past Robben Island, best known as a penal settlement. Soon afterwards we picked up a wind from the south which rapidly hardened into a stiff breeze. In nine cases out of ten, yachts are blown out of Table Bay and into the Atlantic by a south-east gale; we adhered closely to tradition.

For the next four days we lived in misery, resolving, when we had the energy, never to put to sea again. Every night the weather forecast predicted gale-force winds, and every night it was correct. Before the lights of Cape Town had sunk below the horizon everyone, apart from myself, was horribly seasick. Liz, full of Avomine, lay prostrate. The children huddled in their bunks for the most part, occasionally staggering off to the heads to be sick. They were very good about this and behaved wonderfully, but they could not always reach the heads in time. I tried to get them to swallow a few mouthfuls of dry rusks, but they complained that the rusks made them feel worse. At supper-time I heated some soup and made toast, because I was convinced that it is better for the stomach to have a little food to work on, and I was anxious they should hold down the Avomine pills long enough for the system to absorb the drug. The results were disastrous, especially for poor Rachel. In desperation I tried glucose, and to my relief it worked. The cloying sweetness put the children off at first, but surprisingly it did not nauseate them, and though it did not cure the seasickness, they kept it down.

If the crew was green after five months in port, the boat was worse. We had tried to prevent the decks from drying out, but a bucket or two of sea-water sloshed over the boat once a day had not been enough to prevent the planks from shrinking. As soon as we ran into heavy weather water poured into the cabin through the deck seams and between the coach top and decks. Recalling Robin Knox-Johnston's experiences in the southern ocean when his coachtop began to separate from the boat, I became worried that the same thing was happening to us. The dinghy with its heavy load of sails was lashed on the cabin top, and with *Walkabout* rolling through about 60 degrees and back again every three or four seconds the cabin top must have been under great strain. I tightened all the nuts that held the cabin down before realising that the sturdy structure was in no danger whatever. But the water continued to drip in through the seams. I reckoned that about 50 gallons a day were leaking into the cabin, mainly over the bunks and into the clothes nets. Every single garment and scrap of bedding was saturated with salt water. If we had not had a gale up our tail I would have put back to Cape Town.

The following day the wind moderated a little, but again strengthened during the night. The decks were beginning to swell and less water was leaking into the cabin, but there was no possibility of drying anything yet. In all other respects, however, *Walkabout* proved incredibly seaworthy. For instance, with a following wind she steered herself remarkably well. In Cape Town I had made a special transparent spray hood which rolled down to exclude wind and water, and enabled the watchkeeper to keep an eye on the sails and the compass and look out for ships without leaving the cabin. With this aid to carpet-slipper sailing I stayed down below and left *Walkabout* to sail herself. This she did right through the gale on the second night, carrying a reefed main and heavy-duty working jib. Several times she broached, i.e. was slewed round broadside to the seas by a following wave, but on each occasion she recovered and tore on through the night before I could reach the tiller. I was beginning to realise that she was a very fast boat for a cruising yacht. On the second day she covered the remarkable distance of 165 miles with hardly a hand on the tiller or the sheets.

On the third day the wind moderated a good deal and everyone cheered up. The children began eating properly again and went aloft to play in the fresh air. Liz recovered sufficiently to poke her nose out of the hatchway and say, "Ugh! How horrible!" before going below again. In the afternoon Mark suggested that it was calm enough to try our new squaresail. It was a wild sail to handle, but with Kevin and Mark each hanging on to a corner sheet I managed to hoist it into position on the main mast. The mainsail was dropped. Kevin and Mark were delighted with the romantic white sail bellying ahead of the mast.

"It's just like a caravel," observed Kevin with pleasure.

He had been reading of Christopher Columbus and his voyage in the *Santa Maria*.

I watched the sail closely, trying to imagine how the air flowed around it, for there are few people nowadays who understand the squaresail. I imagined I was a little molecule of air. What forces would direct my path over the canvas? I explained what I was thinking to Mark, and together we experimented with the sheets and guys, watching to see how the shape of the sail changed. Finally it dawned on me that the squaresail is not simply a crude wind bag, as I had supposed; it is more of an aerofoil, but a horizontal not a vertical one—rather like a mainsail lying on its side with a yard instead of a mast. This was one of the reasons, I realised, why the old sails were broader than they were high—the aspect ratio was higher. The aspect ratio of a sail is the height divided by the breadth, and the higher the ratio the higher is the aerodynamic efficiency of the sail. I had thought that a squaresail was poor in this respect, but once I realised that it was a sail lying on its side, the sound thinking of the old sailors at once became apparent.

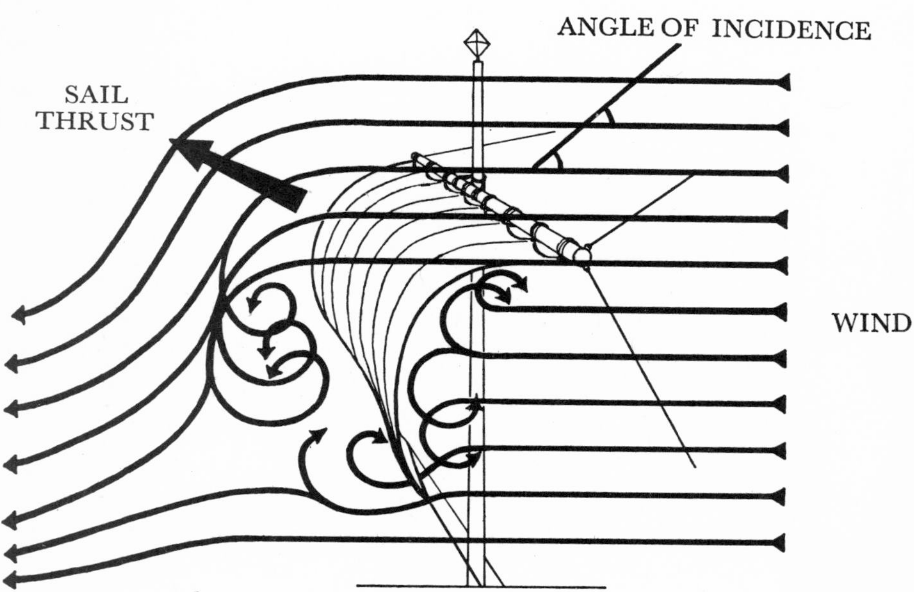

THE SQUARESAIL AS A HORIZONTAL AEROFOIL
(i.e. wind bent through an angle)

One cannot take this line of thought to extremes, because a high aspect ratio sail does not work well when the angle between it and the wind (called the angle of incidence) is too high, and with a squaresail the angle of incidence is always high. Another point about the squaresail is that it is a wonderful lifting sail in a following wind; it does not press the boat into the sea as modern mainsails do, but lifts the vessel up and onwards. Of course it is of little use with the wind ahead, and it needs lots of complicated ropework to control it—fore and aft guys as well as sheets, and a system of raising and lowering the sail without raising and lowering the yard, such as roller reefing on a false yard.

Our beautiful squaresail had only flown for a couple of hours when it blew out. Mark saw it start and shouted, "Daddy, look out. The sail is going." Pop! The first eye on the yard tore out. Then, pop! pop! pop! The rest ripped out, and our poor sail was flogging like a bullwhip and the yard was trying to club everyone off the deck.

"Oh, well," I panted, when we had pinned the sail down and stowed it, "it was only an experiment. We'll stitch it up again tomorrow."

Tomorrow? Not likely. Two crises lay in ambush yet before the gales left us. The first occurred at about two o'clock the following morning. It was a wild night, and the wind seemed stronger than at any time since we had left Cape Town. I reefed the main right down, but the wind eventually became so strong that I decided to take in the working jib and replace it with the storm jib. I am a firm believer in flying as much canvas as the boat can possibly carry, but there comes a point when sail must be reduced. When I tried to get the working jib down I found that the halyard was jammed and no amount of tugging would free it. I called Liz up on deck and fetched the bosun's chair, a short wooden seat with a rope attached like a child's swing. We dropped the mainsail and attached the bosun's chair to one of the halyards.

Then I went up the mast to cut the sail down, a knife clenched between my teeth like Black Beard himself.

The idea of climbing the mast at sea was quite horrifying to both of us. The boat was rolling wildly as she lay broadside to the seas, and I had the greatest difficulty in simply clinging to the mast, let alone climbing up it. Each time the boat rolled I swivelled round to the underside of the slippery mast. I felt like a rat shaken by a terrier. But slowly I inched up, and Liz pulled the bosun's chair up after me so that I could rest on it. *Walkabout* had no winches, so Liz could not winch me up. The worst moment came when I had to stand on the chair to reach the jib halyard. The halyard block, made of tufnol with stainless steel reinforcing, had been completely crushed by the force of the halyard and had jammed the rope. I cut the sail down and returned from orbit. Liz claimed afterwards that it was much worse for her to sit on deck and watch me swing overhead, but when I offered to change places with her next time she declined. From that time on I always made sure that there were a couple of spare halyards on each mast to avoid going up in bad weather.

For the rest of the night we lay ahull with no sail set, and the experience was such a violently uncomfortable one that we swore never to repeat it. Perhaps in extreme conditions the wind is strong enough to press the boat over on the masts alone and thereby hold her steady.

It was the following afternoon, after repairs had been effected, when the second crisis occurred. Liz was swept overboard.

At the time we were preparing to make sail. Liz suddenly stepped on to the wrong side (the leeward side) of the mainsail just as I hoisted it aloft. The boom caught her across the chest and swept her off the deck. My immediate reaction was to rush to the spot and help. I was brought up with a jerk at the end of my safety harness line. Unable to go forward and unwilling to go back, I danced foolishly at the end of my leash. Meanwhile Liz, who was also harnessed to the boat, had disappeared over the side carrying the safety lines with her. In the water she grabbed the main boom, and the next wave swung her inboard again. She was soaked to the skin and absolutely furious. The first thing she saw was her ineffectual husband still bleating at the end of his tether like a nanny goat.

"Stop dithering around like that," she said furiously. "Do you want to get the sail up or not?"

I crept back to the halyards without a word. It had all happened so quickly, it was too much for me. Liz refused to discuss the incident for hours, but she was stiff and sore for days afterwards.

After our baptism in heavy weather, the winds slackened and we had a long period of calms and variables. During the gales everyone had been groaning about the rough conditions. They wished the sea would stop; they wanted to get off. But that was nothing compared with the complaints levelled in due course against the calms. At first it was delightful. We hung everything up to dry—not that things soaked in sea water can be successfully dried, because the salt later absorbs moisture from the atmosphere—and the children ran about and played on deck. As we approached the tropics, the sea became warmer and we showered in the cockpit, using sea-water and shampoo first (soap is useless) and rinsing with our fresh water spray afterwards. The children no longer felt seasick and we all ate enormously—far more than we ate in port. Meals, in fact, became a matter of great interest and psychological importance. Liz never stopped feeling queasy, but this did not noticeably reduce her appetite.

We hungered not only for food but for emotional nourishment too, and Mike Hill's cassettes provided a diet of taped music, somewhat limited in that we had few tapes and knew every one, but satisfying none the less. Each composer fulfilled a different need and matched a different mood. Brahms in the fluctuating complexities of a calm, Telemann in light airs, Bach in the endless variety of a steady breeze, Mozart for the perfect day when every dancing wave plays a pattern in the universe, and Dvorak for Force 6 gusting 7. Beethoven is best appreciated in a gale, and Schubert—Schubert can only be played on those rare days of profound beauty when nature blends all her forces in serene harmony.

But one gets tired of Brahms day after day and, as I have said, calms are often more damaging to the boat and more tiring to the crew than rough weather. The wind may fade, but the sea seldom flattens sufficiently to allow the boat to lie still. The senseless slatting and slamming of sails and gear hour after hour, night and day, is hard on the boat and frets the nerves of everyone on board. We had eleven sails all told, and I hung them every way and in every place imaginable—upside down, between the masts, and out on poles. Progress was, however, tedious and slow, and this is what really upset the children. They took a keen interest in the day's run, and a dozen times a day Kevin would pull out the chart and compute how far we had come and how far we had to go. Every other day Liz baked bread in the tin oven—cautiously at first, hopefully later—but she attracted no gales.

The day's run varied from 135 miles down to 35 miles, depending on the wind, and we reckoned to cover something in the region of 25 to 30 miles per day per Beaufort force. A Force 3 wind, for example would give 75–90 miles a day and a Force 4 100–120 miles, depending on wind direction. When the wind was lighter than Force 2, the self-steering no longer functioned properly and someone had to sit at the tiller. The boys detested this chore, and groaned whenever they were detailed to do it, so to make it more palatable I offered a small prize to the one who could steer the greatest mileage in a day.

We settled down to a rather different routine from the one established round the African coast. The main difference was the watch-keeping regime. Our main enemies were ships and sleeplessness. If we kept a 24-hour watch for ships, we knew from past experience that with the children active all day we could not get enough sleep. Liz and I would become more and more exhausted, until our weariness in itself constituted a danger to the boat. If on the other hand we slept all night, the chances of being run down were much greater (even if we steered clear of the shipping lanes), but we should at least remain alert and healthy. We compromised by each sleeping half the night and keeping a "sleeping watch" for the other half. The person on "sleeping watch" slept on the floor (by far the most comfortable place on a boat) and got up every hour to check course, sails and ships. Kevin and Mark took alternate morning watches from five to seven as before. And we started Bruce on an hour watch every afternoon. Only one ship was sighted, near Cape Town.

One day, however, we were all sitting in the cockpit enjoying a sandwich lunch when Bruce cried, "Ship ahoy!"

"Not again!" said Kevin, and idly thumped him on the head. Whenever Bruce cried "Ship ahoy!" (which was at least once a day) it had become habitual for the nearest member of the family to thump him first and look later—his ships were invariably of the imaginary kind.

"Ship ahoy!" he cried again. "It's going to bash us, I tell you."

We all swung round, and were shocked to see a ship steaming up astern only a few hundred yards away. It was all the more alarming because we had come to assume that we were alone on the sea. We steered away and Mark scurried about hoisting and dipping the ensign. But after passing very close the ship altered course and steamed away without responding. She had merely come to look us over, presumably for salvage fodder.

Bruce and I also eagerly scanned the sea for fish but, apart from flying fish which came aboard at night and were invited to the breakfast table, we saw only one small tunny in the whole Atlantic. We fished every day, and in deep water only succeeded in catching the log line. In shallower water near land, where food is more plentiful, we did catch occasionally. The children made up for this by catching a couple of thousand imaginary fish a day from the dinghy. Nestling among the sails in *Crawlabout* they ranged about the oceans, hauling up great marlin, tunny and dorado. Sometimes the dinghy was a submarine for hunting down international crooks, at other times it was a time-machine that took people back in time to play heroic roles in some dreadful disaster—oddly enough, the time-machine never travelled into the future. I think that the imaginary world on *Crawlabout*, especially for Bruce, was more real than the rather cramped world of *Walkabout*.

The lack of space in *Walkabout* was an abiding problem. But while it undoubtedly caused a lot of friction, it also gave us an insight into certain instinctive human behaviour patterns. Mark's bunk, for example, was side by side with Rachel's and head to heel with Bruce's. Mark's territory was therefore hemmed in on two sides by "alien" territory, and to reach it he had to cross Rachel's territory. Rachel invariably objected, and Mark became more and more irritable, until towards the end of our stay in Cape Town he began to have tantrums with increasing frequency.

It seemed to me that behaviour in cramped conditions could be explained by the hypothesis that everyone has a "personality balloon", a sphere of personality influence that envelops his body and is none the less real for being invisible. When two people approach each other their personality balloons press one against the other and become distorted. This is often stimulating, but after a time it becomes tiring and eventually nerve-racking, and the person needs to be alone for a while. Some people, of course, have more robust personalities than others, and there are special relationships such as man and wife and mother and baby, where the personalities tend to blend rather than deflect. In a very confined space like a boat one needs a territory of one's own, where one can retire to allow the personality balloon to heal. Merely a bunk with a personal shelf will do, but it must be private. The solution, in the case of Mark, Bruce and Rachel, was to provide each of the boys with a curtain to cut his bunk off from the rest of the boat. The results were dramatic. Mark's tantrums vanished, and general bickering, which had been serious, fell at once to a casual level.

Fifteen days out of Cape Town the wind returned and we looked forward at last to trade wind sailing, the carefree slide down the slopes of the steady winds that girdle the earth in tropical seas. Sailors have so often sung in praise of the trades that we expected nothing less than to set the sails and go to sleep for a week. "Wake me up when we get to St Helena," I told Mark. But nothing in nature is that simple, and in fact we did not find the true trades until after St Helena. We did, however, on our way north, pass the sun on his journey south to the Tropic of Capricorn, and on the same day we crossed the Greenwich Meridian and slipped into the Western Hemisphere. Both events signified progress and boosted morale.

In a navigational sense, though, the results were curious. When the day's position had been computed I found that we were miles from where we ought to have been. At first I put it down to an error in calculation because the two crossings had necessitated turning the calculations upside down. But when the sights on the following day confirmed the first results I realised that the sextant must be out. I threw myself into a mild panic and spent the whole day shooting the sun and moon and calculating the results. By comparing the sun and moon sights and also sights before and after passing under the noon sun, I was able to guess that the sextant was 9 miles out. This gave me a nasty empty feeling, because if the sextant was not 9 miles out (and there was no real guarantee that it was not something quite different), then our actual position could be as much as 13 miles out, which, coupled with other factors such as poor visibility, could in turn conceivably cause us to miss the island. After all, St Helena is only about 10 miles across, and the next speck of land—Ascension Island—is 700 miles away. The error had not been discovered before because our daily position was taken from two regular sights—one at noon and one at about 3 p.m. The calculated positions were always therefore correct relative to each other but not in absolute terms.

I decided to stick to the estimated error of 9 miles, and on the eighteenth day from Cape Town I announced that St Helena would probably appear over the bowsprit at four o'clock in the afternoon. A prize was offered to the first person who sighted the island. All day the children were peering eagerly at the horizon from the foredeck, from the end of the bowsprit and from halfway up the rigging. As for me, I went to bed. One patch of ocean looks remarkably like another, and the whole exercise seemed suddenly quite improbable. Witchcraft, I thought as I fell asleep, is our only chance.

At exactly four o'clock I was awakened by a mad drumming of heels on the deck over my head. There were yells of "Land ho!" "There it is!" "I can see it!" "I saw it first!" "No, you didn't." "Yes, I did," and then Rachel's imperious little voice rising above the others, "Really! Will someone please show me where to look?" I rolled out of bed and lurched to the hatch, where I met Liz tumbling down to call me. We became wedged in the hatchway.

"Mike! Mike, we can see St Helena!"

"I inferred something of the sort. Will you please take your shoulder off my jaw?"

"Sorry! Mark saw it first! Isn't it exciting?"

"Yes. But unless you climb off my windpipe I shall stop breathing."

"Sorry. Mark! Come and show Daddy where it is."

"Please climb off my windpipe."

"Sorry. Mike, aren't you coming out to see?"

"I AM TRYING TO!"

"All right, don't get so excited."

The island lay like a small, tastefully designed jewel on the horizon, far away yet wonderfully clear. Every landfall is exciting, but there is nothing to compare with the wonderment of the first one. The spell grew as night fell and the few lights winked through the waves ahead of the bowsprit. And how enchanting it was to sail round the south-eastern corner at dawn the following morning. Mark was on watch with me, and when it became light enough to see we called Kevin to watch the cliffs go by. For St Helena is a real island. Not a low, scruffy, beachy, corally sort of island but a rugged, cliffy, craggy volcanic island, rising square out of the sea to 3,000 feet, cut here and there by green ravines and pocked about the base with mysterious sea caves. We sailed slowly along the leeward shore in crystal green waters until we came to the largest ravine of all. Clinging to the sides of the ravine and dozing in the little valley at its foot is Jamestown, the capital and the island's only town. In the roadstead in front of the town we dropped anchor, and relaxed in the cockpit with a sense of achievement.

We were able to relax for nearly a minute before the children began to agitate.

"When are we going ashore?" asked Bruce. "I want to find a toyshop. And a fishing shop to buy some more hooks."

"I'm going to spend my prize money on a penknife," said Mark.

"Daddy," asked Kevin, "do you think there's a library?"

"I want balloons, all different colours," said Rachel.

"I wonder if there's a shower somewhere," mused Liz, "and a place to do the washing."

"Single-handed sailing seems so attractive at times," I sighed. "Come on, Kevin and Mark, help me unship the dinghy. Bruce, start putting those sails on deck."

As soon as the port authorities had come out to clear us we went ashore. When we reached the landing-stage we found it as rudimentary as the harbour itself, which is simply a patch of sea in front of the town. It consists of several stone steps, over which hangs a rope, and the idea is to surge in on top of a swell, grab the rope and swing ashore. The children thought this a splendid idea, but I believe that on the rare occasions when a cruise ship disgorges a load of tourists the antics of the poor people keep the St Helenians laughing until the next ship arrives. As soon as we stepped ashore Rachel fell down. She picked herself up and walked a few steps, then fell over again.

"Mummy, I keep rocking with the land but the land isn't rocky," she wailed. Just so. We all rocked into town on land that would not rock.

As we walked up the main street everyone turned and stared with undisguised curiosity. "They be yachties," "there go the yachties," they told each other—a fact which required no profound deduction, for a stranger can only reach St Helena by yacht or by ship, and there were no ships. To us they smiled and called, "G'd mornin'," and "Is it today you've come?" Yachties were obviously a common event in St Helena, and it was pleasant to be welcomed as normal visitors for a change rather than as some strange sub-species of the human race.

We were directed to Dot's Café, one of the two or three eating houses on the island. Like most buildings in Jamestown it was a small, lumpy place, half-tunnelled out of, and half-built on to the rocks, as though it could not decide whether to be a house or a hobbit hole. The eating room—which was frankly squalid—was decorated from floor to roof with hundreds of signatures, verse, emblems and even paintings done by yachties over the years, and we spent a happy hour hunting for the yachts we knew. Dot herself is a splendid, big-hearted, bustling woman, and she welcomed us with open arms, hugging Rachel and chaffing the boys. The food—fresh tuna and spicy fishcakes—was superb.

St Helena, we found, suffered from the Rip van Winkle syndrome. The clock had stopped when Napoleon Bonaparte died in 1821 and the attitudes, the institutions and even St Helena's version of the English language were all rooted firmly in the nineteenth century. Napoleon is regarded as the island hero, perhaps because he is St Helena's main claim to fame, or perhaps because, during his internment, thousands of British troops were stationed on the island and St Helena enjoyed its last period of prosperity. Since then various projects have been attempted, and have met with invariable failure. Flax was grown, and it spread over half the island until the bottom dropped out of the market; flax still covers half the island. Then a fish factory was set up, but of course the shoal fish all went away. With no hope of capturing another emperor, the island had gone into a decline and resigned itself to poverty.

Perhaps the people themselves, who number 5,000, are partly responsible for the decline: they are a mixture of various Asiatic, African and European races, blended during the period when St Helena was a popular staging port on the trading route to the Far East; but isolation and inbreeding have made them indolent and apathetic. The island cannot even grow its own food now and exists, I gathered, principally on a British colonial grant and the sale of postage stamps. There is no aerodrome, and the only regular communication with the outside world is by mailship every three weeks. Religious sects and dejected charities are a prominent feature of island life.

This state of affairs is not without its advantages. When I wanted the exchange rate between the American dollar and the pound sterling altered I simply went to see the Chancellor of the Exchequer (Island Treasurer), a most courteous gentleman, and he obliged immediately. The people everywhere are friendly and always have time for a chat. Most refreshing of all, there is little sign of pollution around the island, and fish abound in great numbers. The boys were delighted with this. They went goggling virtually every day, and fishing lines were forever trailing overboard. Hundreds of mackerel and other fish swarmed around the boat, and if you felt like fish for breakfast you simply sat in the cockpit and caught a few. Now and then a big fish like the huge manta ray would swim past. Bruce always said rather wistfully afterwards, "St Helena was my best port ever."

One day Mark, Bruce and I went fishing with one of the few local fishermen. His method of fishing was to harpoon the fish from the bows of his little open boat, using an enormously long, thin, bamboo pole with a home-made harpoon head attached loosely to its end. While I motored the boat slowly forward he would scan the waves for a faint shadow which we could never see but to him meant fish. Balancing precariously on a thwart in the bows he would stiffen, then suddenly hurl the pole forward, and with incredible skill bury the harpoon head in the fish. The head would break off and the line, attended by Mark, would whistle over the side. Ten minutes later the fish would be hauled cautiously to the surface, usually dead. That day the fisherman speared four wahoo, each weighing between 50 and 60 lb., and narrowly missed a tunny and a marlin. We contented ourselves with 5 lb. tiddlers caught in the usual way with hook, line and sinker.

The only other yacht in St Helena was a 50ft French schooner called *La Semillante*, sailed by the Discords, a family with three children—two boys, and a little girl of Rachel's age. The Discords had sold up everything to go cruising, but they had had a rough time. *La Semillante* was specially built for them in France, and after many delays they had set out in mid-winter to sail south. They reached Portugal, and there the yacht was driven on to the quay one day by a gale while the family were ashore. The main damage was fortunately only to the propeller and engine, but it took six months to effect a repair and the engine soon broke down again. They continued, however, to Dakar and thence to Ascension Island. The voyage took a long time, for the sails were all blown out and the rigging damaged in heavy weather. In Ascension they managed to effect some repairs, and then sailed to St Helena. From St Helena to Ascension is 700 miles, and most cruising yachts would reckon to take seven days or less. But sailing the other way, into the teeth of the trades with poor sails, *La Semillante* took twenty-five days. The worst feature of these long, exhausting voyages was Mme Discord's desperate seasickness, which confined her to bed from the moment they set sail till the anchor dropped again. The poor woman looked terribly sick even in port.

Their sails were being repaired in St Helena by a local barman who owned a sewing machine, but the Discords had no money to pay him. Their bank had airmailed money to St Helena, unaware that there was no air service, and they looked forward gloomily to Christmas on the island. They wanted to sail as soon as possible to Cape Town, where they intended to sell the boat and settle down. This worried me a good deal, because sailing direct from St Helena to Cape Town they would again be battling into the prevailing winds, and I tried to persuade Dr Discord to head south-west, perhaps even as far as South America, before cutting across to South Africa. Cruising from Europe to South Africa one should go so far west, in fact, that it is worth while popping into Brazil en route. What route he finally adopted I do not know; we heard later that they had reached Cape Town, but that the voyage had taken nearly two months, which says much for the family's tenacity.

La Semillante and *Walkabout* lay two minutes' row from each other and the children from the two boats were to-ing and fro-ing all day. All day, that is, after the work had been done, for the Discord children, like ours, had to pull their weight aboard. It was the first time our children had met other boat children, and they had great fun—racing dinghies, swimming, diving off *Walkabout*'s bowsprit and swapping Tin Tin books.

For the first couple of day we just relaxed. Then we faced up to a variety of problems that had been simmering unspoken for some time. In many ways St Helena, at the end of our first ocean crossing, was as much a crisis point as Durban had been. As before, the most serious problem was Liz's seasickness. Contrary to expectation it had not disappeared after the first few days, but had persisted in a subdued form throughout the crossing. Apart from the despondency it caused I feared that persistent seasickness would result in jaundice. I had no medical grounds for this supposition, but remembered that David Lewis's wife succumbed to jaundice after long periods of seasickness during their circumnavigation. The children were fine, but we wondered what effect the cramped conditions would have on them after a long run.

The second problem was a technical one. The amount of chafe and wear after less than 2,000 miles was depressing, and I could see that maintenance would stretch our limited resources to the utmost if not beyond. Most of the sails and running rigging were in doubtful condition, and I badly felt the lack of large light-weather sails. We had, for instance, only one big genoa, and that was a cast-off from a 30 Square Meter. If we sailed south to Rio we should have to battle 1,500 miles north again against light head winds and the Brazilian current, and of course we could not use the engine. The alternative was to sail straight to England, stopping only at the Azores, or possibly in the West Indies as well. But to miss Rio, to by-pass the new world after nearly a year on the boat. . . . We pulled out the charts and worked out several alternative schedules. Liz finally solved the dilemma by insisting that we should go to Rio regardless; we estimated that if we kept to a tight schedule we could reach England by the following June before our money ran out. If not, then we could stop and work in Brazil, in the West Indies or even in the U.S.A., and reach England the year after next. Were we walkabouts or were we not? We decided we were.

So we worked to prepare our ship for the next crossing. The squaresail was mended, a new headsail arrangement to reduce chafe was built, a new jib boom was made from a special type of heavy bamboo which the St Helenians call "He-man bamboo", and the sextant was adjusted with the help of Dr Discord, who had the proper tools for the job and knew how to use them. Liz washed and washed until all the salt had been leached out of our clothes and manfully rowed stores aboard. The boys filled the water bags and ferried them over. As always it was a heavy job and they grumbled like stink.

Before we left St Helena, however, we toured the island in an old car that snorted out clouds of steam up every hill. It is a beautiful island, and the high interior where the rain falls is surprisingly lush. Flax grows everywhere, but try to find a fruit tree or vegetable patch! It can only be done through the old boy network. Naturally we visited Longacres, Napoleon's house, which is now a museum, although it feels more like a morgue, for the nondescript house caged an Emperor for the last six miserable years of his life and the rooms are strewn with artefacts from the death chamber. Astounding as it may seem, tiny St Helena has a diplomatic representative in the form of the French Consul. Queen Victoria gave the house and grounds to the French nation, and ever since a consul has lived there to take care of it.

We had intended to stay in St Helena for five days, but in the end stayed ten. On December 10th we raised anchor and set sail, bound for Rio.

IX

BOUND FOR RIO! What a splendid ring there is to that phrase. The reality was just as fine. We eased out from under the lee of the island and at once picked up a fresh trade wind. St Helena quickly became smaller until it was a miniature island, then a little shadow, and finally no more than a doubt upon the horizon. By the end of the day we were alone on the ocean surging towards the sunset over South America.

Our departure lacked the deplorable dramatics in which we had so far specialised. No one was seasick, because the anchorage at St Helena had been so unquiet that we had, in effect, been at sea all the time. There were no gales and nothing broke. It finally dawned on us that we had at last found the trade winds, and I was determined to hang on to them for as long as possible by shaping the right route.

The essential tool for route planning is the Pilot Chart or the Routeing Chart. Such a chart chops the oceans up into 300-mile squares and for each square it gives, for each month of the year, the average direction and strength of the winds, the direction and strength of the currents, and a host of other data, including such things as gale frequencies, incidence of fog and mean temperatures. The Americans publish the Pilot Chart and the British the Routeing Chart. I have used both and prefer the British charts, because they break down the wind data into more detailed patterns and provide information on sea temperatures; when one eats, sleeps and reads below the waterline, the sea temperature is more important than the air temperature. Also the British charts are made of stronger paper—very important if there is a drip over the chart table.

The Routeing Chart of course gives only the probable weather based on thousands of observations over the years, which is not necessarily the weather that a ship will actually experience, but does enable the navigator to plan a logical route. The shortest distance from St Helena to Rio is about 2,100 miles, but to follow that route is asking to be becalmed. To find the winds one must go further north. The route that I finally selected actually passed 120 miles north of St Helena, although Rio is 450 miles to the south of the island. The route distance was increased to more than 2,300 miles, which I reckoned would take about twenty-five days, but in the end we took much less and the longer route paid off handsomely.

It took us a day or two to settle down to a sailing routine (if such a word can be applied to a life governed by the restless kaleidoscope of sea and air) before Rachel popped the inevitable question.

"Mummy, how many days to Christmas?"

"Fourteen, my love."

"Yow! Only fourteen!" Her vivacious face beamed with glee. "We had better hurry up and get things ready," she said anxiously.

"Yes!" said Mark worriedly. "We've got to decorate the boat and—and . . . "

"Roll up, roll up, roll up," I cried. "Only fourteen sailing days to Christmas."

"How many miles is that?" asked Kevin.

"With a bit of luck, 1,500," I replied. "Hurry, hurry, only 1,500 miles to Christmas and not a moment to lose!"

The children took me at my word and began to plan excitedly for Christmas.

"What are we going to do?" asked Mark.

"I'm going to fire off all the flares like Daddy did on Guy Fawkes," said Bruce.

"There are plenty of things to do," I said hurriedly. "For one thing we must start practising carols, and Kevin and Mark must learn their parts on the recorder."

"Why not put on a play?" suggested Liz.

"There's no room on the boat," said Kevin dejectedly.

"Yes, there is," I said. "There is if you make it a radio play."

"What's that?" cried everyone.

I explained. "You don't need a stage. You can hang a curtain across the engine hatch and read your parts from behind it."

The idea was adopted enthusiastically and it was decided

that Kevin would write and produce the play, Mark would copy out the parts and they would all rehearse secretly in the dinghy and present the play as a surprise on Christmas Day. For the next fortnight the old man and his missus were liable to be unceremoniously bundled out of their comfy seats in the cockpit and sent down below during rehearsals, which took place in the afternoons after lessons.

The next preoccupation was with food.

"What are we going to have for Christmas dinner?" everyone wanted to know.

"Hurry, hurry!" I chanted. "Only fourteen flying-fish-frying days to Christmas!"

"Shut up, everyone," said Liz irritably. "It's still two weeks away, for heaven's sake! You'll find out on the day." She was becoming a little nettled by the daily enquiries immediately after breakfast about the lunch menu.

It is extraordinary how important food becomes at sea. Our staple diet was a hard wholewheat bread that Liz baked—4lb. of it—every other day. "She bakes the best bread in the South Atlantic," I recorded appreciatively in the log. We also depended heavily on fresh eggs and fresh fruit—or, failing that, the excellent South African dried fruit. Most of the main courses were some type of stew or casserole which could be prepared in the pressure cooker or a deep, safe pot. But variety, we found, was as important as quantity, and Liz used onions and spices imaginatively to make the tinned food interesting. Too interesting, for we began to suffer from indigestion. This was caused not only by too much food but by the motion of the boat and lack of exercise. When sailors talk of "rolling down the trades" they mean just that! *Walkabout* rolled her scuppers under in a 3-second cycle clear across the Atlantic. Bracing oneself against the motion week after week is very tiring on the stomach muscles but not good as exercise.

It was Bruce who one day solved the exercise problem, at least for the three youngest members of the family. We refused to let them swim for fear of sharks (which we never saw), but one day, when the sea was a little calmer than usual, Bruce begged to be allowed just to dip his bottom in the water. Mark and Rachel joined in, and soon there was a complicated game called "bottoms'ls", which involved plunging oneself as deep

As fast as we foraged the children ate it up. Here I grumpily return from the market in Dominica, West Indies, with another dinghy-load of victuals

Crawlabout was a maid of all work. Here Kevin ferries water bags aboard. Note the lateen rig, the leeboard and an oar used as a rudder

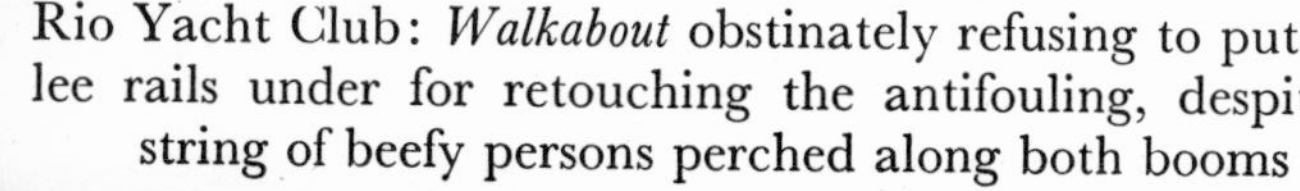

Rio Yacht Club: *Walkabout* obstinately refusing to put her lee rails under for retouching the antifouling, despite a string of beefy persons perched along both booms

Endless maintenance—the skipper despairs

in the water as possible when the boat rolled without actually falling off, all accompanied by obligatory screaming. Oh, for a solo crossing! They used safety harnesses, of course, and I rigged a bamboo toe-ledge over the side. Kevin declined to join in, preferring to lie in the dinghy reading.

Trade wind sailing sounds idyllic, but it is not all beer and skittles, and it took me some time to learn how best to sail *Walkabout*. For one thing, the trades are only relatively steady. The strength fluctuates continually throughout the day, tending to reach a peak late at night or in the early hours of the morning, and unless the sail plan of the boat is perfectly balanced, the self-steering needs continual adjustment. The wind direction varies too, fluctuating over 15 degrees or so, unless there is a major change when everything shuts down for a few hours in the transition. This 15 degrees is often just enough, when the wind is in a critical position astern, to get on the wrong side of the sails and gybe or luff the boat.

So when you have found the trades, what do you do with them? I turned to the most venerable authority of all, Odysseus (I was reading Homer's *Odyssey* at the time). "Would that I could control the winds as Odysseus did," I lamented in my log one night. "On one occasion he was presented with a leather bag by Aeolus, Warden of the Gales. This bag contained the boisterous energies of all the winds and was secured tightly with burnished silver wire to prevent the slightest leakage [says Homer], and with it Odysseus was able to sail right back to Ithaca. But his suspicious crew, seeking unshared loot, opened the bag while their skipper slept and released all the Gales, which promptly drove them out to sea and wrecked them." But how can one look up to a man like Odysseus who, for all his fine talk and impressive string of shipwreck survivals, took ten years to cross a patch of sea that I would have expected to cross in *four days*?

No, I thought sadly, I shall have to look to my seamy old sails and sticks of bamboo, and accordingly I experimented with all manner of bizarre arrangements, even insisting on Liz hanging out the pot rags in a certain way until *Walkabout* looked like a flying felucca with sticks and strings hanging improbably everywhere. The conventional twin headsails, I found, were not large enough—the real power lay in the gaff main. The best arrangement was found to be with the main to leeward and the genoa flying as a spinnaker, with the foot boomed out to windward and the clew lashed to leeward. The mizzen staysail was a powerful sail and could be flown together with the mizzen if the wind was on the quarter. The squaresail I used in lighter winds only, flying from the mizzen mast.

The arrangement, illustrated opposite, was not only powerful, but a stable and well-balanced system which could accept fairly wide variations in wind strength and direction without upsetting the self-steering qualities. The mizzen staysail does not blanket the main because the gaff reaches up to catch the high wind and scoop it down.

The balancing feature of the rig suggested an idea which would have been useful several thousand miles later when we had to reach or close reach (i.e. the wind across or slightly ahead of the boat) for long periods. The development of sail plan over the last century has been concentrated on fore and aft rig for reasons of windward performance, mainly for racing craft. When the wind bears to the beam, the sails are all swung out on one side and all drag the boat along from that side. This gives rise to weather helm, i.e. the rig is unbalanced and self-steering with any system becomes a problem; one can set the course on a particular wind strength by adjusting the self-steering and tensioning the tiller, but as soon as the wind strength changes so does the course. One possibility is to use a swinging bowsprit which will balance the sails and could at the same time provide extra power. The pivot on the bowsprit must be in line with the masthead and bobstay anchor so that the tension of the forestay and bobstay will not alter. The bowsprit would be swung out, of course, for running as well as reaching. (See diagram on p. 164.)

We sailed fast towards Christmas and the children's excitement mounted daily. Everyone was happy and busy, and Liz's seasickness had at last abated to a mild, almost subconscious, annoyance. A few days before Christmas she delved with a secretive smile into strange dark places and emerged—with a Christmas tree! Not a proper one, of course, but a tiny folding silvery thing which we lashed to the battery charger. Hidden decorations were uncovered, and the children decorated the cabin so that one could hardly move without being garrotted

WALKABOUT'S RUNNING RIG

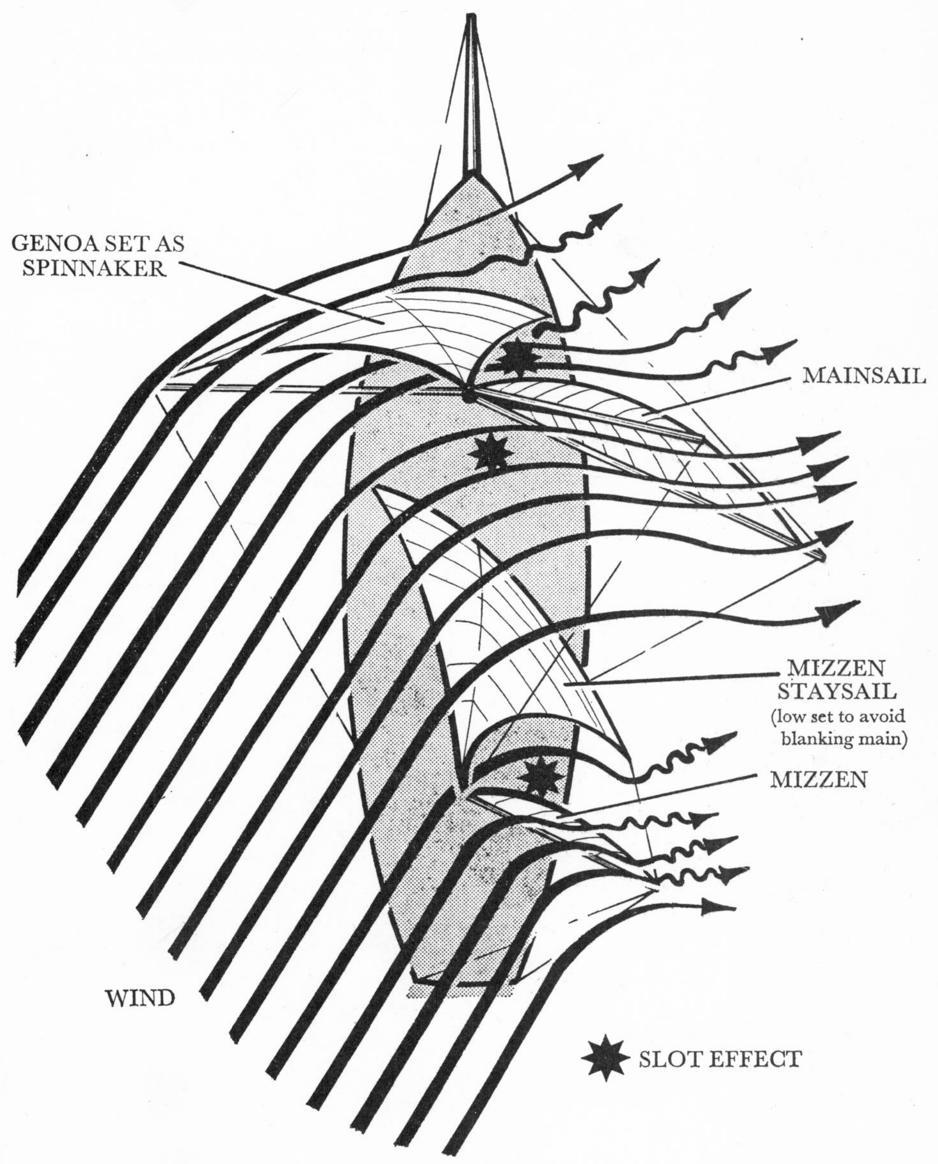

by a streamer. Christmas Eve dawned, and with it Liz's birthday. More burrowing in deep chain lockers and the like, and presents were produced. We all fussed over her, the children insisting on cooking her lunch while Kevin and I made a fine supper of ham with specially concocted mustard sauce and potato salad, with stewed apples and custard to follow. Afterwards we sang carols by candlelight.

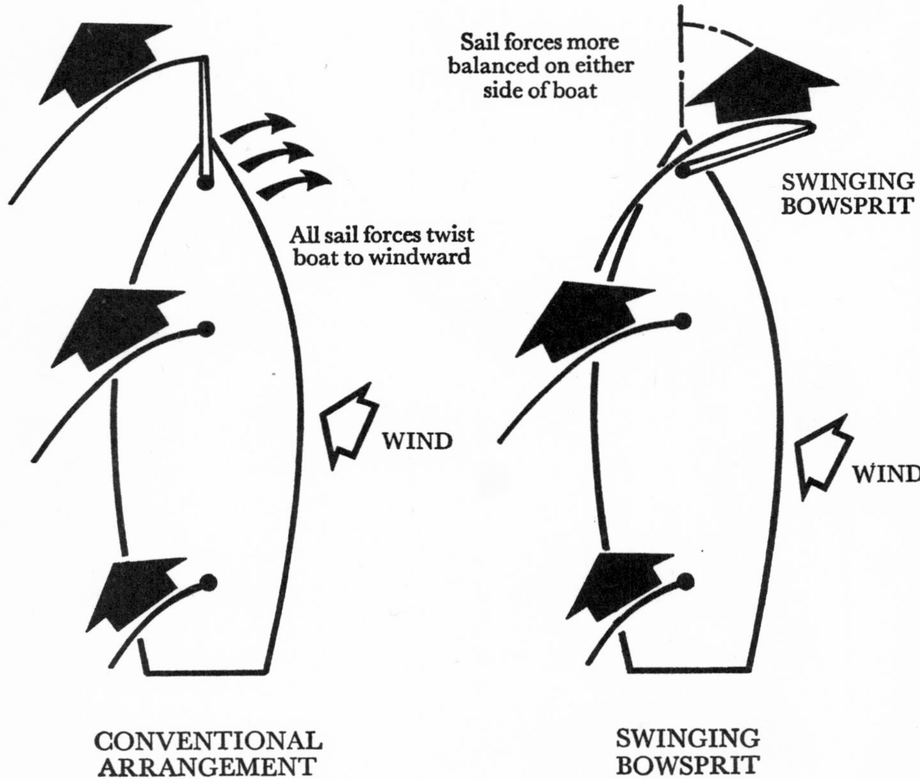

Then the genoa fell down. Alas, the elements did not observe the festivities and the wind had been blowing hard all day. In fact, we covered 142 miles on Christmas Eve. But at least the genoa waited until after the carol service. I recorded sadly in my log that night, "Observe the ink blots. There has been another crisis. Ink blots on the log are always a sign of crisis because the ocean jumps into the boat whenever we weaken. I heard a tapping on the hull and found the big genoa ballooning alongside in the water. The halyard had chafed through and the whole Heath Robinson affair had collapsed. It has taken Liz and me over an hour to sort out the tangled mess of sails, ropes and spars, hoist a new working jib and untangle the log line and Bruce's wretched fishing line."

On Christmas Day the children were swarming around the cabin before daylight. After breakfast more digging and delving revealed further presents, some of which caught even Liz and me by surprise. There is no end to the hidey holes on an old yacht, and our Cape Town friends had been generous. We tried to get the Queen's Message on the B.B.C. Overseas Service, but reception was poor and we only managed to hear a discussion on seasickness, or acceleration sickness as the academic commentator dryly put it. He suggested that the main culprit was the relative motions of head and body, and if only the head and shoulders of the victim could be encased in plaster of paris . . . "No!" shrieked Liz as we advanced on her. "It's the season of goodwill."

In the afternoon a curtain was erected across the cabin for the radio play, and a piece of cardboard on which was written *The Highwayman* came hurtling over the curtain top on a piece of string. The play was short but very good, and we were much impressed by the period language. "Oh, what times we live in, sir! What times we live in!" complained Bruce gruffly as the stagecoach was held up.

We sat down to a magnificent Christmas dinner, so eagerly awaited, so painstakingly prepared and so difficult to eat. The wind was blowing hard, and even an ordinary meal of stew would have been difficult to handle. But a Christmas dinner with several courses posed special problems. We got through the shellfish hors d'œuvres without mishap, but when the guinea-fowl began to fly we were hard put to catch it. A full glass of beer landed in my lap and seeped everywhere. The rum and Christmas pud were solid enough, but the white sauce was decidedly sticky. When we finally put the children to bed and retired into the cockpit with Polish honey wine (given to us by a solo round-the-worlder, Chris Baranowski) it was only diluted a little by the occasional boarding wave.

The next day it was business as usual. Liz stitched up the big genoa and I climbed both masts to effect rigging repairs and then crawled into the bilges to repair the paraffin lines. I do not know which is worse.

The wind held and onwards we sped, Rio drawing closer by the day. But during the night watches, when everyone is asleep, it is calmer, and I read, unhurriedly and with deep pleasure. Sometimes I walk slowly round the decks of our little world—to check for chafe, I pretend, but really to soak in the wonder of the sea and the night sky. I turn off the Tilley lamp to blend better with the wind. I look up to the sails and think I am the wind undulating across the sea, rising and falling as I slowly spin like an astronaut in space. A sail reaches up to scoop me round and I compress, smaller, faster, as I swirl down between the two sails before cascading off the edge of the cloth to carry on across the sea. Now I am standing solidly again on the foredeck and in front of me is the bowsprit. I crawl out along it and sit at the end so that I can look back on the whole boat as she surges down the silver avenue laid by the full moon straight across the sea. How she roars as each wave thrusts her forward in the foam. And how she twists and rolls. At times like this I cannot help thinking of her as a living thing.

On December 28th, just eighteen days out from St Helena, I announced to a cheering ship's company that we should reach Rio the following night if the wind blew hard. On the morning of the nineteenth day we found ourselves lying becalmed near Cabo Frio (Cape Cold), 60 miles from Rio in a green sea. What was this extraordinary green sea, everyone wanted to know? Was the sea not always a fantastic blue? I explained that green sea meant shallow water. Although we could not see land we were on the continental shelf of South America, and if a wind did not blow up we should slowly drift down to Argentina. We all whistled hard and a fresh wind sprang up, blowing so hard that I feared for my sails. But I refused to take down a scrap of canvas and we raced towards Rio like an express train.

At lunchtime we sighted South America. This was for me an intense moment of personal discovery. The fact that Cabral had first discovered Brazil in 1500, that over a hundred million people now live there and that planes commute daily with

Europe was a trifle irritating, but did not nullify this sense of personal discovery. Shadowy mountains loomed in the haze and slowly hardened into a magnificent landscape of green and rock mountains, stopping sheer at the edge of the Atlantic. The impressive scene took all of us aback, for we had not expected anything to vie with the Cape Peninsula. We sailed parallel to the coast looking for one particular mountain, the famous Pão de Açúcar (Sugar Loaf) that guards the entrance to Rio harbour. Curiously enough there was no sign of habitation anywhere. We must have seen and positively identified at least a dozen mountains before the real Pão de Açúcar finally showed up at sunset. We could not reach Rio in daylight, but we decided to press on anyway and enter by night. We also decided that the children could stay up until we anchored, so we ate an early supper and went into the cockpit.

That entry is unforgettable. For Liz and me, at least, the memory will remain with us to the end of our days. After nearly three weeks at sea a city of five million people lay before us. We could hear the rumble of traffic as much as 30 miles away. The lights of the city, obscured by the mountains, threw a glow into the night sky that dimmed the moon. Silhouetted against the light, Sugar Loaf thrust up as boldly as a pillar to guide us in. Our other guide was Corcovada, the titanic neon-lit statue of Christ mounted thousands of feet in the sky, apparently without support. And our shepherds were the dolphins, hundreds of them, burning phosphorescent paths as they criss-crossed like tracer torpedoes under and past the boat. They escorted us to the very entrance of Rio and then, under the shadow of Sugar Loaf, they left us, and for the first time since Cape Town we went forward under motor.

The yacht basin at Rio is an entire bay called Enseada de Botafogo, and the passage into it is easy. But once inside we motored around in circles, totally bewildered by the garish city surrounding us, the flashing neon signs and the roar of traffic. The children gazed in wonderment at the huge Christmas illuminations. "Isn't it super!" they breathed to one another. Shadowy yachts lay everywhere at anchor. At last we found one with a light aboard and approached cautiously. I hailed it and a woman appeared in the cockpit.

"Good evening, senhora," I began in my most fluent

Portuguese. "Can you please tell me where we can anchor?"

She made some unintelligible reply.

I tried again. "We've just come in, you see, and there are so many boats we can't see where to anchor."

"What is going on up there?" called a male voice from down below in B.B.C. English.

In the same tongue his wife replied, "I don't really know, darling. There's a man out here gabbling in Portuguese and I can't understand a word he's saying."

"Dear Lord!" I murmured to Liz. "We've done it again! The first people we speak to in the New World are British yachties. And I bet they've only been here a few hours." They had.

Next day we found ourselves in a land of flash and glamour. Rio itself must surely be blessed by the most beautiful surroundings of any city in the world. It is a city interwoven with the mountains and the sea, the one rising grandly here and there in granite above the metropolis, the other flooding round the edges through lagoons and the coves of the Bay of Guanabara. The Rio Yacht Club occupies a vast site just inside the Bay of Guanabara and under the lee of Sugar Loaf Mountain. It is one of the most exclusive social clubs in Brazil, and one is forever rubbing shoulders with field-marshals and diplomats or apologising to millionaires one has trodden on. The girls who graced the place were luscious. Brazilian girls are in any case an exquisite blend of many races, and one will see Scandinavian blondes with honey-brown skin and chocolate girls with classical features and ice-blue eyes. They dress in revealing garments that flow with their limbs, and wear bare skins more elegantly than any other race I have seen—especially the girls at the yacht club. Liz threatened to let me ashore only with a ball and chain. Amongst this fauna of high society one sometimes saw members of a very much lower species, and I found that when, say, a general was admitted to the membership so were his sisters and his cousins and his aunts, for the family is strong in Brazil.

The club itself occupies several hundred acres of prime Rio real estate and has *pied-à-terre* blocks of flatlets (boxes, as the Brazilians call them), restaurants, a chapel, halls, shops, barbers, a resident doctor, a score of different workshops, some four hundred employees and aircraft hangars full of gin-palace-type motor yachts and sleek sailing dinghies; only a small proportion of boats are put into the water, and an even smaller proportion venture out of port. *Walkabout* looked tiny and old among such a splendid flotilla. All this was guarded by dozens of the club's fully armed guards who patrolled the grounds and manned the gates. They could never stop fingering their pistols, and we were always terribly polite to them.

Despite its eliteness the club extended to us all its facilities, and for all this generous hospitality never charged a cent. There were so few walkabouts that their presence did not unduly affect the members, but I am certain that with the growing number of walkabouts this situation cannot last long.

For the children the star attraction was the swimming pool, surrounded by lawns and coconut palms. When they were not at the pool they could usually be found on *Ilanda*. *Ilanda* was a walkabout, a 48ft steel sloop which had been built in South Africa and bought by Pieter Boshoff and his wife Jean. They had had her fitted out for permanent cruising, and had then sold their business and gone afloat with their four teenage children. We had previously met them in Cape Town; they had sailed for Rio shortly before Bruce's arm broke, and they had been there ever since. The children did their schooling by means of a correspondence course and had just successfully completed examinations. The Ilandas had no definite plans; they were disposed to Argentina and then Spain, but generally preferred port to sea. This was hardly surprising, as the boat was one of the best fitted out for living I have seen, in terms of sensible equipment and economical use of space. But on one matter we never saw eye to eye. Pieter had elaborate radio equipment, including a ham set.

"But what use is it?" I asked.

"You can call for help if need be," he replied.

The only time he had done so, however, had been a farce. When they reached Rio the wind, as frequently happens in those parts, vanished completely, and as the engine was damaged they could only drift with the current, which bore them towards the rocks off Copacabana beach. Copacabana is a skyscraper suburb of Rio, housing a million or more souls; thousands must have been looking at *Ilanda*, the only boat offshore, and thousands more were packed along the beach.

But when she fired distress flares, I suppose they simply thought them pretty fireworks. Pieter radioed the yacht club (which operates its own ship-to-shore station), the harbour authorities and the ham frequencies, all without response. Eventually, when *Ilanda* was only a few hundred feet from the rocks, they lowered the dinghy and towed her into port.

"Well, anyway I like to chat to other people at sea," said Pieter.

"I go to sea," I said, "to get away from people."

There were a number of other boats in Rio, including a lovely Laurent Giles 50ft steel ketch, *Fandango*. Maurice Coreth, the skipper, and his crew were on a walkabout from England to East Africa, and I never failed to enjoy his witty company. He had set out from England with gay nonchalance but in such complete ignorance of sailing that, once south of the equator, he had no idea how to upend the calculations, and placed his position south of Cape Town until they reached Rio. Perhaps because I sailed the well-known *Walkabout*, or perhaps because I wore a beard and a bus conductor's cap, I was deemed to be knowledgeable; and Maurice, after a disastrous attempt to leave Rio with a Brazilian crew, invited me to accompany the boat to Cape Town. I refused with the greatest reluctance, for a voyage back through the roaring forties attracted me like a lodestone, but I could not leave Liz and the children for six weeks. Maurice set out later with other crew and made it, not only to Cape Town but later to East Africa, arriving, no doubt, as experienced an old salt as any.

The most moving walkabout story came from a young couple, John and Karen, who arrived from England some weeks later in a 25ft Vertue, one of the sturdiest little sea boats ever designed. Although they were barely out of their teens, they had bought *Virtue Carina* in Durban, and without any prior knowledge of the sea had quietly prepared her for their voyage in the face of opposition from parents, locals and finally the port authorities. The local salts subjected them to terrorisation by tales of the sea, but they finally left and sailed to England. On the way John had to dive over the side to clear a tangled propeller, and between Cape Town and St Helena they had received a severe thrashing. In England they got jobs, refitted, went to Denmark (where the mast fell down) and had a baby.

Now they were on their way back to South Africa with the 10-month-old baby. After more than fifty days, much of it in the roaring forties, they reached Cape Town and returned to shore life, thereby completing a fine voyage with courage and tenacity.

Liz and I were fascinated by Brazil and everything Brazilian. The first thing that strikes one is that everything is done on a grand scale, from the sports boats which hurtle out to sea and return with more sailfish and marlin than I have ever clapped eyes on to the 1,000-member orchestra. The dominant cultural influence is American, and anything American is automatically right, but the Brazilians are nevertheless strongly nationalistic; they make their own diesel engines, build aeroplanes and manufacture Volkswagens, which they export to Germany. These laudable things are rarely done efficiently, but it is something that they are done at all. One cannot escape the impression that Brazil is a young giant just beginning to flex its muscles, and the language tends to confirm this: although technically identical to Portuguese, it seems to me poetically richer and more flexible (particularly in absorbing foreign terms), both signs of a vigorous young language.

The other side of the coin became apparent to us only after a time. At first we observed only the fanatical pursuit of money and material wealth. In this the Church, which is still powerful, sees no evil, and one might say that in a country where the unit of currency is the symbol of Christ ("cruzeiro" means "cross") there is a perfect marriage of Church and State. Later we found that a deeper malaise afflicts high and low alike. There is a basic lack of personal integrity. A man's word is not his bond, and anyone who thinks so is quaint. Consequently, personal or business relationships are not on a firm footing. Cheating in stores and buses is rife, and it is incumbent on the buyer to be on guard.

Whether this mercenary attitude rubbed off on Rachel I am not sure; but after a week or two she began to return to the boat with coins, and with no very good explanation of how she had acquired them. Liz investigated, and found that Rachel—who so far as we knew couldn't swim—was diving into the swimming-pool to a depth of 10 feet to retrieve coins which people apparently left in the pool. She had, as we learned with dismay, established a thriving little coin-collecting business.

Liz and I spent a good deal of time washing clothes and doing maintenance work respectively, and the children were happy making new friends, but after a couple of weeks we decided we really ought to "do" Rio. Our first little excursion, by bus and ferry across the bay to Niteroi, was the last. The temperature in the shade that day fell a whisker short of 110°F, and the air was as still as an oven. Trailing back to the boat that evening with four sweaty, fretful children straggling behind, we decided that henceforth our touring would be done on *Walkabout*. So a couple of days later we sailed to Paquetà.

Paquetà is a small island situated in the upper reaches of the Bay of Guanabara. No motor vehicles are allowed, only bicycles and horses. We had a pleasant sail up in ridiculously smooth water, for the bay is landlocked except for one narrow passage to the sea, and neatly dropped the hook in front of the local yacht club. As we ghosted into the anchorage, the boat failed to drag the anchor back and dig it in, and this was to have serious consequences.

The first thing we did ashore was to find the showers and take refuge from the heat for a few moments under a stream of lukewarm water. Then the children began agitating for a bicycle ride, so we hired a couple of tandems and they hurtled round the island roaring like Formula-one machines on the race track. It made Liz limp just to look at them. The next day we all hired bicycles for a grand tour.

The island is now largely a resort for day trippers, but there are a number of fine old colonial buildings and some luxuriant gardens. In that part of Brazil, plant life flourishes like Jack's beanstalk; toss a seed into the humid air and it will probably germinate before it hits the ground. We found a man selling iced coconuts and sugar-cane juice. The coconuts were at the green, unhusked stage when the milk has not yet crystallised into the coconut flesh. He punched a hole through the husk, popped in a straw, and handed over the perfect thirst-quenching drink, untouched by human or mechanical hand. When we asked for sugar-cane juice he went to what we were certain was the original machine which had inspired Heath Robinson and, throwing some green cane into a hopper at the top, began cranking. After a lot of horrid clanking the machine began to spit bits of cane out of one side and brown juice out of the other. It looked sticky, but was surprisingly refreshing.

We picnicked in the shade of a big mango tree, and then went swimming. The water was salty, dirty and fully over 90°F. It felt as though one was being slowly casseroled. We returned to the boat, but the evening brought no respite from the heat. January is the stickiest month of the year in Rio, and that year was particularly bad. We would sleep on deck with nothing on, but even in the coldest hours before dawn we would lie in a pool of perspiration waiting for the slight morning breeze.

That evening, in the middle of supper, a sudden gust shook the masts. There was a second's stillness, and then the rain came roaring down. With it came the wind, so hard that the boat heeled over before she swung to face it. I half-rose from the table to check outside. But before I could reach the hatch a curious bumping was felt through the boat.

"I think we're aground," shouted Mark.

"We can't be," I cried, and dived through the hatch.

Outside was complete confusion. Lightning split the air to left and right. The rain drove across so densely that visibility was down to a couple of feet. I stumbled forward to check the anchor warp. It seemed secure, but peering over the bows I was horrified to see a little fishing boat directly under the bowsprit. I recognised the boat as one that was moored near the beach and, suddenly aware of the ominous bumping, I knew we were aground. I hurried aft again, and just as I reached the hatch the first wave broke over the stern and into the cockpit. *Walkabout* was stern on to the seas. It never ceases to amaze me how quickly waves build up in a high wind. What had happened was that *Walkabout* had dragged her anchor, moving backwards until the deepest part of the keel at the stern had struck ground. The boat had then pivoted on the foot of the keel and swung the bows towards the beach.

I tried the engine, but in these circumstances an engine is not only useless but dangerous, for it wastes time. Liz was standing beside me in her nightie, so I left the engine and together we went forward to try to pull the bows round with the anchor warp. Nothing budged. We brought the warp aft and tried to haul her off stern first. She never moved. *Walkabout* fully loaded weighs about 16 tons, and for two people to try to pull her off the bottom against the weight of boarding seas was quite futile. All the while the lightning slashed repeatedly through the rain and the awful pounding of the keel on the beach continued. Every thump jarred right through us as though it were our spines and not the boat's that were on the beach. Waves broke over the stern and the cockpit was completely flooded. Liz glanced below. The children had sensibly cleared the table and were lying in their bunks, reading. They knew from previous experience that the best thing to do in a crisis was to keep out of the way.

At that moment a vague shape appeared over the bows and a figure lumbered into view. It was the owner of the little fishing boat.

"Your bowsprit has been pecking at my boat," he began crossly.

"Sorry," I said. We had to shout above the storm.

He waved this aside. "Have you a strong rope? There is a motor boat coming and I'll get him to pull you off." He pointed to what appeared to be a searchlight glowing astern of us.

I handed him a rope end which he tied round his waist. Then he jumped overboard and swam off in the direction of the light. After a few minutes the rope tightened and we could hear the motor boat roaring as it tugged at the other end. It pulled and pulled until I thought the quarter bits would come adrift, but *Walkabout* never budged. The rope went slack and the fisherman swam back again.

"It's no good," he said. "What shall we do?"

"We must lay out a second anchor, to hold her," I said. "Then at high tide she may come off."

"Maybe," he replied, "but high tide is soon. The water will only rise a few more inches. But you are right. It is the only thing to do."

We laid the second anchor with the dinghy, and as we were doing so the storm stopped. The wind died as abruptly as it had started, the lightning was switched off and only the rain continued. I was amazed but vastly relieved.

"Now at least we have a chance," I told Liz when we got back to the boat. The three of us hauled both anchor warps very tight and then sat down to await developments.

"We might as well have some coffee," suggested Liz. Her

hair was plastered across her face and she was shivering in her nightie. I realised my teeth were chattering. The fisherman looked as strong as a bull, but he nodded. We drank the coffee in the rain and then the fisherman left in *Crawlabout*, saying he would return later.

High tide was at ten o'clock, and by a quarter to ten, when *Walkabout* still had not moved, I was seriously worried and more than a little puzzled. The water had become perfectly calm again and *Walkabout* should have floated off. I decided to dive down and inspect for myself. I swam along the bottom of the keel, feeling my way, for of course nothing could be seen. Right at the stern I discovered the trouble. A huge concrete mooring-block was wedged under the rudder, and the two anchors held *Walkabout* firmly on top of it. Once the trouble had been diagnosed it was a simple matter for Liz and me to slacken the anchor warps, haul the bows round and motor into deep water. The fisherman reappeared and helped us lay both anchors down for safety. I took him ashore and thanked him but he refused to accept any payment or presents, saying, "People of the sea should help each other."

The next day we returned to Rio to examine *Walkabout* for damage. That day sticks in my mind as one of the most depressing of our voyage, for we realised suddenly how vulnerable a walkabout is if his boat is lost. Not only his boat but his home and everything he possesses goes too; very few walkabouts are insured because cover is almost impossible to get for boats that range from ocean to ocean, and if one can get it then the premiums are extremely high. I remain convinced that insurance under the conditions currently imposed by insurance companies is not worth having. The official attitude is odd, for I am also sure that the greatest proportion of yacht accidents occur to boats which are used only occasionally and have no one aboard to tend them.

Walkabout showed no evidence of damage, but until she was pulled out of the water and inspected we could not be sure. I arranged slipping facilities with the yacht club, and a few days later we went up. The slipping facilities were decidedly rough. A number of dollies (heavy grid trailers with small wheels) were available, and the idea was to run these under a floating boat and winch the whole lot up a concrete ramp, keeping the boat upright with wooden props as she came out of the water. These dollies looked fragile to me, and I asked the Master of the Slip—there really was such a man!—for the strongest he had. He inspected *Walkabout*, who was looking low and small in the water, and declared that dolly No. 4 would do.

"But that's too small," I protested. "My boat is terribly heavy."

"Nonsense!" he replied. "I have been Master of the Slip now for fifteen years, and I can assure you that everything will be all right."

"But she's all under water," I tried to explain. "She's heavy . . . "

"Three o'clock this afternoon," he said. "And if you don't want to go up there are plenty of others who do."

When we motored round to the slipway at three o'clock we found two men swimming about in the water.

"This way," they cried. "The dolly is under our feet."

The two men manœuvred *Walkabout* into position and the Master started the winch. As we lurched out of the water there was an ominous crack from the dolly. The front beam broke, and *Walkabout* slipped a little to one side. The second beam took the load, and that cracked too. *Walkabout* heeled further. Liz squealed, I yelled, and all the men on the slipway began shouting instructions at one another. The Master stopped the winch and rushed up shouting, "Calma! Calma! Where is your calma Britannica?"

"The devil take my calma Britannica! What about my boat?"

"Calma! Calma!" he said again, and everyone took up the cry, "Calma! Calma!" in the most agitated manner.

"If they don't stop shouting 'calma' at me I'm going to have hysterics," I said desperately to Liz.

Eventually, as *Walkabout* leaned no further, everyone did calma—even Liz and I. But till the next afternoon we crept around the boat on cautious feet. We found that *Walkabout* had sustained no damage whatever at Paquetà except for a slight notch where the mooring block had wedged under the rudder, and our confidence in the boat strengthened further. We anti-fouled her carefully, principally against teredo, endemic right through Brazil and the West Indian waters, and prepared to refloat her. Where the props supported the boat, however, we were unable to antifoul, and as the teredo can penetrate even the tiniest crack in the defences I asked the Master of the Slip to ease us into the water only as far as the unpainted patches. Then I would rock the boat over to the other side while Liz daubed the bare patches.

The first part of the operation went according to plan. *Walkabout* rumbled into the water while Liz and Mark circled about in the dinghy, brushes at the ready. The boat was rocked and the patches painted. We had just restarted our downward journey when one corner of the dolly fell into a deep hole. *Walkabout* lurched, and I found myself clinging to a steeply angled deck with the bowsprit aimed over the top of a nearby roof. The winch strained to pull us out, but the dolly was stuck fast, and eventually with an alarming crack the winch stalled.

"We must quadruple the cables," said the Master, and he sent men wading in with heavy blocks and tackle. They began to work out of sight under the boat.

"What does it look like?" I called to Liz, who was still nervously circling the boat in *Crawlabout*.

"It looks quite terrifying," she answered. "The aft deck is under water and the whole boat is sort of twisted over and up."

"What are these two clowns doing underneath us?" I asked.

She gave a small cry, and then began to laugh. "They're crossing themselves!"

"What!" I leaned out and peered down at the two men. They were fixing the tackle to the dolly underneath the water, and before every dive they would mutter a short prayer and cross themselves. So much for the Master's supreme confidence! We collapsed in helpless laughter.

When the tackle was ready the Master engaged the winch again and about twenty men strained on ropes. *Walkabout* trembled, teetered, then lurched out of the hole and up the ramp. This time, notwithstanding the damaged dolly, we were hauled right up to the top of the ramp. The Master placed chocks under the wheels, then disconnected all cables.

"Now you go right in without stopping," he called. "Are you ready?"

I stood by the tiller, which I had lashed, and nodded. All I wanted was to get back into aqua firma. A man stood by each chock with a hammer.

"Now!" cried the Master, and the chocks were all knocked out.

Walkabout rumbled down, slowly at first, then faster and faster till she fairly flew down the ramp. We struck the water with a spectacular splash, and *Walkabout* catapulted off the dolly and into the water. A cheer went up on shore. Liz and I were never so thankful to be off dry land.

Of course the problem of unpainted patches remained, because in jumping off the dolly the fresh paint had been scratched. I solved the problem quite simply. I collected seven of the beefiest club members I could find, swung out the main boom and mizzen boom at right-angles to the boat, and perched all seven, together with the whole family, along the booms. They looked like twelve partridges in a pear tree. *Walkabout* heeled over, and I was able to row round in the dinghy and touch up the antifouling.

But the excitement, together with the stifling heat and a surfeit of millionaires, made us feel we needed a break from Rio. We decided to visit Ilha Grande, a group of lovely islands some 60 miles west of Rio. We made the boat ship-shape, and at about two o'clock one morning we sailed past Sugar Loaf out to the open sea once more.

X

ENGINES ARE NOT essential for cruising—but they are essential for happy cruising. We were soon to discover this the hard way. It was pleasant to be away from Rio, away from the heat of the city and the stench of its traffic. It was pleasant just to look at the lights from the sea. When we ate breakfast in the cockpit next morning we were still able to pick out all the familiar buildings, having covered only 7 miles through half the night.

I should explain that the weather system around Rio in summer is the very worst for sailing boats. The predominant characteristic is a sultry calm. Morning and evening, sea and land breezes stir the waters for a short while; they can be strong, but are more often fickle. From time to time the pattern is disrupted by savage thunderstorms that build up titanic clouds during the day and break in the evening, often bringing winds of 60 knots or more. It was such a storm that had driven us ashore in Paquetà.

So it was that by evening we had managed to coax barely a dozen more miles out of old *Walkabout*. Had we been able to use our engine we should already have been riding contentedly at anchor instead of hurtling along in a thunderstorm like a bat out of hell. The storm had come down on us at sunset, so suddenly that I had only half-woken from a cat-nap. Now I hung on to the tiller still dressed in my underpants. Everyone else scuttled down below and stayed there, calling out fatuously from time to time, "Are you all right?" Actually I was enjoying the excitement. We had experienced several of these storms in Rio, and I had got their measure by now. The high wind invariably lasted a very short time, and usually vanished completely when the rain set hard.

This storm was no different, and within the hour we were lying becalmed in heavy rain. Throughout the night, while the children lay in enviable slumber, Liz and I nursed the boat through a succession of head squalls and calms. The big genoa which had drawn us across the Atlantic blew out, and I was very upset. The next day was no better. Everyone got soaked and seasick and began to mutter mutiny.

"Don't you want to go exploring strange tropical islands?" I demanded impatiently, but wisely did not wait for a reply. In the afternoon we sighted Ilha Grande between squalls, and a couple of hours later came under the lee and nosed our way over glass-smooth water into the little bay of Abraão. It looked a fascinating place, and everybody came out into the rain to watch as the steep, smooth rocks slipped by. A sheer wall of deep green jungle silently slid past, so close that it seemed as if one could lean over the rail and touch it, and through the rain we could smell an exciting primitive odour.

The next day was fine, and we began to explore the island. I had been brought up in an area of Africa where the thick bush grows, but never have I seen such tropical luxuriance. Dense jungle swept up from the edge of the beach and over the lovely mountains. We crept into the jungle as though through the looking-glass, and found ourselves in wonderland. Plant life uncoiled from the rich, warm earth and swarmed skywards to blot out the sun, and hundreds of exquisite orchids drooped from almost every tree fork.

Habitation was so sparse that we could easily imagine we were on a desert isle. One day, in a tiny cove, Mark jumped into the dinghy with a faraway look in his eyes and sailed for some rocks. Who he was I cannot say, but he flung commands to his men, lifted an imaginary telescope to his eye and was evidently on the point of discovering a new continent. Presently he dropped sail, picked up the little folding anchor, and with a grand gesture cast it over the bows. It was unfortunate that the anchor was not tied on. Poor lad! In a second his new continent had shrivelled away, leaving only a vengeful father swearing from the foredeck. We dived for hours, but never recovered the anchor.

The last bay we visited was Arroeira, where we encountered a numerous and hospitable American family. Here we lazed for several days, eating bananas from the land and mussels from the rocks. Mark and I found a grove of splendid bamboos and cut ourselves a jib boom apiece—a big one for *Walkabout* and a little one for *Crawlabout*, the "He-man" bamboo from St Helena having proved to be a he-man of straw. But I knew that if we did not get away soon we should simply lose the will-power to move and would have to retire on Ilha Grande, so reluctantly we set sail for Rio.

It took us over two days to get back. The current was against us and the wind, when it blew, also came tearing down the coast. Sail after sail blew out, until only the heavy-duty jib and a small staysail were left. We were very depressed, and I quoted the irrepressible Slocum to cheer us up. "At 3 p.m. the jib was washed off the bowsprit and blown to rags and ribbons. . . . Let it go! After all, I had need of pot rags."

One reason for our sails blowing out was simply that they were old and tired, like the ropes in the rigging. The other reason was peculiar to *Walkabout*. When beating into a head sea, the waves flung up by the bows would crash into the low-cut headsail, literally "washing it off the bowsprit". In light headwinds the waves were too small to do much damage, and in high winds I used the small, heavy-duty jib, cut with a foot so high that the waves could not reach it. But in average winds up to Force 6 *Walkabout* relied on big headsails for ability to drive into the wind. When at last we got to Rio I went off to find the yacht club's sailmaker. He shook his head over the sails but, encouraged by a bottle of Scotch, made a fair job of repairs. I also managed to buy an old genoa from another walkabout. It was the wrong shape, but it was at least a second big headsail, and I felt happier for having it.

We now concentrated on making ready for sea. Our policy was always to lay in food, water, fuel and spares for sixty days—although the food, I think, would have lasted for ninety days—on the grounds that you never knew what might happen. A mast could break and you might have to limp into port with a jury rig. In Rio this policy was a little difficult to put into practice because of the lopsided economy. They made aeroplanes, but kitchen paper was unknown; gin-palace yachts were more common than fleas on a dog, but try to find a spare compass bulb! Tinned stuffs, especially, were few and costly.

One happy diversion from these mundane activities was the finish of the Cape to Rio yacht race, which took place just

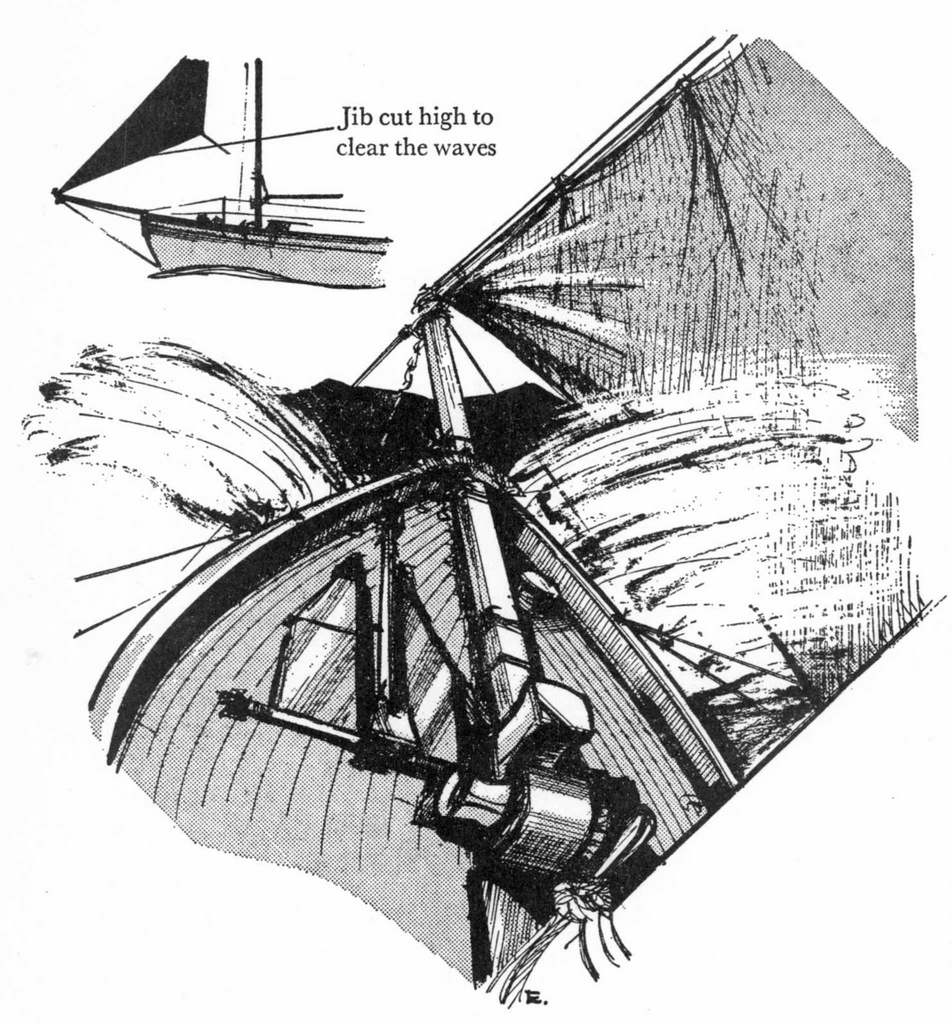

WASHING THE JIB OFF THE BOWSPRIT

before we left. Although the race causes about as much stir in Rio as a frog in a pond, we nevertheless enjoyed watching the yachts come in, and the children, at least, enjoyed the television cameras that followed them and, to Liz's deep embarrassment, caught her energetically scrubbing our laundry on *Walkabout*'s foredeck. We sailed a couple of days later, once again saying those sad farewells to all our Rio friends which are a poignant part of a walkabout's life. Slowly Sugar Loaf Mountain dissolved in the haze of the afternoon heat, and with it the city of Rio. To the north lay Recife, and beyond that the West Indies and England. To the south lay Cape Horn.

"Turn left for Recife," said Liz crisply.

"You notice everything," I complained. "Why go north when the wind is blowing north? And the further north we go the worse it will get. Beyond Recife lie the doldrums. But the further south we go, the better it gets. Cape Horn is only a few thousand miles away," I went on persuasively. "We'll just nip round, up the other side and through Panama and . . . you'll hardly notice the . . . "

"Turn left for Recife," repeated Liz, warningly.

"I thought we were walkabouts and could go anywhere we wanted," I said bitterly.

"Turn left for Recife," said Liz, threateningly, and all the boys backed her up. "Who wants to go to Cape Horn? Filthy storms and cold." I sighed, and put the helm over.

For two days we tacked doggedly into the fitful head winds which we had expected. But I had grown cunning. Near the shore, almost within the surge of the breakers, I found a favourable counter-current, and we hugged the beach day and night. We never knew the depth under the keel, because our echo-sounder had long since given up the ghost. During the day we could judge our distance from the shore by eye, but at night the moonlight was deceptive and we sailed by ear alone, listening tensely to the breakers a couple of hundred feet away, ready to put about at an instant. We would have given a lot for an echo-sounder (though not as much as it would have cost us to buy a new one, of course), and at various times I had inveigled several learned electronic gentlemen into examining the sick instrument. They had all pored over the little nest of transistors for hours and then hurried away, muttering such shameful excuses as, "I haven't got my testing oscilloscope with me today".

Anyway, the echo-sounder was unimportant in accomplishing our sailing strategy, which was this. We would cling to the coast, which runs due east for 60 miles to Cabo Frio. At this point the shore swings sharply northwards. To gain against the predominant winds and currents which are from the north we would head easterly, standing off at least 300 miles into the Atlantic, where the current weakens and the winds become more easterly. I hoped there to find more favourable winds to sail to Recife, roughly 1,000 miles to the north. That was the theory, but in practice I was unsure how well *Walkabout*, with her old-fashioned gaff rig, would perform to windward on a long voyage, or how we should take it, for that matter. So far neither of us had done too well to windward, but it takes a wide variety of seas and winds to learn how to charm the best from your boat. Look how *Walkabout* had sped before the trades after teaching me. Had I possessed a crystal ball I should have seen us beating to windward for nearly 5,000 miles, but fortunately I had not. And just as fortunately I did not know that within hours we should be facing the severest test of any boat and her crew—a full gale on the nose.

On the afternoon of the second day from Rio we saw Cabo Frio, and at once the wind began to harden and raised a steep head sea. With our heavy genoa we were able to punch our way through the waves, but towards evening the wretched sail ripped clean across the clew. I was peeved by this inauspicious start to the voyage, and replaced the torn sail with the heavy weather jib, determined to foil any further vandalism by the waves on the headsails. It was as well that I did so, because the wind continued to stiffen as we approached the cape, and the waves were vaulting across the bowsprit and landing on the deck.

To my surprise nobody was seasick and we all enjoyed a substantial, if somewhat violent, supper. After supper, when I stepped outside to stand first watch, I found the wind blowing very hard indeed. Cabo Frio, rising high and black in the moonlight, lay close off the port bow and protected us somewhat from the heavy seas. Then the wind started to warble in the stanchion pipes and I knew it was time to call Liz on deck.

By the time she had clambered into her oilskins and crawled into the cockpit we had edged around Cabo Frio and into the full force of the gale. Liz took the tiller, and while she held the boat against the seas, trying to keep the sails just barely ashiver, I managed to drop the mizzen and lace the frantic sail to the boom to quieten it. Then I crawled forward to reef the main further.

We could not do it. The wind had reached such a pitch that my strength could no longer match that of the canvas. A wave threw us over on our beam ends, and for a moment I found myself lying along a nearly horizontal mast which a second before had been a leaning post. I decided then to run for shelter under the cape and reef down there. We wore about and raced for shelter at a horrifying speed, seeming to catch the waves and dive over the crests.

Reefing under the lee of Cabo Frio was still something of a battle, but at least the waves were smaller. When the job was done we close-hauled and headed out again, shaving the cape so close that the lighthouse winked down on us from the cliffs. Conditions outside seemed to have worsened, if anything, and wave after wave washed clean over us. The lee deck was buried and the cockpit permanently filled. Liz did not like it one bit.

"How much more can the boat stand? Shouldn't we try and take shelter?" she shouted, but I had difficulty in hearing her above the shriek of the wind and the sea.

I shook my head. "The wind doesn't have to shift much to put us on a lee shore. We must clear the land."

I did not admit it, but I wanted to see whether *Walkabout* could claw off a lee shore in a gale, and although this was not a true lee shore a day might come when we had no option. I sat back and left it to *Walkabout* to sail her best.

She exceeded all my expectations. No progress could be discerned by looking at the welter of foam alongside, but the forbidding silhouette of Cabo Frio in the bright moonlight gradually contracted and the lighthouse sank closer to the horizon. We drew steadily out to sea.

The gale continued for a day and a half, sometimes abating a little, at other times rising to a new intensity. All that time we were driving into the seas, carrying as much sail as I dared. The noise below was frightful. The waves thudded against the hull like sandbags fired from a sling, and the crack of the bowsprit striking the seas sent a shudder through every timber. Most of the time we remained below, each one wedged in his or her favourite spot, reading or playing chess, or with the three younger children playing make-believe games which sounded like the purplest sort of thriller. Everything was soaked, of course, and because we had to keep the forehatch locked it became hot and stuffy. Ventilation in heavy weather in the tropics proved to be a real problem. We chased the children into the cockpit once a day and tethered them firmly to the mast. Kevin grumbled about this, but Bruce and Rachel loved it. They shouted encouragement to every wave to board us, but the ones they liked best were those that knocked them off their feet and swirled them down on to the floor. Afterwards they would come down demanding food.

Food was difficult to prepare, but Liz managed somehow. She had to, because no one felt seasick. Watching the family during the gale I knew that we had finally learned the sort of endurance-seamanship needed on a small boat. We had at last become "old salts".

Part of the reason, no doubt, was the absolute confidence we now had in *Walkabout*. People have spoken of the alarming creaking made by the fabric of a wooden boat in a storm, but I never heard the boat creak, though I listened for it anxiously enough. When the gale died, which it did quickly, one morning, and I was able to take sun sights, I found we had beat a remarkable 170 miles to windward in 35 hours. The decks had been scrubbed as white as a washboard by the seas but nothing had been damaged or lost, apart from a fishing gaff and some rods that had broken free from their lashings. But down below we found that the violent motion had flung all the fresh water out of the tank through a tiny leak around the filler cap.

There was still thirty days' fresh water supply in the plastic water bags, but Liz and I spent an anxious couple of hours dismantling the plumbing system to check for leaks. Then Kevin discovered water coming out of the paraffin pipe, and that system also had to be dismantled and cleaned. Meanwhile Rachel and Bruce hung up the clothes and bedding to dry while Liz baked bread. Mark and I pulled out the torn genoa and began stitching patiently.

This sort of wound-licking activity was quite normal after a bout of rough weather. We delighted in the hot sunshine and calm seas, and settled down quickly to enjoy the rest of the voyage.

The voyage was one of the most pleasant we made, mainly because we all fell into a placid yet busy rhythm of shipboard life. One thing we all enjoyed was the life in the ocean around us, which was more plentiful where we were sailing, a couple of hundred miles off the Brazilian coast, than it had been in mid-Atlantic. Soon after the gale Bruce discovered a score of tiny striped fish swimming furiously in our wake. When we slowed up they swam alongside or took up a position an inch or two ahead of the stem, riding on the bow wave. Bruce made a small net and caught one. We counted the spines and rays (soft spines) on his fins and identified him from a standard work we always carried, Professor Smith's *Fishes of Southern Africa*.* He was apparently a Naucrates Ductor, Family Curangidae, Genus Naucrates—in other words, a pilot fish. I believe a famous member of this species was called Pelorus Jack, and for years piloted ships through the Bass Straits and was known to hundreds of mariners. The fish are said to live on sharks' excreta and to make good pets. I came to know one of the little fish quite well from his markings, and would anxiously watch him for hours as he struggled to keep up, buffeted by the slipstreams.

"It would be a kindness, really, to catch him and fry him," I said to Bruce. ". . . No, no! I was only joking. Let's see how long he keeps it up."

He kept it up for the incredible distance of 1,000 miles, leaving us near Recife! Who am I to give myself airs as a voyager in face of such a feat?

Another voyager who accompanied us to Recife and all the way beyond, to the West Indies, was my good friend Captain Slocum, who, 85 years before, had sailed this very route with his wife and two sons in the little *Liberdade*.† The *Liberdade* was a 35ft canoe-like boat built by Slocum from flotsam and local timber (including one called batetenandinglastampai, he says) after they had been made destitute by the wrecking of their

* *The Fishes of South Africa*, by J. L. B. Smith (privately printed).

† *Voyage of the Liberdade*, by Joshua Slocum (Rupert Hart-Davis).

ship at Rio Grande, a couple of hundred miles south of Ilha Grande.

Liz never wholly believed Slocum. "He spins a good yarn," she conceded, "but you can't expect me to believe that he sailed round the world using an old alarm clock instead of a chronometer. I ask you!"

"But he boiled the clock in oil," I said.

"Oh, in that case, my apologies," said Liz. "Tell me more."

"He sailed in fear of reefs in the West Indies because a goat had come aboard at St Helena and eaten his charts. That was on the *Spray*. On this voyage, at Cabo Frio a whale came up under the boat and scratched his back on the keel." Liz just snorted.

When we drew level with the Abrolhos, however, my faith was severely shaken. The Abrolhos are an archipelago, interlaced with numerous reefs and banks, and I longed to go there. The Brazilians are hardly aware of these islands and know little of the fascinating Brazilian coast which, stretching from the Amazon to the luxuriant south, must be one of the finest cruising grounds in the world. Here we were, sailing past, basically because our boat was too small to serve as a permanent home and we had to reach England. I sought vicarious satisfaction from Slocum, who had stumbled one night into what he forecast would be the harbour of the future. He gave the precise latitude and longitude, so I unfolded my charts to place it. Imagine my distress when I discovered the harbour was 20 miles inland!

As well as fish there was also a fair amount of bird life, including a brown bird with a curved beak that looked like a skua. One evening, while Liz and I were wedged in the cockpit enjoying our after-dinner coffee, one of these creatures began circling above the sails. He stayed with us throughout the night, but proved to be a bird of low intelligence. First he wanted to rest, but instead of finding a solid perch he set his mind on the gaff boom. The wind was light and the seas lumpy, so the gaff, slamming to and fro, presented one of the most difficult perches on the boat. He clung to the end, flapping and squawking, then shrieking piteously when thrown off. Finally we could bear it no longer. Liz went to bed, and as usual I hunched under the dim light on the chart table to read and write. After a while the racket aloft ceased, and when I looked up a little later the bird was trying to sit on the self-steering vane. If anything this was more difficult than the gaff. The vane swung continuously and its thin edge offered no grip whatever. The bird flapped furiously, silent and grimly determined to make a success of this one. I climbed out into the cockpit.

"Shoo, you senseless bird," I cried. "How can my self-steering work if you keep tampering with it?"

He flew off into the darkness and I returned to read. Half-an-hour later *Walkabout* suddenly sheered off-course and gybed. The sails went back, and I rushed out to see what was wrong. The bird had obviously brought the vane under control and forced it down with his weight. He sat foursquare on the horizontal vane with an expression of immense satisfaction.

"Begone, you bird of evil!" I cried. "Look what you've done! Have you no sense whatever?" He looked back at me smugly and ruffled deeper into his perch. "I don't like using force," I replied, "but you goad me too far." I pushed him off the vane, and with a surprised cheep he fell into the sea.

I put *Walkabout* back on course and returned to the chart table, keeping an eye on the wind vane. Sure enough he was back in a few minutes, trying to take up his former perch. I shooed him away but he persisted, and this went on for some time. Eventually he gave up and disappeared, and I forgot about him till the end of my watch, when I made a tour of the deck. He was back again, sitting near a shroud on a perch as unstable as ever; the length of slack rope that served as a safety line swayed under him and he wobbled on it like a tipsy tightrope walker, his tail towards the cockpit and his beak over the sea. I leaned close and addressed his back.

"You are a bird of remarkably weak intellect, as I think I mentioned before. There are dozens of comfortable perches on this boat, and yet you have selected the three most precarious. Not that I mind you sitting there. Please don't misunderstand me. You're welcome to sit anywhere you fancy apart from the steering vane, and you're welcome to sit as long as you like. But it's the principle of the thing. If all your friends and relatives are as stupid as you are, what future is there for your species? If I encourage you now you'll be trying to nest in jet engines next."

He had been gazing into the dark, ignoring all this completely, but now he turned his head slightly and glanced at me over his shoulder.

"Yes! And another thing. Why do you assume I am not hostile? I've been chasing you all night. And if Mark and Bruce were awake they would be asking whether you are good to eat. Come to think of it, it is fortunate for you that I have dined well, else I might be contemplating skua pie."

I reached out and gently tweaked the feathers in his tail. He turned his head further and glared coldly at me out of one eye.

"Well, all right, it was only a joke. But just think about what I have said. Good night."

I went below to call Liz on watch, and they entertained each other for the rest of the night. He flew away at last before dawn, perhaps a little suspicious of my final remarks.

Halfway through the voyage Rachel became ill. At first we thought it was 'flu, for we had left Rio during a 'flu epidemic, but when the illness persisted Liz diagnosed a urinary infection. We gave her a course of broad-spectrum antibiotics called Unicycline, and in a day or two the trouble cleared up. This was one of the few occasions when we used antibiotics, but it was comforting to have this heavy artillery of medicine aboard.

As we pressed further north we became increasingly irritated with the weather, which refused to conform to the pilot charts. A tongue of north-easterly trades licks down from the northern hemisphere into the region of south-easterly trades, and my intention, as I have said, was to stand out from this area to find the latter winds. Instead, however, we found ourselves always sailing up the edge of the tongue in a convergence zone where the two systems met. The characteristics of the zone were identical to those of the doldrums—calms interspersed with fierce line squalls that blasted us with terrific force for a few minutes before dissolving into a still, heavy rain. On average we were hit by two or three squalls a day, and always the wind came from ahead. On three occasions the headsails were blown out and had to be mended. So we felt we had not done too badly when on the sixteenth day, nearly 1,300 miles from Rio, Bruce cried, "Land ho!". It was a spot called Tamandare, about 40 miles south of Recife.

The coast of north-eastern Brazil is flat and featureless, but we bowled along happily in the afternoon sun while I repaired the navigation lights and tested the boys on their English lesson for the day. Rachel, quite recovered now, prattled incessantly in the dinghy. Liz once asked her whether she ever stopped talking, and she replied, "No, I can't. I don't know why I do it and I've tried and tried to stop, but I simply can't."

After supper, when the lights of Recife were already twinkling off the port bow, the trade wind which we had been looking for blew hard at last. We put the children to bed, promising to wake them up when we neared port. It was a rough night, and *Walkabout* was thrown repeatedly over to port. Suddenly a big wave caught us and threw us over harder than usual. We heard a thump in the cabin, followed by crying. It was Bruce, who had been thrown out of his bunk and across the cabin. He had landed on the opposite seat and caught his eye on the metal beading. When we got to him blood was streaming out of the split eyelid and dripping to the floor. We dressed the wound and gave him a Ponstan capsule to calm him. He seemed perfectly all right, but the next day he passed out on deck with a face the colour of mouldy cheese. He looked ghastly. Fearing concussion, Liz and I made him lie very still in the shade, sponging him with fresh water to keep him cool and dressing the gash every two hours to ward off infection. Thankfully he recovered in a day or two, but it was a nasty experience, and we wondered how he would have fared had we been in a rough sea during that time.

Our main concern that night, however, was to make port, so after Liz had put Bruce back to bed she woke up Kevin and Mark. Navigating the approaches to Recife in strong onshore winds proved a tricky business, for Recife has not been given its name (meaning "reefs") for nothing. The main difficulty, however, is one that is common to many ports nowadays. The city was illuminated by such a blaze of lights that we could not distinguish the navigating lights on the buoys and beacons; flashing neon signs were the worst, for they were always confused with flashing red marks, and there were so many that we wondered whether this was the start of the famous Brazilian four-day carnival, due about then. With the help of Liz's and Mark's keen eyesight we finally passed through the harbour entrance into calm water, and dropped the sails with relief.

When we started the engine Bruce and Rachel came up, and the whole family stood outside to share the fun of entering a new port.

The yacht club in Recife is situated some distance up a shallow lagoon, and in a boat of our draught it can only be reached at high spring tide. I could find no chart of the area, and all we had was a Rio Yacht Club menu, on the back of which a yachtsman friend had scribbled a few notes: "Proceed to the end of the harbour and, at the top of the tide, turn hard to starboard and feel your way along the channel in the lagoon with the echo-sounder. The far end of the channel swings to port and leads into the yacht basin. It is marked by sticks pressed into the mud."

"Everyone I know has gone aground," he had added, "so it's best to wait for the harbour authorities to guide you in."

But we happened to arrive at the entrance of the lagoon at 1 a.m., at the height of the tide, and we decided to press on so that we might sleep the rest of the night in a safe place.

We crept forward at a snail's pace, Liz at the tiller and myself at the bows, sounding with the lead. Kevin and Mark stood on either side to keep a lookout. Most of the time there was barely a foot under the keel, but we successfully negotiated the channel and began to pick our way from stick to stick at the end. Beyond the sticks there seemed to be a great deal of noise and a lot of coloured lights, but it was impossible to tell what they meant.

We had reached the penultimate stick when *Walkabout* went aground and stopped with a slight lurch. I put the engine astern but she was held fast. We had carefully worked out a procedure for such an eventuality, and when I called, "Heel her over now!" everyone knew what to do. The main boom was swung out and secured with a guy. Then everyone quickly crawled out along it, first Liz, being the heaviest, then Kevin, Mark, Bruce and lastly Rachel, perched nervously close to the shrouds where she could hang on. *Walkabout* heeled a little, lifting her keel from the mud. I put the engine astern and slid back.

Scarcely had we come free than we went aground again, this time at the stern. "Heel her over now!" I called, and the de-grounding procedure was repeated. Once free I did not know

Rolling down the trades—a unique game called "bottom s'ils" played on calm days and accompanied by obligatory squealing

Smiles to welcome the sun after a couple of days of filthy weather. Kevin, Bruce, Rachel and Mark

Mark up the mast—running repairs at sea

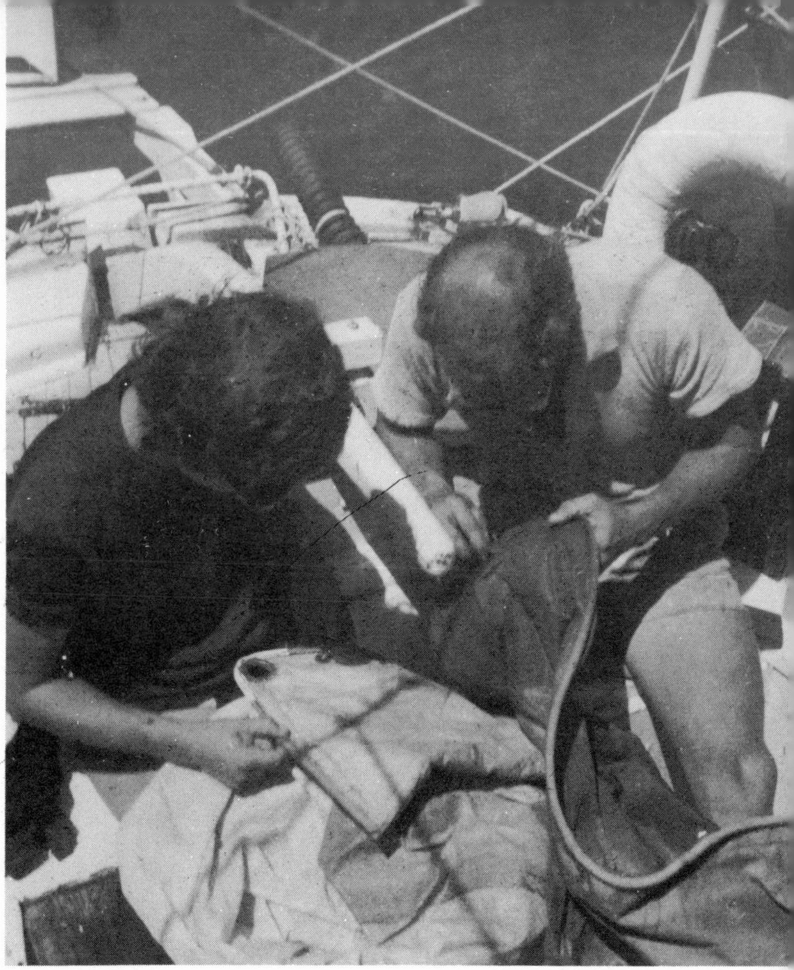

We did not sail across the Atlantic, we stitched our way across

where to go. The channel seemed almost to have disappeared, and we were bewildered by the flashing coloured lights around us, the throbbing dance music and the hundreds of people who could be seen swirling between.

"The only thing to do," I said, "is to throw out an anchor and wait for morning. We'll be left high and dry at low tide, but we shouldn't come to any harm."

But the trade wind was blowing hard down the lagoon, and we dragged immediately and went aground. I hauled in the anchor and it came up full of black, sticky mud. Again we heeled the boat and tried to anchor a second time, but the result was the same. There was nothing for the anchor to bite into.

By now we were all exhausted. We were slippery with sweat, for it was a hot night, and we were, one and all, plastered from head to toe with black slime. We looked towards the yacht club where, not a hundred feet away, five hundred revellers were pulsating in mass abandon to the samba, whose hypnotic beat throbbed through the tropical night. We learned later that this was the opening ball of the carnival, and the social event of the year in Recife. All we needed was for someone to point to the yacht basin entrance, but no one did, for not a single person on shore was aware of our predicament. It was a bizarre situation.

"Mike," said Liz suddenly, "I think I can see the entrance. There! Just to the right of that pole."

"The one where the girl dressed in streamers is dancing. Yes, I think you've got it. Let's go anyway."

We made straight for the entrance. As we reached it we touched bottom, lurched, and then we were inside the tiny basin. Suddenly people saw us and began to gather.

"This way, this way!" they called.

We edged to the wall, made fast and all stepped ashore. We looked like coal-miners from the pit-head on a steamy day. Around us gathered a crowd of perfumed revellers, the men in brilliant loose shirts, the gorgeous olive-skinned girls nearly naked.

"Where have these people come from?" asked a girl.

"I'm not sure," replied her man. "By the look of them I should say they come from Africa."

XI

WHEN WE AWOKE next morning the sun was burning down through the hatchway and the wind had died. All that remained of the carnival ball was a forlorn debris of coloured paper and broken glass which ragged-looking men were sweeping away. The tide was out, and when we saw where we had come the previous night we were horrified. A filthy ditch meandered through the mud banks which stretched down the lagoon, and when I looked over the side I found we were aground even in the yacht basin. It is amazing what can be accomplished if one is sufficiently ignorant.

Kevin and Mark were dispatched to find milk and bread, and Bruce scampered off to spy out the land before he could be given any work to do. He returned with the joyous news that there was a club swimming pool, but we took one look at his bloated eye and put the pool out of bounds. The Pernambuco Yacht Club, we soon found, was a complete contrast to its sumptuous Rio counterpart. There were a couple of fine modern buildings, but they had a faintly derelict air about them and they sat on a small unkempt site. As for the yachts, it was difficult to find one larger than a runabout. For once *Walkabout* did not lower the tone of her surroundings.

Recife is, in fact, much poorer altogether than Rio, and everywhere one saw the poverty that is normally relegated to the back streets of Rio. The north-eastern corner of Brazil is dry and relatively infertile compared with the rest of the country, and we were told that the land is in any case apportioned into vast estates owned by a handful of sugar barons, and the peasantry have little to live on. They are malnourished and uneducated—ineducable, said some, because diet and endemic disease have depressed the level of intelligence. There is unemployment, and people hang around the cities hoping for work. The spiral of problems, each aggravating the others, had a depressingly familiar Rhodesian ring about it, but I think that the situation in this part of Brazil is worse than Rhodesia. When a man can sell only half a banana to his customers, then you know that hunger and poverty are real. Yet we found the people friendly and more genuine than those in Rio, perhaps because they did not worship the cruzeiro quite as ardently. They did, however, share the blind nationalism and fierce loyalty to their country displayed by every Brazilian we ever met. If you want to be declared *persona non grata* in Brazil there is no need to foment revolution or plan an assassination. All you have to do is take a cup of coffee in a public place, raise it to your lips, hesitate, sniff it, sip it and then put it down, saying loudly, "This coffee is black, it is strong, but it is quite tasteless. Colombian coffee is better."

"Colombian coffee *is* better," insisted Liz, looking round surreptitiously. We were standing in the crush round a coffee stall in the market. As ever, our prime concern on reaching port was to buy fresh food, and our first morning at Recife found us jostling through the market with great baskets on our arms.

"Hush! You can't afford to go round saying things like that! We have a boat and four children to support. Anyway," I went on, "look what else is available here. This is a fantastic market."

It was indeed. Liz and I love markets, and a good market, we found, is not only a convenient place to buy food but a meeting place for rich and poor, concentrating the flavours of a community so that they can be sampled all at once. Recife market is the tastiest we ever found. The fish square was checked off into dozens of slabs on which were displayed sailfish, dorado, lobsters, tunny, barracuda, grouper, prawns, shellfish and sharks. There was a corridor devoted to nothing but eggs and poultry, and another to cereals and suchlike, where one could dip into sacks of black beans and chick peas and cashew nuts. Alley after alley was filled with basket work, wood carvings, tooled leatherwork, textiles, and the rather fine, hand-made hammocks which are a speciality of the area. We averted our eyes, for the stuff was mostly expensive, and passed on to our main interest, the fruit section. Here we loaded up with oranges, grapefruit, mangoes, guavas, custard apples and several other tropical fruits we had never seen before. Most of them had weak, rather elusive flavours, but we tried them all anyway, for we worked on the principle that one should live off the land and eat what the people eat. Then we went to the tobacco kiosks, and bought for a few dollars a carrier bag full of evil-looking cigars to break up for pipe tobacco. On our way out I was waylaid by a man at a booze kiosk. He dragged me to his counter.

"Just try this, senhor! Cane spirit, a speciality of the region. And very cheap, too. Only half an American dollar a bottle. Once you have tasted this you will never drink anything else."

He poured me a paper mug full of yellowish fluid that looked like nitric acid. I swallowed it in one gulp as roguish Old Salts are expected to do. The man was right; it was very nearly the last drink that passed my lips. I was still gasping when Liz helped me into a taxi a little later.

"Live off the land, eat what the people eat. Drink what the people drink. I can't understand," she said innocently, "why you didn't buy a bottle."

When we got back to *Walkabout* we found the children trying to launch the dinghy. As it was too heavy for them to lift over the side they had rigged up a tackle on the main boom, and Mark was busy at the top of the mast clearing a fouled halyard. The system they had devised was a very good one, and I adopted it thereafter for shipping and launching the dinghy. The skipper of the boat next to us was much impressed by the children. He was a tinsmith, and so it was natural that he should build his 37ft boat, *Zwerver*, in steel. She was crude but strong and effective, for he had sailed her with his family and two other crew from Australia via South Africa. They also were on their way to the Caribbean, and were thinking of selling the boat there and flying back to Australia.

The only other walkabout in the basin was a Californian, Earl Koepke, who was sailing around the world, accompanied part of the way by his son and his son's fiancée. The boat was a 30ft ketch called *Renee Tighe*, and carried a rig exactly like *Walkabout*'s. It was the only rig I ever saw that even resembled our own, so it was interesting to talk to Earl about handling and performance. He was satisfied with the rig, particularly in heavy weather, and told me that he had been rolled right over during a storm in the Bass Strait but had come up virtually undamaged. I doffed my cap to skipper and boat.

While we were in Recife we were generously entertained by an American family who took in Liz's laundry and had the children to sleep over for a night or two. Bruce and Rachel were so thrilled at sleeping in a house they could scarcely get to sleep at all. It was a year since they had last spent a night ashore, and Rachel could only vaguely remember ever having slept in a bed. The boat was as peaceful as the cloisters without them.

Our time in Recife was mostly divided between carnival and cockroaches. Carnival carried on for four days and we went into the city to watch the festivities, expecting, after the first night of the carnival ball, a mounting orgy of revelry. We were disappointed. The processions were dutiful to tradition, the bands restrained, and although great crowds turned out they did not generally participate, but watched quietly and looked bored.

Our cockroaches, on the other hand, were as lively as ever. The founder fathers of the colony, as it were, had come aboard in Durban, zooming low over the harbour and landing on deck. If you threw them overboard they simply swam off to some other boat and probably swam back again at night. They had had a hard time of it during the Cape Town winter, but when we reached the steamy coasts of Brazil they multiplied and prospered. We blasted them whenever we saw them, but there are many places where a cockroach can hide on an old boat, and the poisons seemed to have, if anything, a beneficial effect on the vigour of the species. They never appeared to do any harm apart from displaying a catholic taste for literature—any sort would do as long as there was plenty of glue in the binding.

"The cockroach is a much maligned insect," I told Liz once. "I've just read that they don't carry dirt and disease like flies. They have very clean insides."

But Liz did not respond favourably to such propaganda, and eventually I too became fed up at carrying so many non-paying passengers and we decided to fumigate in Recife. We removed from the cabin everything that could be contaminated, shut the place up tight and left it for a day, filled with toxic vapours that nearly did us in. When we opened up and found cockroaches dancing the samba on the engine hatch we admitted defeat. I consoled Liz by reading such philosophical excerpts from the cockroach poet, Archie, by Don Marquis,* as "humans appear just as unnecessary to cockroaches as cockroaches do to humans", and,

"germs are very
objectionable to men
but a germ
thinks of a man
as only the swamp
in which
he has to live."

Actually the cockroach colony did go into a decline after that, and eventually withered away.

We remained ten days in Recife, just long enough for us all to have a rest and do some necessary maintenance, and give the children time to exercise the normal healthy colour back into their cheeks. On March 13th we cast off in the morning and motored gingerly down the lagoon in the company of *Zwerver* and *Renee Tighe*, all bound eventually for the Caribbean, though they were stopping first at Paramaribo. Our destination was Barbados, 2,150 miles from Recife.

March 13th

It is 10 p.m. and everyone is fast asleep, all suffering a little from first day queasiness and the sedative effects of the Avomine I administered at supper. It's better this way. Formerly Liz would try to stick it out and help me sail the boat, but it was misery for her and not much help to me. Now she takes a pill straightaway and goes to bed; in a day or so she gets her sea-legs and life returns to normal. The kids are quite unpredictable—chirpy one minute, seasick the next and bouncing again the third. If they show any signs of prolonged queasiness they get the same treatment as Liz, and they too get their sea-legs in a day or so. Another trick we have learned is to make a fine stew in the pressure cooker before we leave. If the pressure weight is left on the pot draws a vacuum when it cools, which preserves the stew even in this heat, and if necessary the vacuum can be

* "random thoughts by archie", from *Archie's Life of Mehitabel* (Doubleday and Co. Inc.).

renewed by reboiling. In this way we eliminate all cooking problems for the first three days.

We were up with the first light this morning, and the kids set about departure preparations with a will. We have been discussing the Caribbean and they are very keen to get there, but more as a stepping stone to England than for its own sake. They scrubbed down the dinghy, swung it aboard, stowed the sun awnings and sails, and lashed everything fast. They worked so efficiently that by 8.30 everything was shipshape and we were ready for sea.

I have just checked to see that Bruce's canvas leeboard is properly hooked across his bunk. We don't want another accident like his eye injury. He is such a clumsy child, always lurching across the cabin or tumbling down the companion way, shrieking with mock indignation and then dissolving in giggles at the bottom. I usually give him an absentminded thump to remind him to be more careful; that makes him really indignant, and he invariably pipes up with what we have come to recognise as a Brucism—a remark that is designed to put him in the right and you in the wrong.

"I only fell because I was rushing to tell that the genoa is tearing, and you go and hit me," he wails accusingly from a tangled position on the floor. Of course it turns out to be a fabrication, but he is a very observant child and you can never tell.

Together with *Zwerver* and *Renee Tighe* we crossed the bar and straightaway ran into a swell and head winds. I could hardly believe it. The winds are supposed to blow from the south-east, not the north. We began to tack away from Recife, watching a little enviously as the other two yachts motored off north in search of fair winds. But a school of dolphins came to visit us and we felt happier straight away.

In the afternoon Mark spotted a sail ahead and we slowly drew level. It was a saveiro, a local sailing craft used for fishing and coastal trading. It was an open boat about the same size as *Walkabout*. The interesting thing about these saveiros is their rig, which consists of a triangular mainsail, longer than it is high, laced to a bendy mast and stretched out by a boom mounted about a third of the way up. They carry a jib so tiny that it can only serve a symbolic purpose. The sails look very pretty, but I guesssed they would be neither handy nor efficient, and so it proved to be. A point or so closer to the wind, *Walkabout* nevertheless overhauled the other boat and showed her a clean pair of heels.

We stood out to sea about 15 miles, and then came about at sunset and bore north. We are now pounding towards Cape S. Roque, the north-eastern corner of South America. Once round the corner I hope to find favourable winds to take us as far as the doldrums near the equator. There should be no real problem crossing the doldrum belt, which is very narrow and ill-defined near South America, and beyond that I would hope to reach across the north-eastern trades. That may prove a little rough but reasonably fast, and altogether we should be able to cover the 2,150 miles to Barbados within three weeks. It doesn't seem all that far, but you never know what might happen.

March 17th

So far only one thing has happened, and that was really more drama than action. Though, thinking back on it, I wonder if the event has not signified something of considerable importance—namely, the crossing of the doldrums.

This afternoon, for the first time since Recife, the wind fell light over a restless sea. Around the entire circumference of the horizon a dark woolly roll of thick clouds gathered and began to close in on us in a perfect circle. Overhead the spotless sky turned a hard blue. The amphitheatre of cloud rolled nearer and higher until it drew quite close. Then it stopped and the thunder began to mutter. I said uneasily to Liz, "I feel like a Christian in the arena of a Roman circus, waiting for the act to begin."

She looked round uncertainly and asked, "What's on the programme?"

"I don't know, but if history is anything to go by it's bound to be unpleasant."

After a while I grew so uneasy that I changed down the headsail to the heavy genoa, but nothing did happen till after dark. Till after Liz had gone to bed, in fact. Then the south-east trade piped up, as brisk as though it meant to take us to Barbados. Immediately the amphitheatre of cloud, which I could see quite clearly in the moonlight, contracted around us until it closed overhead and shut off all light from the night sky. The wind at once stopped, and a minute later a fierce squall swooped down from the north. The change in direction was so abrupt that it took me by surprise, and I did not really appreciate the significance of a northerly wind in an area of south-east trades.

Anyway, I had my hands full. I jumped into the cockpit and took over the tiller from Muncher, who, although capable in a thick, dogged sort of way, is a little slow on the uptake in these situations. We tore along at a frightful speed, lee rail under, and driving into great sheets of spray. The jib boom (the bamboo pole from Ilha Grande) snapped like a piece of dry spaghetti, and a little later the luff wire on the genoa broke. The sail rumpled up and began jerking horribly, but the worst of the wind was over by then and the rain poured down. Liz, woken by the squall, came crawling through the hatch, looking like a pantomime duck in her yellow oilies; she silently handed me mine but I was soaked already, so there was little point. She helped me to replace the damaged sail with another, a job which proved quite difficult as the broken sail had rumpled up out of reach. In future I shall attach the bitter end of the halyard to the head of the sail to act as a downhaul.

Afterwards Liz returned to bed and I to my chart table to read again about the doldrums. It seems that the proper name is Intertropical Convergence Zone, and the weather is not well understood. The basic pattern is caused by the sun which heats up a belt near the equator and causes the hot air to rise. Cooler air rushes in from either side, but because the earth is spinning the cooler air does not flow directly from the north and south but deflects eastwards. In this way the trades are formed—the north-east trade in the northern hemisphere and the south-east trade in the southern hemisphere. The two trades meet in the doldrum belt, and this is the bit I can never understand. Where on earth does all that wind go to? Millions of tons of air must rush in every day and what do you get? Dead calm! And the odd squall. All this air must get out somehow, and as it cannot go down and does not go sideways it must go up and return whence it came, otherwise there would not be anything left to breathe on the north pole by now. And that apparently is where the meteorological distress arises, because the upper atmosphere is fiercely turbulent and makes the weather down below unpredictable. Our experience of an hour ago seems to bear this out, for we appear to have crossed the doldrums in about 60 seconds.

If this is true then it is a pity, because the wind was blowing nicely from astern—for the first time in 1,500 miles. We swept up past Cape S. Roque and beyond; 133, 135, and today 155 miles. Not that it has been champagne and caviar all the way, I hasten to add. You can't do this sort of mileage *and* be comfortable, and we have had our fair share of squalls. Yesterday we had one that gave some amusement—to me at any rate. Several squalls had passed over during the morning, and I saw Liz eyeing each one through the plastic hatch cover and looking at the clock, obviously wondering whether to dash out and take a freshwater shower. She laid out all the soap and shampoo and towels in Rachel's bunk, and when she saw a squall approaching about noon she was ready.

"Come along, everybody, shower time," she commanded. "Off with your clothes! Out you go! Rachel, don't forget your flannel. Come on, Bruce, here's yours." She stripped off in a jiffy and hustled the protesting children out into the rain. I was out there already, braced against the tiller because of the strong wind, but dressed against the wet in oilskins.

"You take off those oilskins and get undressed this minute," said Liz firmly.

"I have a feeling," I said, "in my bare right toe, that this shower is not going to last as long as the others."

"Oh, do hurry up, Mike. The truth is you just don't want to get wet." She began lathering herself and the children from head to toe. Or rather, trying to lather them, for the boat was rolling and they were horsing around and slippery as eels.

She was right, of course; I felt too lazy to shower, but I got up, muttering, "Very well, don't listen to your wily skipper. Go your own way. I'll be ready to bail you out when you're in trouble."

I picked up two buckets and went forward to fill them at the gooseneck, where a good proportion of the rain that drove against the mainsail dribbled down. I had barely managed to fill the buckets when the shower tailed off and receded to leeward as a solid grey wall. There were cries of real anguish from the cockpit.

"Where's the rain?"

"There's soap in my eyes."

"Somebody pass me a flannel, quick."

They were all soaped from head to foot and groping around with eyes screwed up.

"The rain has gone and there isn't another shower in sight," I told them.

"Oh, Mike, you can't mean it! Stop fooling around and . . . Oh!" Liz wiped the soap out of her eyes. "The shower has gone! Quick, chase it!"

"What on earth do you mean?"

"You must alter course and chase that shower. We're all covered in soap," she wailed.

"Don't be daft. We can't go chasing clouds all over the sea. Anyway we wouldn't catch it. We can't sail faster than the wind."

"What are we to *do*?"

"Ah-ha!", and I produced the two buckets and brought the whole affair to a happy conclusion.

I feel less happy now. There is a sail to be mended tomorrow, and right now we are pounding to windward in a rough sea. The sky looks ominous. Dark rags of cloud are scudding low across the sky and it looks very squally. I'm afraid neither Liz nor I will get much sleep tonight.

March 19th

My fears were justified. We slept hardly at all two nights ago—was it only two nights ago? It seems much longer. Slept very little last night, too. It has been very rough the last couple of days, but more of that later.

Today's headline news is the crossing of the line. I have always had the vague notion that the equator would be marked by a neat white line, or perhaps just the odd signpost on a buoy saying something like "The Northern Hemisphere welcomes careful mariners." The truth is more remarkable. The equator is marked by a canal of boiling sea-water or, to be more accurate, a number of parallel boiling canals.

What happened was this. I had worked out the previous

night that, provided we kept up the same speed and assuming the current continued at one knot, we should reach the equator at about eight in the morning. Normally Liz and I try to catch up on sleep in the early part of the morning while Kevin and Mark are on watch; we hope that demands for breakfast do not become too insistent before 8.30, and the previous night we had had such a picnic with gale winds that we could happily have slept the whole day. But I suppose I must have had the equator in the back of my mind and slept restlessly. At about seven o'clock I woke up suddenly with the feeling that something was wrong. The motion of the boat was wrong. The crashing of the seas against the hull had ceased, and I could no longer hear the brittle roar of water racing by on the other side of the planks near my head. Kevin was on watch, sitting on the companion steps and peering out through the plastic hatch cover. I asked him what was happening.

"I don't quite know," he replied. "The wind has just died."

"What is the log reading?"

"Er . . . 50. And the compass is 290. About 10 degrees off course."

"Well, that puts us 4 miles from the equator. I'd better get up and look at the weather."

I crawled out of my bunk and we both went outside. The surface of the sea was remarkably calm, although a heavy swell still rolled us this way and that. While we were standing there, wondering uneasily what this sudden change meant, we heard the distant roar of breaking water. Looking ahead we saw a mass of white, troubled sea stretching across our path. A few minutes later we were suddenly in it, and both Kevin and I were knocked off balance as *Walkabout* bounced in the turbulent water like a pea in a boiling pot. The waves were only a few feet high, but they jetted up so sharply that the peaks fell every way and often split and fell two ways at once. They slapped the sides and jumped into the cockpit, yet there was hardly a breath of wind. It seemed so unnatural that I felt the hair on my neck rising. Liz and Mark stumbled up then and, thoroughly frightened, we all clung to the mast and the coamings while the terrible little waves set their teeth in *Walkabout*'s flanks and shook her until I thought the fastenings must fall out.

The boiling canal proved to be only a few hundred feet wide, and a little later we passed abruptly into perfectly smooth water. In its way this was just as uncanny. The belt of smooth water was roughly the same width as the turbulent patch, and beyond was a second canal, somewhat less violent than the first, but the boiling, roaring water was just as creepy. We crossed four canals in all, each one just a little less turbulent than the last, and each one separated from the others by a band of flat water. The queer thing was that the dividing line between rough and smooth water was as sharp and as straight as a pavement kerb.

There are, no doubt, prosaic people who would attempt to explain this strange phenomenon in terms of currents or winds, but we who were there know better.* 0° latitude, alleged by geographers to be the real equator, was passed about an hour later.

We were going to celebrate the event in traditional style, but the weather blew up so rough afterwards that we could face nothing more orgiastic than a pot of popcorn that Liz had the bright idea of making. The wind as usual blew from ahead—not directly from ahead but something like 60 degrees off the bow—and we sat around crunching hot popcorn and grumbling about the weather.

We had plenty of legitimate grumbles, considering this is meant to be a fairly steady trade wind area. It started two nights ago after the squall that drove us through the doldrums. The wind blew hard from the north and a second squall struck about an hour later. It was stronger than the first, and with Liz's help I reefed down the main and the mizzen. When the next squall arrived I took down the mizzen altogether and reefed the main as far as it would go. The trouble was that between squalls the wind was still nearly gale force, and we drove into 15ft and 20ft seas all night and for most of the next day. Heeled over so that one's world is always at an angle of 20° or 30° is disagreeable enough, but in these seas every other wave heaves the boat over on its side and every seventh throws her really hard. About once in an hour you get a really big one

* We later met the yacht *Rigadoon*, sailing from St Helena to Barbados, whose skipper had observed a similar phenomenon some miles further east about a day later.

that breaks right on the cabin top with an awful crump, which makes everyone duck instinctively.

In these circumstances it is impossible to keep dry. The decks have been permanently under water, and although the leaks are not severe they are enough to soak the bedclothes, the pillows, the carpet and our clothes, and keep them soaked. We try to protect things with plastic sheets, but to little effect. Kevin and Mark have been complaining bitterly about leaks over their bunks.

The most distressing thing of all, however, is the heat. We overtook the sun yesterday on its journey north and passed directly underneath its orbit in the late afternoon. Since before Recife the sea-water temperature has been a constant 86°F. The temperature in the cabin varies little from this norm. During the hottest part of the afternoon it may rise to 90°F, and in the chill hour before dawn the thermometer sinks to a frosty 83°F. If only we could get some air through! Yesterday I rigged up a double splash sheet with an old sail over the fore-hatch, and it worked splendidly for a while. We were able to crack open the hatch and breathe again. Then one of the big ones came over and buckets of water cascaded through the galley and our bunk. We decided that sticky heat was preferable to sticky salt water, but I wonder. In a day or two we'll be steamed to a turn like tinned sardines. Rachel is already suffering from a sweat rash under her chin and in the creases of her arms and legs. Mark and I have started salt-water boils where we sit and where we lean.

One way of escaping the heat is to sit near the main hatch, where the plastic spray hood is doing a splendid job—though it too cannot keep out the big ones. Yesterday I sat by the hatch all day, mending the sail that was damaged in the "doldrum" squall, and after his schoolwork Mark sat by me and helped. The galvanised luff wire, which is plastic-coated, had broken at the root of the splice, where the rust had eaten deep. The fault lies squarely with the sail-makers, who apparently cannot grasp conditions at sea from their still, dry lofts. The seizing around a splice, which looks so fine in the loft, serves only to retain the salt water at sea.

I have noticed that there is frequently a lack of understanding of important detail on the part of boat-builders and designers, even on expensive yachts from famous stables. I suppose that part of the trouble is that the people who build boats are too busy to go to sea, and the people who sail are too lazy to work. Anyway, Mark and I spliced in a new piece of wire and stitched the sail up again, making a strong job of it, although it took us all of yesterday and most of today. I also had to reeve a new jib sheet. The old one parted this afternoon, mainly because the manila is rotting; the new rope is not much better.

March 21st

The northerlies have if anything grown more determined in the last two days, and conditions in the cabin more distressing. Perhaps I am driving the boat too hard? Yesterday, for example, we covered 144 miles, only 11 of which was current. Maybe I am, but everyone wants to make a fast passage if only to reach port more quickly, and under these conditions *Walkabout* is fast; her masts are stubby, her shape seakindly, and her great weight gives her momentum to carry through waves that would stop a lighter boat dead. I remember how fast her sister ship, *Svaap*, was when Robinson sailed her round the world over 40 years ago. *Svaap*, at that time, was the smallest boat ever to circumnavigate the world, and Robinson drove her hard in all kinds of weather. And I know *Walkabout* can take it.

But what of the crew? They are bearing up, but the children are beginning to look pasty in this confined space and Liz is looking very drawn. Like me she is only managing to accumulate about three hours' sleep out of the twenty-four, but, unlike me, she has this problem of seasickness to contend with. She also takes the brunt of the cooking crises, which are so frequent now that they are no longer remarkable. As we are always heeling to port and the galley is on the starboard side, it slopes towards the cook. It is as if one's kitchen is hinged and tips up capriciously at various angles, tossing pots and plates at you. The galley stove—built in Rhodesia about a million years ago—is gimballed and has adjustable pegs to grip the pots, and if the boat merely heeled it would work well. But it cannot take the jumps. Neither can anyone nor anything else.

This jumping, in fact, is largely responsible for Liz's seasickness as well as the galley crisis. What happens is that the boat climbs up a wave and falls down the other side. Falls rather than slides, because with the wind against the current the waves are steep as well as high. Then we hit the trough with a jolt before climbing up the next wave. The jolting invariably accelerates at meal times, and not a meal passes without a bowl of cornflakes or mug of soup being upset. For some time now we have been using a damp towel as a tablecloth—a tip we picked up while I was reading Arthur Ransome's *Peter Duck* to the children. It prevents things slipping and soaks up a good deal of the mess when food is spilt. Actually we use two table towels, one on the table and the other always towing astern to clean it. They are swapped over when the table one gets too revolting.

If the effects of the boat's motion on the meals are aggravating, the effects on the cooking are often disastrous. This morning, for example, a jug of milk catapulted off the draining board and struck Liz in the midriff, drenching her. She burst into tears. And last night a pot of hot stew jumped at least 12 inches above the stove and then landed where the stove wasn't. Liz, grimly silent, insisted on heating something else rather than falling back on bread and snacks.

She is quite right, of course. One should not let things slip too far, regardless of what rubbish is flying around outside. We insist that the kids clean their teeth, wash their faces and so forth, and carry on with their lessons. They have at least to write up their diaries, work a couple of pages of sums and do a little English. We are too tired to help them much, but it is the principle of the thing that counts—like dressing for dinner in the jungle. Also it keeps them busy. Kevin is no problem; he simply buries his nose in a book. And Bruce's stamps are a blessing. Strictly speaking, they are shared between Mark and Bruce, but neither is allowed to sort them in port. They collect them in port and paste them at sea, very carefully in a stamp book with maps and a potted history of each country, and this keeps them happy for hours. Today Mark brought his electronic set out from the toy locker, but, alas, the damp had got at it and it did not seem too healthy. He is becoming quite competent, and in Recife built a transmitter with a range of about 2 feet. Now the apparatus will not work so he has another legitimate grumble. I put him on to making a new toaster (a sort of shallow open box that sits upside down over the primus) from a spare piece of copper sheeting, and that absorbed his attention for several hours.

As usual I have been occupied in maintenance work myself. This morning another jib sheet parted. I am running short of spare rope, and if there is much more trouble I shall have to start splicing the old stuff. Then the compass light packed in for the fourth time in as many days. Being situated under the tiller it is always wet and the copper wires corrode rapidly. Now I am mending the mizzen, which tore along the foot in a squall just before dawn. The cloth is getting weak—this terylene fibre rots away in a few years of tropical sunshine—and it is no longer safe to stitch. I glue the repair patches on with contact adhesive and stitch well back from the edge. This method is stronger than stitching alone, and avoids weakening the cloth along the line of needle perforations.

I have just seen a most extraordinary thing. I stopped writing and poked my head up into the plastic hatch cover to check for ships. Ships worry me in this weather, because half the time the seas are large enough to hide our boat from them, and the other half we cannot see more than a few hundred yards ourselves. We have only seen one ship since Cape S. Roque, and when Liz spotted her she was far too close for comfort. I hope she picked us up on her radar. We cannot carry navigation lights because the electric ones are too greedy, and the Tilley, while it is showerproof, cannot take green water. Anyway, I saw no ships but I did see a moonbow—the first I have ever heard of, let alone observed. It was like a rainbow, only it was more tightly curved and showed no colour, only a gradation from light to dark grey. I wonder what it portends? Everything is taken as a sign nowadays.

We are now halfway across the mouth of the Amazon river—though standing off some 200 miles—and the Routeing Chart does show a higher percentage (5 per cent) of gale force winds for this region. We appear to have collected the one chance in twenty. But the frequency of gales diminishes quickly to the north, so I should imagine that in a day or so we shall be clear of this rubbish and sailing free in the easterly trades.

March 23rd

The strong winds have not diminished at all in the last two days. We are still thrashing into heavy head seas, decks awash.

The weather pattern is similar every day. Dawn breaks through heavy cloud and gale force winds intensified by periodic squalls. After each squall there is a short period of slack wind, so the tiller demands constant attention. The squalls become less frequent as the morning wears on and the clouds begin to scatter. Shortly before midday the wind too gradually abates, until it is blowing only Force 5 or 6 in the late afternoon. At this point we hopefully ease out the reefing only to regret it soon after, for at sunset the wind pipes up again. It blows harder and harder through the night, the squalls become more frequent, and things generally reach a climax at about four o'clock in the morning. Then a new day begins.

Liz wanted to call in at Cayenne today. We are both red-eyed and do things slowly, unwillingly. Liz admits to losing her pioneer spirit. She thinks longingly of living in houses and travelling by aeroplane. So when I told her we had just passed the northern border of Brazil at midday and would be level with Cayenne tonight, she asked, "How far away are we?"

"About 100 miles out to sea."

"So with this wind behind us we should be there tomorrow, shouldn't we?"

"Yes, but . . . "

"Please, Mike, let's go in. I'm so weary and the cabin is so sordid. We desperately need a rest and a clean up."

I was tempted. We have the charts, for we originally planned to pay a visit. Cayenne, known also as Devil's Island, is the capital of French Guiana, and from reading about the place we imagine a dreadful hole—mosquito-infested swamps surrounding a miserable town with naked, half-starved children racing cockroaches across the pot-holed streets. Maybe we are wrong and there is a twenty-storey Hilton Hotel and shady avenues. But it sounded so horrible that we felt we must see it. Studying the charts and the *South America Pilot*,* however, thoroughly alarmed me. Stretching for many miles along the coast and several miles out to sea there is a huge bar of shifting

* *South America Pilot*, Vol. I (Hydrographer of the Royal Navy).

mudbanks with maximum charted depths of a couple of feet at low tide, and the river itself appears to have only one small mudhole to anchor in. In moderate conditions it would have been feasible, but now it would be madness to run on to a lee shore. Even if we came in safely we could well come to grief getting out, especially with a doubtful prop shaft. Joshua Slocum nearly met with disaster on a bank somewhere to the south when he ventured too close in the *Liberdade*. He struggled to beat off, and came so close that he could "smell the slimy bottom of the sea" and "taste the salty sand". He wrote afterwards that, "Any weather one's craft can live in after escaping a lee shore is pleasant weather—though some may be pleasanter than others."

"I know it doesn't seem like it, but our present weather is pleasanter weather," I said to Liz after explaining the position.

"At the moment, I can't imagine anything worse than this," she replied. She was very upset.

The kids seem to be coping better than us in many ways, probably because they get their full quota of sleep, even if it is in damp bunks. Rachel takes her alphabet very seriously and pesters us for tuition, which we grudgingly give. She is always asking questions about death—why, I don't know—but she startled me today. She was singing (rather incongruously):

"Row, row, row your boat,
Gently down the stream,
Merrily, merrily, merrily, merrily,
Life is but a dream."

"That's nonsense!" she exclaimed. "Life is but to die."

I do not know whether her comment was cynical or prosaic. I tend very much towards a prosaic philosophy in these conditions of ceaseless discomfort. It is interesting to see that Alexander Solzhenitsyn, in his novel *First Circle*, which I have just finished, arrives at a similar conclusion. He points out that the life sentences dealt out during the Stalin regime were not necessarily destructive to life, as commonly supposed. The tortures, interrogations and hardship suffered by the prisoners did not always have a dramatic, soul-destroying effect. Rather such experiences constitute a pressure that changes a man's life, sometimes beneficially. Removed from social and family pressures as well as from illusions of happiness and most pleasures, a man may more clearly come to terms with himself and life in general. A process of purification by deprivation, in fact. The point is that suffering is not dramatic, and neither is tragedy.

Our circumstances are trivial compared with those of Solzhenitsyn's characters, but there are similarities. Scaling the argument down to us, it is too commonly supposed that great courage and stamina are required to cross oceans. Certainly one should be able to inject these qualities at short notice, but the demand is infrequent, and the ability to endure a wet bottom and the third plate of stew in one's lap is the deciding factor. I think a cruising man must expect anything to turn up, and endure or enjoy it until it changes. The most important single quality, in short, is phlegm.

Yet despite the wretched conditions of the past week I personally would not have it any other way. Not because I am masochistic, but because circumstances like these are the bricks and mortar from which adventures are constructed, and adventures are becoming so few these days. I confess to feeling envy as well as admiration for Robin Knox-Johnston, who has accomplished the last great sailing adventure—the first single-handed non-stop circumnavigation—done in a boat very similar to *Walkabout* and with resources similar to my own. It is no use crying over spilt milk, but one cannot help shedding the occasional tear over the empty bottle.

We are all suffering from painful salt water boils, which, as much as anything, are responsible for this outburst of philosophy. We have long since found that synthetic fibres are unusable next to the skin at sea. In some way they manage to aggravate skin irritation. If we must be wet we use either wool or cotton, depending on taste. I should imagine that pure silk is best, but we have never been rich enough to buy it.

We have maintenance problems inside the cabin as well now. The primus stoves are corroding from repeated drenching and we are rapidly consuming our stock of spares, though the trouble is due in part to the poor quality of the Brazilian paraffin. The heads, too, are upset by the thrashing outside, and keep getting airlocked at critical moments. Last night the gaff boom fell with a crash because of a broken halyard. I climbed the mast and reeved a new one—too light, but the heavy rope had run out. Then the outhaul on the bowsprit broke and had to be respliced. This sort of thing wears you down.

As if that was not enough, today the sextant was also slugged by a wave. We have found that there is only one way to take sights, and that is to run downwind. At first we tried heaving to, but there was still too much spray coming aboard. Now Mark or Kevin takes the helm and runs before the seas while I shoot a snap sight when we are on the top of a wave (the only time one can see the horizon); Liz sits by the chronometer. This morning, however, a piece of sea caught the sextant fair and square and I spent hours cleaning it and oiling it, as lovingly as a sharpshooter would his gun. I don't think it is damaged.

There have been no unusual portents or signs today, so we are hoping that the high winds will soon be done, or at least blow from the proper quarter. Seven days of rubbish is surely enough to satisfy any god.

March 25th

Two further days of misery, and there is no sign of a change. Last night we had the worst squall ever. I luffed up as much as I dared without flogging the sails to rags, but *Walkabout* still raged on at 8 knots, with so much water tumbling aboard that I could not see boat for sea. The mainmast arched forward like a fishing rod, and I waited in fascination for the splintering crack. The squall fortunately abated quite quickly, but I am certain it was a close thing. The mast is a stout stick of solid spruce, planted through the deck on to the keel and braced with bronze knees, but there is a limit to what it can stand. Running backstays must be fitted in the West Indies, for the North Atlantic is worse than this, or so we are led to believe.

Liz and I no longer react to crises like this one. We are more like zombies than sailors. When we are not dragging ourselves about our duties, we are very irritable with the kids. There has been only one bright spot during this dismal voyage, and that is our high speed. Our excellent progress has been the strongest tonic of all. Yesterday we crossed the time zone and put the ship's clock back an hour, which is a pleasantly tangible sign of progress. This noon our position was 8°-32′ N. and 53°-26′ W., just 455 miles from Barbados. The winds can blow, we don't care. We shall be in port in a few days, and we have become so used to a state of exhaustion that it is as natural as breathing.

March 27th

I think the gales are over! The wind began veering a little this morning and the squalls diminished. Now, for the first time in what seems like a decade, the wind is no longer blowing against us. We are too tired to care. Liz and I feel as though we have sand in our eyes, and we move around like slugs. I have difficulty in controlling my saliva.

Today I could not work out our position. I struggled with the calculations and got into such a state that Liz came and helped. Her navigational theory is hazy but she knows the recipes I use, and we went slowly through each step together. In the end we discovered that I had been looking up the wrong month in *The Nautical Almanac*. I felt like resigning.

The kids were in a roisterous mood all day, which is very trying. The reason is the proximity of a landfall. Kevin has been working out the distance to Barbados every day, and declared this afternoon that we were only 170 miles away and should reach port tomorrow. They have been capering around ever since.

March 28th

It is 10 p.m., but nobody is asleep. They are all outside, looking eagerly at the lights of Barbados sprinkled in the sea ahead.

We had hoped to make port before nightfall but the wind fell light today—just when we needed it—so we shan't get in before midnight. I took a number of sights, including moon sights, during the day, and predicted a landfall in the late afternoon. Kevin climbed the mast after lunch and claimed he could see land, but we didn't believe him. When your eyes are searching every segment of the horizon you see islands by the archipelago, so he was told to find an island that everyone else could see too. At five o'clock Mark shouted, "Land Ho!" and there it was, quite definitely not a cloud.

I must confess to a feeling of relief. Even I have had my fill of the sea for a week or two, and it goes without saying that the rest of the family are hungry for land.

As for *Walkabout*, she too needs a rest. She has covered 2,150 miles in 15½ days in foul weather, and the effort has cost her. The decks need recaulking. They have been under water for so long that moss is growing on them. Her mast rattles. It has worn out the deck sleeve and must be re-wedged; and the rigging must be completely renewed. Every rope is stranded, chafed or rotten. The sails don't bear thinking about. Down below the water and heat have damaged our gear. How badly we don't know yet. When Liz pulled some clothes from the cupboard she found they were beginning to rot; the stove, tin openers, bread tins and tools are all encrusted with rust, and I am sure that our undeveloped films have been damaged by the heat. The sea is much cooler here, thank heaven; the cabin thermometer is down to 76°F.

Has it been worth it? The question occurs to me, but I am too weary to think of an answer. Tomorrow, maybe, when we are riding safely at anchor, we shall feel a sense of achievement. Right now I just feel pulped and cannot think much further than my salt-water boils, which are agonising. Anyway, we still have to reach port, and . . .

I have just heard a crack above. There is a familiar flapping noise on the foredeck, and Mark is singing out some story about broken halyards. There will be no peace till we are riding at anchor.

XII

THE FIRST DAY in Barbados passed in a daze. We collected our mail, the first since Rio, dissolved enough salt off our bodies to raise the salinity in the bay by several degrees, and in the evening slid into sleep as deep as the ocean.

While we slept a three-masted barquentine sailed through the last night of her voyage from France. In the early morning she bore round the headland of Carlysle Bay and brought up near us. On *Walkabout* four pairs of youthful eyes gleamed with excitement at this grand sight, for, unlike us, the children had been up since dawn. The unfortunate Frenchman scarcely had time to drop anchor before the children were alongside in the dinghy, asking pointed albeit polite questions about the ship. A few questions were sufficient to produce the desired invitation. A Jesuit priest leaned over the rail.

"Come aboard, *mes enfants*, and see for yourselves."

They swarmed aboard and were shown over a real ship, *Le Bel Espoir III*, built originally as a cattle-trader and later on roughly converted for human cargo. Afterwards they invited Père Alain for breakfast, and he was rowed over by a man with such a horrible, blood-thirsty appearance that he would have been taken for a pirate anywhere in the world. He proved to be quite docile, however, and told us he was one of the crew.

The ship, it seemed, was now being used for a rehabilitation project run by the French government and the Jesuits for drug addicts and delinquents. The "rehabilitatees" were of both sexes, aged from roughly eighteen to thirty; about twenty were taken on a cruise from France through the West Indies and back again. Whether the treatment was successful or not is doubtful, but Père Alain said that it helped and was good fun anyway. We greatly enjoyed his witty company, and when *Le Bel Espoir III* left a couple of days later we were sorry to see her go.

There were few cruising yachts left in Barbados by the time we got there. Some months earlier the annual flotilla of eighty-odd yachts had floated in from Europe, but most of them had dispersed around the Caribbean. One which remained was *Baus*, a 44ft Colin Archer built in Norway in 1890 and converted, regrettably, to modern Bermudan rig. Aboard was an American family—Bob and Chris Clark, their two children and a young Moroccan lad. In a sense they were all infant walkabouts, for they had not yet sailed anywhere. They had given up their home in the States, had flown straight to Barbados, and intended now to make their way very slowly to Honduras.

"What then?" I asked.

"Gee, I don't know," drawled Bob. "First ya gotta learn to be a real slowed-up person."

He had not learned yet but he was working hard at it (which, of course, tended to speed him up), and whenever we met we would greet each other with the solicitous enquiry, "Hi! You real slowed up yet today?"

For all of us it was a holiday. The water was crystal clear over the corals, and the colourful sailing dinghies darted round the bay like butterflies. In the careenage we found, to my surprise, inter-island trading schooners which still carry cargo regularly round the West Indies. Their skippers are fine seamen, but apparently experience the occasional difficulty in reaching Barbados because it is the only island that is not visible from any other and is, moreover, directly up-wind. A common technique is to go first to Martinique, further north, then to sail hard on the wind on a south-easterly course until Barbados appears. There is a story that one skipper who did this failed to find Barbados, and after sailing hard on the wind for four days gave up and turned back to look for the West Indies again.

"Ah done sail to Barbados," he complained afterwards, "but she wasn't there."

What surprised us even more than the traders was the number of sailing ships we encountered, most of them now chartering or training. There is nothing to set off a harbour like a three-masted tall ship with her magnificent rigging whispering and clicking in the trades.

But after a few days we moved on. We had only come to

Barbados because we had been totally ignorant about the West Indies, and the island is the ideal jumping-off place to any other island. But if our anchorage was pleasant the shore life was not. The islanders and officials were disagreeable, even on occasion threatening, and the policy towards visitors, who were mainly Americans, was to wring from them as many dollars as possible. The deciding factor was that fresh food was scarce and formidably expensive. Apparently all cultivation is given over to sugarcane. So after washing every scrap of cloth aboard, by kind courtesy of the cruising club, and loading up with fresh water, we left for St Vincent, where we had been advised to go for food.

St Vincent lies a paltry 100 miles downwind of Barbados, and we drew into Kingston Harbour the following day. Everyone thought it just a nice length of voyage, except for Liz, who felt it was a trifle too long. We pulled off into the harbour, dropped anchor, and went to the market to see what the locals could offer. Not a great deal, it appeared, despite St Vincent's proud boast that the island is "the fruit basket of the Caribbean". We did, however, discover some strange varieties of fruit and vegetables. Jostling through the crush of yelling mammies, we would reach a stall piled with what looked like dead roots.

"What are these called?" I would ask.

"Dasheen, skip."

"How do you cook them?"

"Peel 'em and boil 'em, skip."

"And this one?"

"Dat's de bread fruit, skip."

"How do you cook that?"

"Peel 'em and boil 'em, skip."

"And this one that looks like a giant banana. I suppose you . . . "

"Dat's right, skip. Peel 'em and boil 'em."

"I can see that cooking in the Caribbean is not going to present any problems," remarked Liz.

Bananas at least were plentiful, and we never sailed anywhere without a stalk lashed to a stanchion near the cockpit, so that anyone feeling peckish had only to reach out and pluck a fruit.

Unlike Barbados, which is low and somewhat featureless,

St Vincent and the other islands are volcanic and possess some impressive scenery. St Vincent has a simmering volcano called Souffrière (anything with a volcanic air about it in the West Indies is called Souffrière), which could never be seen because it always had its head in a cloud of steam. We went up to the lighthouse because the children wanted to see *Walkabout* from the light, for a change, instead of the other way about. And before leaving we paid a visit to the Botanical Gardens to see the actual bread-fruit tree planted by the notorious Captain Bligh. It was during the mission to transport bread-fruit from the Pacific to the West Indies that mutiny occurred on the *Bounty*; the bread-fruit plants themselves were said to have contributed to the mutiny by consuming too much fresh water.

After a couple of days we sailed for Bequia, the northernmost island in the Grenadines, where we planned to refit. Bequia is less than 10 miles distant, and clearly visible, and the trip was a great attraction to the children. Here was a passage they could easily grasp.

"Can we sail *Walkabout* there?" asked Kevin.

"All by yourselves?"

"Yes, I'm sure we can do it," said Mark excitedly. "But you mustn't help us or tell us what to do."

"Very well," I agreed. "There are the charts. She's all yours. Wake us up when we reach Admiralty Bay."

Kevin took command, and apart from raising the anchor the boys got the ship under way and made sail by themselves. They laid a course and trimmed the sails to it, and would have negotiated the passage entirely on their own had we not run into strong winds and a tide rip. I had to add some muscle to the ropes, but we sailed safely into Admiralty Bay a couple of hours later. I asked Liz whether the voyage was short enough for her this time. She felt it could with advantage have been a trifle shorter.

For nearly a fortnight we lay at this very still anchorage, close by the village of Port Elizabeth, licking our wounds. The place boasted a chandler (one of the reasons we went there) called Lully's. Legend has it that Lully was shipwrecked many years ago, swam ashore and started selling fish hooks. One thing led to another, and now he sells wares so dainty that to re-rig our boat we had to dig deep into the ship's purse; even then we were forced to splice old manila tails on to Lully's new rope. Because of the North Atlantic crossing, however, there was a limit to the corners we could afford to cut. We were dreading the voyage, knowing that it would be much colder and convinced that it would be stormier than the last leg.

Kevin and Mark were put on to re-caulking the decks. They had been caulked a year before with two-part polysulphide rubber, which was now peeling up like elastic tape, although we had carried out all the maker's priming instructions. This material, which is now universally used for caulking, is another example of the divide between boat-builders and sailors. On even the most highly crafted new yachts I saw the bond between this rubber and the wood failing after a few years in the tropics. Kevin and Mark were given old-fashioned caulking cotton and they sat in the sun every morning, tapping it into the seams. They did very well until they had completed the areas over their respective bunks, when enthusiasm waned to a negligible level.

During the afternoon the children could do whatever they wanted. The sea was their backyard and the reefs were their garden. Stepping over the side of the boat was as natural to them as opening the front door, and they spent as many waking hours in the water as out of it. When they were not swimming or diving, Bruce and Rachel could usually be found on the beach or helping the fishermen with their gear, while Kevin and Mark preferred to sail *Crawlabout*. In the afternoon and evening Bruce and Mark would row round the bay visiting yachts from different countries to ask for stamps, and many friendships were made in this way.

Admiralty Bay was a favourite spot for cruising yachts, which passed through in bewildering numbers. Hitherto, a foreign yacht coming into port had been an event of significance, but in the West Indies they came and went like caravans in a holiday camp. Most of them were American boats cruising for a few months on their doorstep, as it were, or charter yachts which were often no more than sailing caravans. But there were hundreds of beautiful vessels, and the blatant superiority of so many elegant confections in stainless steel and fibreglass gave us all something of a complex.

However, a comforting percentage of walkabouts could still

be found, the smallest of which was only 22ft. One thing that interested us was why people should take to the sea as a way of life in the first place. What factor had walkabouts in common? Were they all courageous or adventurous, for example? They were not. Were they all intelligent and resourceful? Patently not in many cases. Perhaps they all liked sailing? Again, rather astonishingly, not. Many boats we met preferred port to passage, and some would go to any lengths to avoid putting to sea more than once a year. The shameful truth is that walkabouts have only one thing in common. They abhor work. Not, I hasten to add, that sailing and maintaining a yacht is not work. It is hard work and the hours are terrible. But walkabouts do not mind that. What they hate is regular, organised work of the nine-to-five sort.

And what do they talk about? Apart from boats and all the frightful storms they have weathered, the main topic of conversation is money. They like to reminisce about the ridiculously low price of pineapples in the Honduras or oysters in Indonesia, and compare them with the high cost of living in their present port.

Having come to these disgraceful conclusions, we swapped all our old books for new ones, left Bequia and sailed to Savan Island, a little to the south. We were tired of working all day on the boat, and anyway the food on Bequia was frightfully expensive.

Like many other small islands in the West Indies, Savan has no permanent water supply and no one lives there. We arrived one morning in mid-April, sailing fast over a rough sea and dodging between the coral reefs, which made Liz jittery. We sailed straight down a narrow sand corridor and dropped anchor not 15 yards from the steep, cream-coloured beach. I laid out a second anchor because of a swell that was so heavy that not another yacht came near the place. Apart from a little group of Bequia fishermen camped ashore, we had a West Indian island all to ourselves for a few days.

It was delightful. The children dived and swam until I fancied they were growing gills. The corals were gorgeous to look at but here, as elsewhere, they were denuded of fish. This did not deter Bruce, who swam ashore and charmed bait out of the fishermen, earnestly assuring them of a percentage of his catch. To everyone's astonishment, apart from his own, he caught quite well and was able to tell us the local names of all he caught.

"How do you want me to cook them, Bruce?" asked Liz.

"Peel 'em and boil 'em!" chanted everybody.

We explored the island, which was little more than a cliffy hill above the sea, and the boys demanded to go camping.

"We want to do it all ourselves," said Mark, "to see if we can survive in the wild."

Liz demurred but I said, "Let them go. I also want to see if they can survive without us."

They went off in the dinghy with a saucepan, a box of matches, some water, their fishing gear and a blanket each, and they stayed ashore for two days. We found later that the fishermen had been secretly helping them with a canvas awning against the rain, and showing them how to broil their fish and crabs over a fire. One of the fishermen, a sturdy old Bequian with a kindly, chocolate-brown face mazed with wrinkles, came to see us and found Liz and me pinned to our bunks with a bad dose of 'flu.

"Don't worry 'bout dem chillen," he assured us. "Dey tougher den us fisherfolk and dey knows everything. Now I brought you dese." And he gave us four precious eggs which we gladly swapped for coffee. Later he returned with a plateful of hot fried fish for our supper so that we should not have to get up.

We left Savan Island with regret, for not only was it a happy place but it marked the beginning of the end of our voyage. Here we counted our cash and at last finalised our decision to reach England the same year; with care it was possible, we reckoned, to leave the West Indies fitted out and provisioned and with £100 to spare. We had been a little unfortunate with money, for twice the action of a remote politician had knocked down the value of the ship's purse—once when the South African rand was floated with the British pound, and once when Nixon devalued the dollar. As for carrying the money, we had tried several methods and found that the most satisfactory way was to stuff dollar notes under the mattress. Any method that involves a bank circumscribes one's independence.

Reluctance to tackle the North Atlantic made us dawdle.

First we sailed back to St Vincent and anchored in a pretty place called Young Island for several days. The next island to the north is St Lucia, and Good Friday found us sailing the channel, our bowsprit tossing the spray into a brisk trade wind; the children knelt on the deck exclaiming as big grey dolphins undulated across the bows.

Sailing in the Leeward and Windward Isles is marvellous. The chain of islands runs from north to south, and across the chain, from east to west, the trade wind blows nearly every day. There is an old wives' tale which says that sailing up the windward side is highly dangerous; one should sail up the leeward side, keeping "two pistol shots from the shore", as the old pilot has it. It is true that the windward side is usually rough and there is an onshore current, but I suspect there is a deeper reason; the windward side is the Atlantic Ocean, whereas the other side is merely the Caribbean Sea. Concluding that either side would drown us equally well, I always preferred sailing the windward side, for trying to sail under the lee was too exasperating for a boat with no engine.

As nearly every island is visible from another, navigation among the islands is perfectly painless—except where the reefs lie. On one reef we saw the new bones of a French liner, the *Antilles*, and they served as a warning. We became fair-weather sailors. If we could not raise anchor after breakfast and drop it in time for supper, we felt hard done by.

The shore life in the West Indies was as ugly as the sailing was fine. The open resentment for whites can possibly be explained away by a colonial past and the current invasion by American tourists, but the political and economic mess is all their own. Reduced to the simplest terms, it appeared to us that the West Indians are too idle to support themselves. In Dominica we discovered mangoes flourishing wild on the fertile, volcanic soil, but because the fruit had not yet fallen to the ground it was not available on the market. We found that eggs had to be imported from Britain, onions from Canada and frozen fish from Cape Town! The West Indians, meanwhile, sat on the pavements and passed the word around on how badly the world was treating them.

We passed a couple of days in Vieux Fort, the little banana harbour in St Lucia, and sailed off early on Easter Sunday, hoping for good winds to carry us to Martinique before nightfall. The heavy sky, however, threatened rain and squalls to interrupt the trade wind, and soon after we started Liz and I agreed that we should probably have to find some anchorage in the north of St Lucia that night. The prospect was not displeasing—if we did not reach Martinique that day we should reach it the following day, or perhaps the day after that. And in the meanwhile there was always the chance of finding a deserted little spot to anchor with a nearby reef to examine.

I reclined in the cockpit with a cup of coffee in one hand, a pipe in the other and my foot on the tiller. I could not be bothered to fiddle with the self-steering, especially close to the mountains here where the wind shifted erratically. There are few cruising pleasures to compare with exploring an unknown shore, especially a scenic one, and St Lucia has some of the grandest scenery among the islands. In a boat one always has a panoramic view, and one, moreover, that is always gradually changing as the boat slides slowly forward. We watched the far peaks ease one behind another, then drift out the other side, watched valleys unfold little by little, and picked out the occasional cluster of buildings that told of a village. There was always a bluish headland to gaze at and the next one to anticipate. Suddenly a faint line would appear next to the headland, and before long a further cape would inch out over the sea, to be identified on the chart. The tiny village of Souffrière, clinging to the steep shore of a miniature cove and guarded at either hand by two great peaks, Grand Piton and Petit Piton, sweeping upwards almost from the eaves of the outlying houses, presented an exquisite scene.

Our dreamy contemplation was spoilt when the wind died away completely and then sprang up again from the west. A west wind in April in the Caribbean is rather like snow in England in June, but with our propensity for finding freak winds I suppose it was inevitable. The west wind brought heavy rain, which in turn cut off the wind, and the weather turned fretful. Land was at once blotted from sight. The whole day was spent blundering to and fro in torrential rains which shrouded the boat in a dark grey curtain. We had to change course so frequently that we lost all sense of position. Once the rain thinned momentarily to reveal a headland looming over the bows. We hurriedly came about and beat away.

The crew began to mutter, "It's too rough and too wet. We want to anchor for the night. Start the engine." I held out till the afternoon, and then capitulated. From the chart it appeared that there were a couple of likely anchorages in the vicinity. How to find them was another matter, for we could hardly see beyond the tip of the bowsprit. It became very dark.

All at once I smelt hot oil. I glanced instinctively at the oil pressure gauge. It was flickering just above zero! I stopped the engine and began to look for a leak. It was not difficult to find. A copper pipe had corroded and burst, and the engine had pumped its black blood over the engine hatch, making a frightful mess. Hot oil was everywhere. Books were covered in it, a pile of clothes was steeped in it, and Rachel's bunk mopped up the rest.

We had by now evolved an emergency procedure to deal with crises like this. Immobilise everyone and cordon off the contaminated area to prevent spreading. Deal swiftly with the core of the infection. Work inwards with cleaning weapons, at the same time establishing a rigid disposal corridor. Transfer victims of contamination to special institutions (like detergent buckets). In a remarkably short space of time the place was ship-shape again and the broken pipe was being repaired. The lesson to be learned here, I reflected, was to install an alarm buzzer for low oil pressure. One cannot sit all day watching the gauge, and a sense of smell is not reliable enough.

The engine was started again and we pressed on through the drumming rain. By now we were thoroughly wet and cold, and I decided to close the shore to try to find out where we were. Liz stood at the bows peering forward, while I removed my useless spectacles and gazed at my fingernails.

"There's a headland!" cried Liz. "We're almost on top of it." I took her word for it. "And there's another one on the other side. Careful, we're just about between them."

And suddenly we were out of the sea and gliding over smooth water between a narrow gap in the cliffs. We motored slowly up what was almost a little fjord, and drifted to rest round a corner at the end. The rain thinned away and we found ourselves in a tiny pond, as still and remote from the sea as a

Scottish tarn. The hills flowed to the water's edge under a carpet of rich green vegetation, while here and there the pretty houses dug themselves into the slopes and hid under tall trees. Marigot Harbour—for that was its name—was the perfect port in a storm, so serene and lovely that we named it "Stop-the-sea-I-want-to-get-off".

We left regretfully next dawn for the bustling port of Fort de France, the capital of Martinique. Here we went foraging for French food in a town so much like France that it was faintly ridiculous. The prices were even more that way inclined, for, like the neighbouring states, Martinique leans heavily on outside subsidy. It was enjoyable, however, to potter around the busy yacht harbour, chatting to other boats. The children befriended a rather lonely little boy on a German walkabout we had previously met in Bequia, and we encountered a charming young couple who had sailed across from France in a weatherbeaten little sloop only 24ft overall, called *Ostrevent*. Alain and Irène Galtié had decided to sell *Ostrevent* and fly back to France. When they heard of our problems with headsails being washed off the bowsprit they gave us one of *Ostrevent*'s old sails, which was cut high to clear the waves. The sail must have drawn thousands of horse power from the wind in its time, for before *Ostrevent* it had belonged to an old cutter which had eventually gone down off Morocco. But it was a real cart-horse, made as a cruising sail should be with cloth that was not too heavy, terylene luff rope instead of a wire luff, heavy-duty hanks and eyelets and massive reinforcing around the stress points. The generous gift made all the difference to our sailing; from then on we could beat to windward in any strength of wind.

When we left Fort de France we did so with style. Not for us the boorish engine, blunt tool of lesser seamen. Not for us the shouting and hysterical fuss of the amateur sailor. Aware that many pairs of eyes were upon us, each member of the crew stood by his sheets, alert to the quiet signal of command. We sailed out our anchor and began to pick our way out of the crowded harbour. *Walkabout*'s heavy bowsprit swept close to many gleaming topsides, only fractionally whiter than their owners' faces, and *Crawlabout* towed dutifully astern.

Everything went according to plan and we were almost clear

of yachts when I became aware that *Walkabout* was not responding well to the helm. We seemed to be moving rather slowly. In fact, I suddenly realised, we were not moving at all.

"What's happening? Who's doing what?"

"Daddy, look! The dinghy's caught!" Kevin gestured astern.

"Oh, good grief!" The dinghy was snagged on an anchor chain and we were dragging behind not only the dinghy and the chain but the yacht that belonged to the chain as well. When the chain was fully stretched the whole procession stopped and *Walkabout* started to swing downwind, completely out of control. In a few seconds it was obvious that we should grind up against a dainty little fibreglass yacht.

"Cut the dinghy loose," cried Liz.

"No!" I swung round, grabbed Kevin and gave him an urgent instruction. Then I picked him up and hurled him into the water. He swam like a torpedo to the dinghy, leapt aboard and hooked her free. We moved off, gathered speed and eased past the dainty yacht with inches to spare, trying to appear as though we sailed everywhere towing Kevin in the dinghy. It is always the same. You can execute the most elegant manœuvre a dozen times in solitude, but let there be one mistake and half the world is there to see it.

Dominica, the next island to the north, is the best for fresh produce, and naturally we went foraging. Dinghy loads of green groceries were ferried aboard, but as fast as we foraged the children ate it up. Dominica is also one of the least spoiled islands, and wild Indians, the remnants of the original Caribs, are alleged to live in the rugged interior. I doubt this, however. In any event, all Liz and I found in the hills was a goat.

From Dominica we pressed on north, for time was slipping by, and we did not stop until we dropped the hook in the miniature harbour of Port Gustavia in the French island of St Bartholomew, St Barts for short. The island is something of an anomaly in the West Indies. First, it once belonged to Sweden, and Port Gustavia has the quaint aspect of a Swedish village transported to the tropics, complete with steep roofs to let the snow slide off. Then it is uncharacteristically clean, orderly and quiet. So quiet, in fact, that I never managed to clear the ship, for every time we went to the gendarme's office it was shut. St Barts celebrates seven Sundays a week, the manner of celebration being the same on every day, namely, adding to its considerable prosperity by quietly trading in vast quantities of tobacco and liquor. "Booze and smokes" say the shop signs blatantly, and the yachts slip alongside the Quai de Général de Gaulle, one after the other, and fill their lockers. The fact is that St Barts is a free port. We watched open-mouthed one day as five strapping crew from a big German yacht lugged case after case of booze and smokes aboard for two whole hours. Not only yachts but smugglers' schooners come to St Barts, fill their holds with booze and sail down to places like Grenada, where the liquor tariffs allow them to smuggle at a profit.

The children liked St Barts for the good swimming and the interesting walks, so we lingered there, using maintenance and the well-stocked chandlers as an excuse. The chilly North Atlantic somehow lacked attraction when we contemplated it from our berth in the sleepy careenage. But at last we tore ourselves away and sailed west to the Virgin Islands, to the American island of St Thomas, 120 miles away. We had no special desire to visit St Thomas, which has a poor reputation amongst yachties, but it was apparently the best place to victual for the long crossing ahead.

So we set out, but I very nearly did not make it, being attacked by a fish halfway across. Not a shark or barracuda but a meek flying fish. It was dark at the time and I was standing next to the starboard navigation lights, while Liz sat at the tiller. Suddenly a big flying fish came winging over the boat at great speed and struck me at the base of the throat. We both fell to the deck and thrashed about; I recovered but he did not. I have felt ever since that a more ludicrous way to die could not be devised.

When we did get to St Thomas we were nearly thrown out.

"Passports, please, captain," said the beefy immigration official, who looked like one of those Irish New York policemen so beloved by detective writers. He scowled at the passports. "Where's your visas, captain?"

"Visas? We have no visas. We're on a yacht."

"Listen, sailor! I don't care if you're on a tricycle. If you enter any territory of the United States of America, you gotta

Above: Priest-bread on the island of Pico in the Azores

Right: A great sperm whale rotting on the factory slip in Horta, Azores

Left: "And then, just when the wind reached hurricane force, this huge shark bit the rudder . . ." Bruce and Anna Price stretching yarns on *Domino* in the Azores

Below: Walkabout nearing the end of her long voyage lies travel-stained at the Azores

have a visa. The territory of the United States is only permitted to aliens permitted to carry visas. Got it?"

"Oh very well," I sighed. "I'll buy half a dozen, then."

His complexion took on the appearance of freshly sliced beef. "You-cannot-buy-visas-on-the-United-States-territory," he said, enunciating each word separately. "They are only issued abroad. Now listen to me, bud. You take yourself and your boat outta this harbour as soon as you can. If you want to come back, you can get visas from the United States Consulate in the British Virgins."

The whole affair seemed a ridiculous storm in a teacup. All we wanted to do was to buy provisions and make ready for sea. So I declared the ship unseaworthy, which was in a sense perfectly true. The official went off to consult his superior and returned with a compromise. It seemed we should be placed "on parole" for five days, during which time we could nibble the verdant pastures of United States territory. If we were found in territorial waters after the end of that period, I gathered that we should probably be gunned down with six-shooters.

Why officialdom is so anxious to keep St Thomas exclusive is difficult to understand. It was unquestionably the most disagreeable port we had ever visited. The town is without grace of any kind, and the hills, scarred by bulldozers, are ugly. Relative prosperity has not made the people less sullen, nor has it kept the Black Power movement at bay; instead, American occupation has created a chromium and plastic slum.

There were, however, huge supermarkets, and we were able to stock up on tinned foods and staples. In addition to supermarkets the marina at Yacht Haven boasted a seedy launderette, the first we had ever come across in a harbour. This heady discovery unbalanced Liz, so that when we left she forgot all our washing in a machine, a fact that was not discovered until we were well on our way.

We worked hard every day at our lists and final maintenance but in the evenings, when the children were in bed and we had to get out of the cabin anyway, we were able to row about, visiting. There were a number of walkabouts dotted amongst the luxury yachts, several with children aboard. One we had come to know well from other islands was *Horizon Seeker* from

New Orleans, a 29ft sloop, in which Bill and Carol Wright and their 10-year-old son had been cruising the Caribbean for over a year. They were on their way back to America, where they planned to swallow the anchor and make plenty of money, if necessary by working. My friend Bob "Baus" would have shaken his head sadly over this failure to become "real slowed-up persons".

On May 12th, when our five days' parole expired, we spent the entire day running around the island with cans looking for diesel fuel. The marina's pumps had corroded away and not one petrol station sold the stuff. Eventually I managed to persuade the man at the oil depot to unlock his great tanks and leak out sufficient fuel to fill mine. Then, quite exhausted, we sailed from St Thomas round to Honeymoon Bay, a few miles away, to get ourselves ship-shape.

The principal task was to scrub off the bottom, which had accumulated a quantity of marine growth. This was specially annoying, as we had gone to a great deal of trouble and expense over this crucial matter of antifouling in the tropics. Following the recommendations of an international paint firm, the hull had been taken down to bare wood, thoroughly primed and painted with a hard copper paint, i.e. one that must dry hard before the boat is launched. The paint was supposed to keep the bottom clean for a year, but after three months there was a growth of weed and goosenecked barnacles. The boat had been antifouled again in Rio and now, little more than three months after the second antifouling, the bottom was encrusted with large patches of heavy shell and weed growth. Other patches were clean, showing that the paint was not homogenous. Unless one is certain that a particular brand of paint will work well in tropical waters, the safest approach is to use a soft paint with a good percentage of copper in it and paint it on really thick—at least three coats.

While the children had their last swim in the Caribbean, I dived under and scrubbed *Walkabout* clean—with a nailbrush, Rachel having lost all the scrubbing brushes over the side. Then Liz stowed everything very securely down below while the boys and I double-lashed the dinghy and made ready the heavy trailing warps that would be used in the gales which we fully expected in the days ahead. My last job was to throw all unnecessary junk overboard. This consisted mainly of model boats made from coconut husks, for the boys were still going through a boat-building phase. We kept the best and discarded the rest.

At last we were ready. Liz and I looked at each other.

"I think that's it," I said. "I can't think of anything else to do."

"Neither can I," said Liz. "I'm afraid we'll have to go."

"We could wait until tomorrow. After all, it's the 13th today."

"Only half of it. It's past noon."

"Yes. There's nothing else you want to do?"

"Nothing."

"All right, lads! Come and help me heave up that anchor warp."

The boys began singing, "Heave away, oh! My bully bully boys, For we're bound for Australia."

Log entry: 13/5/73: 13.30 Zone Time.
Left Honeymoon Bay, St Thomas, bound for Horta, Azores, approximately 2,600 miles distant. Provisions and stores aboard:

Foodstuffs and consumable stores 2/3 months
Adequate spares and gear for same period
Water 110 gallons
Paraffin 12 gallons
Methylated spirit (alcohol) 1¼ gallons
Diesel 38 gallons
Petrol 4 gallons (batteries fully charged)
Ship's purse $250 U.S. exactly

XIII

THE FIRST NIGHT out from St Thomas we came closer to being run down by a ship than ever before. So close, that even now I can recall exactly the terror of the moment. And the worst of it was that I have only myself to blame.

It was quite rough at the time, and had been that way from the moment we had poked our bowsprit round the corner of St Thomas and beaten past Cockroach Island. Not only was the wind blowing fresh but it was—inevitably—blowing from east-nor'east, so that we were close hauled with sheets just started. We were sailing, though, in fine style. With the new sail from *Ostrevent* mounted as a staysail and the old, heavy jib on the bowsprit, we were driving through the waves at great speed, throwing up sheets of spray and occasionally taking a green one over the bows. That, I suppose, was half the trouble. Under these conditions you could not see a great deal of the sea around you.

Because of the shipping lanes, we decided to stand two-hour watches throughout the night. I came on watch at 1 a.m. and, too sleepy to read, sat on the companion steps with my head just below the hatch. Every five or ten minutes I would poke my head up into the spray hood to look for ships' lights. We were carrying nothing ourselves, for the Tilley lamp would have been quenched, and the electric lights would have flattened the battery in a couple of nights. So we relied on spotting any ships in good time, and we made sure that we looked about when on the crest of a wave, for only then could the horizon be seen.

At about 2 a.m. I glanced at the clock. Nearly time to take another look; ten minutes since the last one. I had seen nothing, and to get a better view had even poked my head over the top. All I got was an eyeful of salt water. Give it another ten minutes, I thought.

At that moment a searchlight slashed through the porthole and blinded me. It jolted me like an electric shock. In a spasm I had wrenched the helm over, with no recollection of how I had reached the tiller. I could hear the ship's engines above the noise of the seas, but I could not see her. All I could see was a blinding white searchlight shining down on me. It was this that was terrifying. The searchlight was burning *down* on us, not shining over the water. I stood there like a rabbit in the headlights, unable to do anything but hang on to the helm. Seconds later the ship's wash struck us and we were swept from stem to stern. In the reflected light from a wave I caught the flash of turbulence from the great propeller. Then the searchlight was astern and the danger was past.

They kept the searchlight on us for a few minutes longer, then switched it off, and the stern light could be seen drawing away. I am eternally grateful to that ship's watch for keeping a good radar look out, for that is how they must have seen us.

This problem of avoiding collision at sea is a serious one for little yachts sailing short-handed. I have explained the difficulty of carrying lights at all times, a difficulty that is recognised by the International Regulations for Preventing Collisions at Sea, which allow sailing boats of less than 40ft in length to exhibit a light "in sufficient time to prevent collision" if the light cannot be permanently fixed. Many boats carry a light at the mast head only, but if it is powerful enough to be of use it is too greedy with electricity in a small boat on a long crossing. Radar reflectors are essential, and it was clearly our reflector that the ship had picked up. Another line of defence is to use an instrument that can warn the yacht's crew of the presence of a nearby vessel by detecting the ship's radar beam, and can also indicate the direction of the ship. Probably the best solution is a big storm-proof oil lantern, although it is rather a costly item.

As for me, I was incapable of sleeping after that night unless someone was awake and on watch. We changed our routine so that I remained awake for the first half of the night and Liz for the second. Kevin and Mark took slightly longer watches in the morning and Bruce in the afternoon, so that Liz and I could get an adequate ration of sleep.

The logical route from the West Indies to the Azores is

not quite so self-evident as the route we had followed across the South Atlantic because the winds are more variable in the northern ocean. There is an area of high pressure south of the Azores where the winds tend to be light, and it is advisable to skirt northwards round this region. But one has to go rather far north to clear the horse latitudes properly and to pick up the prevailing westerlies and the Gulf Stream, and even here the weather is variable. I decided in the end to sail in a north-north-easterly direction until we drew level with Bermuda. If we were too tired, or needed provisions, we could call in there. If not we would gradually swing east and carry on to the Azores.

It would be a long voyage, the longest so far. We felt that something was needed to break it in the middle. Christmas had been such a success in the South Atlantic that we decided to have a similar celebration in the North Atlantic. There was no suitable holiday to hand so we invented one and called it Mid-Atlantic Day. Before we left the West Indies small presents were sneaked aboard and hidden, and Liz planned secretly the menu for the Mid-Atlantic feast.

The length of the crossing did not perturb us unduly, however. Our greatest fear was the cold. Our clothes were in rags, our oilskins holed, and we had one pair of waterproof boots (leaking slightly) between six of us. So while we cared not a fig for gales (perhaps just a little fig, to be truthful), the thought of cold grey seas and chill grey skies was quite horrifying.

Gentlemen, it is said, never go to windward and never, never sail outside the tropics. And here we were, flying on a close reach, towards the Tropic of Cancer. How we flew! For six days the wind blew hard and *Walkabout* picked up her skirts and leapt, almost from wave top to wave top. Her motion at times was that of a skater, sheering swiftly from side to side in order to drive forward. Before three days were out we had crossed the Tropic of Cancer and every day grew slightly colder than the previous one. Soon we were rummaging for forgotten guernseys, anoraks and woolly caps at the bottom of the stowage net. In a little over six days we had drawn level with Bermuda, having averaged well over 140 miles per day, and that with a cross-current, too.

Then the wind became tricky, boxed the compass and stopped. We had lost the trades and reached the horse latitudes, and *Walkabout* slowed down to an unladylike waddle of 50 miles a day. The new climate was announced by a depression which brought a couple of days of chill drizzle and sharp winds. One of these ripped the lovely old genoa clean across from foot to leach. It was a major repair job that took more than a week to do and consumed most of the spare sail-cloth and glue.

After that the sun came out and drew from the cabin an amazing display of soft ware. Mattresses were strewn over the cabin top, sleeping bags hung over the booms, and the ship was dressed from stem to stern with *Walkabout*'s ensigns—laundry hung out to dry. There was so little wind that we dropped all sails and lay across the Atlantic swell as though our only purpose in getting to this spot in mid-ocean was to dry laundry.

Everyone was very glad of the rest. The first week had been fast but exceedingly uncomfortable, and we felt that we had earned a holiday. Mark lounged against the mast splicing new lanyards on to the fenders. Kevin fixed protective copper sleeves over the new dinghy oars which we had been forced to buy in St Thomas, after the old ones had been broken in an incident when Kevin and dinghy had been rolled over together in heavy surf. Liz was down below baking bread when Bruce cried, "Ship ahoy! She's coming up astern."

The ship, a small Liberian tanker, passed only a hundred feet astern of us. There was a man standing on the bridge and another in the bow. The man at the bow was obviously puzzled. He sketched a question mark in the air and raised both thumbs (are you all right?). We waved back cheerily and answered with the thumbs up sign (we're fine). He gestured to all the laundry and sketched another question mark (what the hell are you doing, then?). We pointed to the sun and to the washing lines and stretched our arms in enjoyment (we're drying out and enjoying ourselves, of course). He raised one arm as a mast, joined the other to it as a boom and swept them forward (why no sails?). We jumped up crossly and waved at the sky and the sea, then flung out arms in a despairing gesture and tapped our heads (there's no wind, you nut. Tankermen must be crazy to ask such silly questions). He pointed questioningly to the west (are you going to America?). We shook our heads and pointed to Europe (no, the other way). He flung his arms to heaven and joined them in the shape of a ship's bow pointing to America (then why the hell are you pointing at America?). We were agitated by this and jumped up again, waved at the sky and the sea and shrugged our shoulders (what does it matter which way we are pointing if we're not moving?). He was drawing away and becoming difficult to make out, and the last we saw of him he was tapping his head (yachtsmen are crazy).

We sailed for some time through the Sargasso Sea, which delighted the children, especially Bruce and Mark. Soon after we left St Thomas bands of seaweed had appeared across our path, and I had been forced to take in the towing log quite early in the voyage. There was little profit in towing clumps of seaweed across the ocean. The bands gradually grew broader and more frequent, and even during the first week, when we were driving into stiff winds, they drew Bruce outside like a magnet. He and Mark made special "Sargasso gaffs", long sticks with wire hooks seized on the ends, and happily spent all their free time hauling seaweed aboard. They popped each clump in a bucket, and when the bucket was full they would, together with Rachel, sort carefully through it to find all the crabs and shrimps, which would then be transferred to the aquarium, another bucket full of sea-water. Rachel gave all the creatures names, and talked to them for hours.

I secretly found the Sargasso as fascinating as the children did. The weed, which was a yellow brown in colour, was kept afloat by little pockets of air the size of a wheat grain. The inhabitants were mainly small crabs and shrimps, but there were also many wriggling creatures, some of which I thought might be elvers, the young eels which come from all over the world to breed in the Sargasso. How many tons of seaweed were taken aboard I do not know, but for months afterwards the stuff was found, wedged in the most unlikely places. I could not help noticing during this time that Thor Heyerdahl's observation was true, that not a day passed without a sight of some item of man-made garbage.

The easy routine of ship-board life was disrupted, however, by some filthy rubbish that scudded over from America. We had reached the north-eastern corner of our curved course, only 20 miles south of the iceberg limit, which dips down from Newfoundland at that point, when a depression passed over, giving us a taste of the true North Atlantic. The wind blew hard from the north-east, so that for two days we slammed into head seas. The wind brought icy rain and we huddled down below, wrapped up like old grannies in blankets, trying to keep the cabin warm with the primus stoves. We abandoned all attempts to keep up lessons, and put the children to bed for the two days. They disliked it but they were very good, and kept themselves amused with games and books. Liz was seasick and I never stopped shivering. The vang broke and the weary old mizzen blew out once again. Yet for all that the gale was a light affair compared with winds we had weathered before, and although we were relieved when it stopped we felt that if the Atlantic could do no better we should have to go elsewhere for our fun.

May 27th, Mid-Atlantic Day, dawned chill and gusty. We celebrated with presents, a play and the last of our Cape Town victuals. The Festival was not to be compared to Christmas, but it was a useful milestone in the voyage.

One night, shortly afterwards, we had a nasty experience with fire. I was on watch at the time, experiencing a great deal of trouble in fluky winds. First I had to climb the main mast to free a jammed halyard, then the mizzen mast to untangle the vang, and finally halfway up the forestay to unravel the genoa, which had somehow twisted itself into a sausage. I had just succeeded in sorting out the mess and was shuffling back to the cockpit when I noticed smoke billowing out of the main hatch.

In less time than it takes to tell I was through the hatch and hunting frantically for the fire. The cabin was thick with smoke but no one had woken up. The fire did not take long to find. Smoke was pouring from some plastic-covered cables behind the battery charger, and small flames were licking at the main fuel pipes.

I doused the fire quickly, ripped out the cables and threw them into a bucket of water in the cockpit. What had happened was that the cables which charged the batteries had shorted across and the plastic insulation had caught fire. Another ten minutes and the boat would have been ablaze. Electric fires are the most treacherous of all because they can start at any time, whether one is aboard or not.

Immediately after this, as though the fire were a finale to crises of all kinds, the glass rose, the wind faded to a cool but gentle southerly breeze and the waves quieted. Never had we encountered an ocean so smooth. Normally even when the wind dies there is a swell which keeps one rolling, but after a few days the sea was so marvellously calm that we might have been at anchor, except for the whisper of water stroking the hull as *Walkabout* glided forward.

Life gradually took on a dreamy, insubstantial quality. Liz and I spoke seldom to each other, not because we had nothing to say but because we knew the trend of each other's thoughts and there was no need for speech. We found that we lived greatly in the past, especially in the dark hours when everything was quiet and we felt too sleepy to read. Scenes long forgotten, trivial and significant alike, marched in procession through our minds with the vividness of a stage production. An outsider might have said that we grew a little abnormal, but I do not think that this is so. We are all slightly abnormal because our concept of the world around us is a little different from the real world. Insanity is, therefore, a matter of degree, but there comes a point when an individual's concept of the world is so far from reality that he cannot make reasonable deductions of cause and effect. When he can no longer make decisions that are rational enough to enable him to survive in society he is recognisably insane. But the dream world that Liz and I inhabited was more a re-examination of reality than a shift away from it. Free from the pressures of others around us, with no compulsion to wear any sort of social mask, we found that we could think more clearly and find peace in doing so.

Time took on a strange quality where its importance was in inverse proportion to its weight. Hours were of casual interest, for example, because they roughly divided the routine of the day. Minutes were more important because they delimited certain tasks. Seconds were vital, for navigation; they positioned us in space as well as in time. But days were of no consequence, and weeks were only noticed when Rachel reminded us that Saturday was sweet night.

We wondered sometimes whether the children were similarly affected, but Liz thought not. They lived, in any case, in a world largely of their own making wherever they were. Bruce, for instance, hunted Portuguese men-o'-war (of which there were now hundreds) in much the same way as he would have hunted tadpoles—that is, by treating them both as dragons. The fact that the jelly fish often stung him severely only made them a worthier foe.

Although the days passed in this placid fashion, we were never for one second bored. There was the reality of the elements; we had to be alert to every little change. No set of conditions is exactly alike, and each had to be used to help us on our way. Navigation, cooking, lessons and endless maintenance jobs filled the day.

The only thing that upset us was the food. We had left St Thomas poorly provisioned with fresh food, and what little we had went bad very quickly. Eggs started to go off in a few days, fresh fruit rotted, and in little more than a week we were taking vitamin tablets. Even the potatoes ran out, and all we had left in the end were a few miserable onions which had to be rationed, although the children loved them raw and thinly sliced. American tinned food, we discovered, is so bland that after a time it becomes indigestible. It is wholesome enough, but eventually we found it difficult to swallow and began to dream of fresh strawberries and yellow cream, crisp apples, juicy oranges, succulent plums, fried eggs and crackly bacon.

"Stop it!" cried Liz. "I can hear what you're thinking."

Eventually it became so bad that we broke open a sealed container of spare life-raft rations, just for something different. With cries of delight the children fell on the tasteless biscuits and glucose cubes as though they were manna from heaven.

"Lovely," crooned Rachel ecstatically as she munched. "I wish we were shipwrecked and could eat these all day."

The last few hundred miles passed very slowly in light airs, but finally, on June 7th, we sighted land—the high island of Flores standing away to the north. Our destination, however, was the next island, Faial, so we carried on. No one, apart from Rachel, could stay below for long, for we could not take our eyes off the land. It is the saddest thing to pass by an island at the end of a long crossing. All next day the children suffered from raging land fever, a sort of fretful impatience alternating with bursts of wild hilarity. But although my calculations showed that we were less than 20 miles off Faial by evening, we saw no land, and the wind grew lighter and lighter till *Walkabout* drifted forward at barely half a knot. This was quite insupportable, so throwing caution to the winds I started the engine.

Liz spotted Horta light shortly before midnight, and we hove to a few miles off. Before daylight Mark, who was on watch, woke me up and we motored to the island, then turned and ran close along the shore. As the light of our twenty-seventh day at sea spread up from the eastern horizon, shadowy headlands took shape and patches hardened into fields. As soon as the sun crept over the edge of the world we woke everyone up and we all sat in the cockpit and drank in the sight of still earth. It was lovely. Every square foot of ground on the easy slopes was divided into neat fields, each separated from its neighbours by an orderly hedge. The terraces climbed to the top of every hill, and even from that distance one could see the love that had been lavished on the soil. This was no unruly island in the new world. This was an old land, peaceful, orderly and traditional, a far-flung piece of Europe.

"What are those low trees between the fields?" Mark wanted to know. He had never seen field hedges before.

As soon as we rounded the breakwater of Horta harbour Kevin and Mark spotted *Leona III*, the boat that had lain by us all winter in Cape Town. They had beaten up direct from St Helena and Ascension, and we had a boisterous reunion.

A courteous and efficient man came aboard to clear us. "Ai, caramba!" he exclaimed when he caught sight of us. "This is not a yacht. This is a crêche!"

"Senhor Commandant," he said when he had finished, "you are free to go ashore. We are honoured to have you on Faial, and I hope you will like us. The island is yours."

Faial is one of nine volcanic islands spread over several hundred miles that comprise the Azores archipelago. The Azores were discovered uninhabited by the Portuguese in the fifteenth century, although they are shown on Genoese maps of the fourteenth century. They were colonised by the Portuguese with some Flemish influence, and are now politically a part of metropolitan Portugal. Horta, the capital of Faial, is one of the few safe harbours among the islands, and it proved to be, without question, the most delightful of any port we visited. The town itself is so clean and neat, the houses whitewashed and the pavements scrubbed, that it is a pleasure to walk through. The public baths, situated close to the yachts, are spotless; for a couple of pence we were given a freshly laundered towel, a cake of soap and as much hot water as we wanted.

The other luxury was—the perceptive reader may have guessed this already—fresh food. Vegetables, meat, milk, cheese and fruit were plentiful and cheap, for Faial lives mainly by agriculture and fishing. The countryside is beautiful, similar in many ways to the south-west of England. When we arrived there spring was phasing into summer, and wherever we chose to walk we were refreshed by green hedges, wild flowers and the singing of birds. The climate, too, is similar to the south of England, though a trifle milder. We soaked in the scents and sounds, the sights and the touch of this tranquil land, and were content.

But the greatest asset of the Azores—or at any rate of Faial and neighbouring Pico—is their people. Quiet, industrious folk, they are generous to a fault, and the community maintains a standard of integrity and honesty that arises as much from an absence of greed as from anything else. In this they are quite out of step with the rest of the world, and they will, I suppose, fall into line sooner or later, probably as the result of increasing tourism, which has already corrupted so many peasant communities.

While we explored the island, the islanders studied us. Never have we seen so many Lookers. We were lying against the quay, which made it easy for them. There were never less than half a dozen of them sitting patiently on the wall until late at night, and once we counted twenty-two. On another occasion a young male Looker arrived before breakfast and settled in with sandwiches. He remained all morning and through lunch, then he dozed off, waking with a start, however, whenever we moved. Just before supper he dozed off too deeply and fell into the water. He climbed out, and to our amazement settled down again. He was still there when we went to bed, but had vanished by the following morning. Perhaps he drowned, a martyr among Lookers. What made us a special curiosity was, I suppose, the fact that we had four children aboard and flew the Portuguese flag.

On the afternoon of our arrival a battered little car drew up beside the boat. A dumpy priest bustled out and addressed us.

"Are you the yacht from Mozambique? The one with four children aboard? You are! Good, good! The word gets round quickly in our little town, you know." He chuckled. "Here's a little present for the children." He handed down a basket of vegetables, and another one full of strange looking bread rings. "The bread," he explained, "is a speciality of Faial and Pico. It is festival bread made only at this time of year, and it's meant to be given away."

He rushed off without introducing himself, and left us stuttering our thanks. The bread was a dense, sweetish type made with baking powder, and nobody liked it much. But we felt it would be churlish not to eat it, so we dutifully chewed through the loaves, which we dubbed priest-bread.

Two days later, when all but half a loaf had gone, a family drew up by the boat and the father called us up on deck. His face wreathed in smiles, he handed down a basket containing about a dozen loaves, each as heavy as a solid rubber tyre. As they were driving away he leaned out of the window and called, "*Adeus!* We'll come back the day after tomorrow and bring you some more."

As we settled down gloomily to our bread Liz had a sudden idea. The day after next there was a festival on the island of Pico, a few miles away. We would escape there for the day. A young carpenter called José, who insisted on accompanying us, told us that this was always a festival of gay abandon. Also, he said mysteriously, fine presents would be distributed to all the visitors afterwards. Our vision of dancing in the streets and wine flowing in the gutters turned out to be some distance from reality, for the islanders' idea of wild abandon was for both women and men to dress in sober black and shuffle in solemn procession. At their head was a rather fine band (the locals love their music), then came the women, each bearing on her head a huge basket of priest-bread and flowers, and finally the men. Two pubs daringly served stew and wine.

When it was over José turned to us and beamed. "Did you

not like that? Was it not exciting? It is a great festival, and visitors come from far and wide. People even come from America to see it. And now for the presents." He rubbed his hands gleefully.

We looked at the hundreds of baskets of priest-bread stacked on the wall around the cemetery, and had a horrible premonition. Our fears were only too well founded. Ropes were stretched across the entrance to the ferry wharf, and no one was allowed to leave the island without accepting a loaf. Even Rachel had to take one, and the man was so taken with her vivacious pleasure that he pressed another one on her despite my protests.

"Well, maybe this marks the end of the priest-bread season," I sighed on the ferry over. "Do you know, I estimate that the women of Pico baked 8,000 loaves for this afternoon? There can't be any more flour left!"

I was wrong. When we got back to *Walkabout* we found that some anonymous well-wisher had placed half a dozen loaves on the cabin roof!

Apart from the priest-bread, the children enjoyed Horta enormously. Near the yacht was a slipway used for building and repairing fishing craft, so there were plenty of wood scraps around. The boys abandoned their coconut boats from the West Indies and began to build more sophisticated craft. Before long *Walkabout* began to resemble a lumber yard. I tried to enforce tidiness, but it was a losing battle. Things were getting out of hand when attention was diverted by the whale.

Whaling is an important industry in the Azores, and we had already climbed to the churches on the hilltops where they keep a look-out for whales. When a school is sighted the whaling boats, small open craft propelled by only sails and oars, are launched and towed out. They approach the whale silently and harpoon the creature by hand.

One morning Bruce came rushing into the cabin, panting with excitement. "There's a whale in the next bay," he gasped. "A huge whale. It must be at least a million feet long. And it's lying half in the water with its tail out, and the tail is bigger than *Walkabout*, and it's got huge teeth and its eyes are tiny."

Not even Bruce would tell a story as tall as that, so we all went to see. It was just as he said, though the dimensions were perhaps a trifle exaggerated. A large female sperm whale had been killed and lay partly out of the water on the slip, ready to be dragged into the factory. The children were at first excited, then they grew curious and inspected the animal all over. Finally, however, they fell silent and stood looking at the mournful sight of the huge creature, becoming shapeless now that the tissues were dead, lying in the blood-stained water. There was something very tragic about death on such a gross scale, and something very evil about man who could do such a thing for no sound reason. Virtually only the oil is used, and there are many vegetable oil alternatives.

"You wouldn't think," said Liz quietly, "that such a huge animal could die from that tiny hole in its back. It doesn't seem right that people can kill so effortlessly."

The really tragic thing about the whale was that it died in the end for no reason whatever. The following three days were special festival days, so no worker would butcher it, and by the fourth day it was bad. They towed the stinking carcass far out to sea and left it.

A happier side of Horta was the camaraderie of cruising yachts, which the children enjoyed as much as Liz and I did ourselves. All the yachts were visitors to the Azores, so all had sailed at least one ocean. Mostly they were on what is somewhat unfairly known as "the milk run"—a one-year cruise from Europe to the West Indies and back again.

Domino was one such yacht, a sturdy 37ft teak sloop, sailed by the youthful Price family: skipper David, an accountant, his wife Clare, David's brother Arg, a newly fledged marine biologist, and their younger sister Anna. As usual it was the children, by now completely at ease with fresh faces, who made the first contact. We found them one day, happily ensconced in *Domino*'s cockpit, sipping orange juice and spinning yarns about their adventures. They soon became firm friends. The Dominos took the children round the island and taught them how to sword fight, then came back and played a dice game which raised the children to an emotional fever that is normally found only in the gambling dens of Monte Carlo. In the evenings, when they were asleep and it was too cold for Liz and me to sit in the cockpit, we would go over to *Domino* to talk and to sing, accompanied by Liz on her recorder and Arg on his guitar. Other yachties with their guitars would usually drop in, and we would sing into the early hours.

Then we would talk, and talk would invariably come back to the same topic—what are we going to do when the voyage ends? The majority of yachties (120 boats called at Horta that year) had saved up for their year's cruise and had homes, if not jobs, to go back to. They could not, therefore, be regarded as true walkabouts, but the disease had seized them none the less and made them unfit for normal life. Liz and I, of course, had long realised that the real motive of a voyage is not to reach a particular place but simply to try to get there. For months past we had been mulling over our future plans with increasing anxiety, hopeful that somehow, as we neared the end, the fog would clear and reveal a shining Aim in Life. But here we were after nearly two years of planning and voyaging, at our last port of call before England, and the fog was as thick as ever.

"Several people I know," said David pensively, "were advised to go by parents, wives and so on—and, mind you, we're in exactly the same position ourselves. 'Go ahead and do the voyage,' they were told. 'Get it out of your system. Then come back and settle down.' Of course there are many who never get past the first port, but those who stick it out never seem to want to settle down. We just want to carry on cruising."

"You're dead right," said Liz. "Everyone goes around asking everyone else what they intend to do as if they expect to find a guru with the perfect answer. 'What are you going to do when you get back?' has become a sort of sick question in this harbour. The fact is we are all in the same boat. We don't know what we want to do when we grow up."

For me it was quite simple. I wanted to do a solo circumnavigation and double Cape Horn, that Everest of sailing achievement. To my astonishment, everyone who heard this thought I was mad.

"What, sail alone!" they said. "Go round Cape Horn! You must be crazy." Liz agreed with them, and my only ally was Rachel, who always said stoutly, "If Daddy wants to go round Cape Horn, I'll go with him even if nobody else will."

Not all the yachts were on the milk run. One day Mark, who was on the foredeck sawing out a keel for a new model boat, jumped up and cried, "Daddy, there's *Raireva* coming in.

I'm going to get the foghorn to welcome her!" *Raireva* was a beautifully fitted-out 36ft steel sloop which we had last seen in Durban. Her owners were a German couple, John and Leni Muller, who were then working in Durban to save up for the voyage home. We had always remembered the yacht as one on which everything was immaculate. Some years before John, who had longed to sail from boyhood, threw up his job as a well-known electrolytic engineer, and the couple had taken delivery of their new steel yacht from a Dutch yard. They sailed the Atlantic, through Panama, across the Pacific and Indian oceans by stages, and now, after cruising through the West Indies, they were on the last lap home after seven years. Beside them we were mere infants, and we listened enraptured while they spoke with a faraway look in their eyes of the Pacific. It seems that once a walkabout has trod the islands of the Pacific every other place falls short of perfection.

This was confirmed by another circumnavigator who came a little later, the irrepressible Frenchman, Dr Emile Lopez. With him were his wife, Annette, and his three-year-old son, Pierre, who had joined him in Madagascar. His boat, a 34ft wooden sloop called *Han Rymic*, was more interesting than immaculate, but during his seven years of circumnavigation nothing seemed to have got him down. He had been wrecked near Dakar, but as he said, "*Pas de problème!* I take ze boat out on ze sand and wiz Spanish carpenter—pop pop, pop pop, knock all ze nails and zings in and she eez okay. We carry on. *Pas de problème.*"

"But, doctor," I asked, "what about this great hole in the cockpit where the tiller sticks out? If you get a wave over doesn't it go straight into the boat?"

"*Pas de problème!*" he shrugged. "Eef water comes in—pomp pomp, pomp pomp, I pomp it out again. All places we go like zis."

The only thing that he could not take in his stride was coping with Pierre on the boat. Pierre was, in truth, a more than usually boisterous child.

"He ees like monkey and firework and terrorist all togezer," groaned his father. "Only one year and already I am *fou.* You have been nearly two years wiz four children. How do you manage?"

"*Pas de problème*," said Liz and I, airily.

The days slipped by too quickly. I remember sitting on deck early one morning, legs stretched out on the smooth planks, splicing a wire rope with methodical satisfaction. It is cool and the air tastes fresh. On the seat is a basket of plums, newly picked, the dew still glistening on them. Every now and then I take one and pass another to Mark, absently humming a horn concerto and absorbed in his electronic set on the foredeck. Bruce and Rachel have gone exploring in the next bay, and some time ago Liz and Kevin rowed across the harbour to buy milk and cream. I glance up and catch sight of them between two fishing boats, rowing slowly back and enjoying the sunshine. A yacht drifts round her moorings in the quiet air and they are lost to view. I return to my unhurried work and take another plum. The moment seems to epitomise the Azores as well as cruising life, and I wonder how many such moments of perfect tranquillity one can expect in a lifetime. Very few, I think, but it is enough to be blessed at all. The secret of tranquillity is lack of ambition, so I cannot wish for further moments without destroying this one. Yet we should be happy to linger in the Azores if we could. We want for nothing of importance, and the medicine chest has become rusty from disuse. But soon we must leave.

The day of departure was set at June 25th or thereabouts, depending on the weather. For several days before gales blew from the north, and we had no desire to begin the last lap thrashing into a head gale. But on the 25th the gales abated and the wind began to veer. There was no excuse. We had to go.

Water, fuel and staple stores were already aboard. The dinghy and the sails were lashed in position. I had dived down below and scrubbed the bottom again. All we had to do was take aboard last-minute fresh provisions and have our last hot shower. Mark and I walked into town to do the shopping. But first we had to say goodbye to Peter, for no yachtie has ever called at Horta and missed Peter. His real name is José Azevedo and he owns the friendly bar, Café Sport. He is the yachties' friend, counsellor, interpreter, helper, bank and unofficial post office. Since 1929 José, and before him his father Henrique, have played host to every yacht that has visited the port.

After we had bought our bread and eggs and fresh fruit and

taken our shower there was still one thing left to do. I sent a telegram to Eric, Liz's father, a telegram that he had patiently and no doubt anxiously been awaiting for many, many months. It read: "Sailing today, June 25th, winds brisk, contrary, loaded whales' teeth plums goatsmilk cheese."

Within the hour we were under sail.

XIV

WE SAILED OUT of Horta harbour with many a honk from friendly foghorns to speed us on our voyage. The bright sun warmed the decks and a light breeze eased the ship on her way. This idyllic scene lasted less than half an hour. Then the sky was painted black all over, the wind freshened and backed, and once more we found ourselves beating into a head sea.

"This is roughly the five thousandth mile to windward since Rio," I noted in the log with irritation. It was such a commonplace condition that everyone merely tut-tutted and wrapped their bedclothes in plastic sheets.

Nevertheless, England seemed close now. This last leg of the voyage was a trivial 1,300 miles—sixteen days if the winds were poor, only ten days if they blew fair. In fact the weather turned waspish after the first two days, and for most of the voyage we were treated to chilly skies, intermittent drizzle, and wind that changed its mind about strength and direction every hour. The children hardly noticed. England filled their horizon and they talked of nothing else. We gathered from their conversation that they pictured a land of glorious snow and ice (they had never seen snow), where grandparental blessings fell ceaselessly like gentle rain and model aeroplane parts were sold for a song. It stood to reason that any place that took nearly two years to reach must be wonderful.

For Liz and me it was different. We wanted to reach our destination, naturally, but we also knew that as soon as the voyage was over real problems would start. With increasing dismay I watched the log ticking off the miles.

As for *Walkabout*, she had done us proud, but she was very travel-weary and all moving parts needed refitting. Rudder pintles, prop shaft, blocks, running rigging, were all worn, the bilge pump had grown tired of sucking sea-water, the dinghy leaked and the paintwork was streaked with rust from the stanchions. Running repairs were now as much part of the daily routine as the noon sight, and everybody helped. When a halyard parted these days it was nearly always Mark or Kevin who nipped up the mast. They bent with us over the eternal task of mending sails. Just as the Fates in ancient times could be found at any reasonable hour of the day at their spinning wheels, so we could be found stitching sails. We did not sail across the Atlantic—we stitched our way across. Kevin and Mark were proficient sailors too, and now handled most of the sail work during the day, unless it was too rough.

"Daddy, the wind is veering to a close reach and it's blowing a bit harder," Mark would say. "Shall we take down the mizzen staysail?"

"Yes, please. Better change down to the heavy genoa too," I would answer, and Kevin and Mark would go for'ard, grumbling at the mariner's lot.

Every day the family held a noon ritual, which seldom varied. I would take a noon sight, or, if the sun was obscured at the crucial moment, an ex-meridian sight which necessitated Liz noting the chronometer reading. Kevin often worked out the noon latitude, and I would check it and find our position. The children would each guess the previous day's run and the winner would perform a little victory dance. Then I would announce the course for the day and everyone, except Rachel, had to commit it to memory.

The days slipped past without distinction, and the tropical blue of the ocean gradually gave way to the grey-green of the Western Approaches. One night we picked up the B.B.C. Radio 4 for the first time, and England was suddenly just over the horizon. The boys wrote compositions on what they expected to find when we landed. Their notions were of the vaguest, but Bruce revealed much when he chose to write about a journey he would make from Falmouth to Leicestershire, where his grandfather lived. He would travel by car, he wrote, starting after a good breakfast and making sure he had plenty of stores aboard, because he estimated that it would take at least two days. He drove all day, but at night he set up the self-steering lines on the steering wheel and went to sleep.

"You can't do that," explained Liz. "There are all the other cars whizzing past."

"I'll keep my headlights on," assured Bruce.

"But the car will wander off the road."

"No, it won't," said Bruce. "My steering gear is very accurate. The lines are made of pre-stretched terylene, you see."

The only thing the children regretted was that we had not seen any live whales, and we had not sunk. Their complaint was heard, and although we were only two days from England the matter was attended to. The sinking came first, and a comical sinking it proved to be.

That very night, when I ought to have been quietly reading, an evil thought entered my head to pump the bilges. The bilge pump was a great brass cylinder sunk into the aft deck, and was operated by stooping low over the handle and pumping between ankle and knee level. It was a back-breaking chore, rather like touching toes with a 50lb. dumbbell. I pumped a hundred strokes, which normally took me to the limit of my stamina. The bilges were not yet dry. Odd, I thought, they usually needed only about thirty strokes. I gritted my teeth and pumped another hundred strokes. Still the bilges were not dry. If I had been properly awake I should have smelt a rat. But it had been rather rough for a couple of days and we had not slept much, so I never stopped to think. I pumped another hundred strokes, then I could no longer think at all. The water continued to splash out of the pipe. I could hear it over the side. Another hundred? It was not humanly possible. But I did it. Then another hundred, then another. Six hundred strokes altogether.

At this point I became dimly aware that if I did another stroke on the pump I should have a stroke myself. I crawled down below and collapsed like a sack of soggy potatoes. When I could move, I groped to the floor and lifted a board. The bilges were more than half full! Now I knew with utter certainty that *Walkabout* was sinking.

I sat down to think. The first thing to do was to try and bale her dry with buckets. I decided not to wake Liz till she was due on watch. She would need all her strength. I sat and waited for the water to rise over the cabin sole.

At 1 a.m. I woke Liz. "Get dressed quickly," I said dully. "The ship is sinking."

"What!" She shot out of the bunk.

"The ship is sinking." I repeated.

She looked at the floor. "I see no water."

"It's only sinking slowly."

I told her the whole story, and when I had finished she burst out laughing.

"A sinking ship is no laughing matter!" I said, offended.

"But, deary me, six hundred strokes on a pump that is probably faulty," she chuckled. "No wonder you couldn't think."

I was beginning to see the funny side myself, but I said, "You don't know the pump is faulty."

"What else could it be? Let's bale her dry with buckets and I'll watch it like a hawk. Then you must sleep. You must be exhausted."

She was quite right, of course. Next morning I found that the suction pipe had split, allowing nine-tenths of the water to fall back into the bilges. The water had originally come in through a leaking prop shaft.

The whales were sighted in the English Channel on the eve of our arrival. They were small, as whales go, but they were whales none the less, and the children were ecstatic. We sailed cautiously up to the herd and watched their ponderous play, the boys gripping the stays with excitement and Rachel tittering with fear in the dinghy. After a time the whales did a curious thing. Six of them suddenly rose from the water and stood in a circle with their heads upright. They all faced inwards, as though having a conference. They held this pose for ten seconds or so, then slid under again. A little later one big fellow humped his back and began thumping the water with his flukes. We took this as a warning and moved off, perfectly satisfied with this splendid finale to the voyage.

That night, the fourteenth out from Horta, we picked up the Lizard Light. The night was clear and cold and very still. We dropped the sails and drifted, a few miles off the Lizard, waiting for the dawn. Liz and I sat in the cockpit with mugs of hot cocoa, enjoying our last night at sea. We talked quietly of the voyage.

"It's hard to believe that in a few hours it will be over," said Liz wistfully. "I have to keep looking at the Lizard Light over there to remind myself. We'll miss the life terribly, won't we? Oh, I know, there have been dozens of occasions when I swore

Walkabout close reaching in style. Note the vang from the gaff boom to the head of the mizzen mast and the way the genoa and mainsail luffs lie parallel for best performance

Walkabout cups a fair wind and humping her transom thrusts out to open ocean

Sailing free, *Walkabout* sweeps under billowing canvas out to sea

I'd catch the next plane, but then we'd reach port and become bloated with achievement. It's funny how soon you forget the terrible bits in between. The reason, I suppose, is that you're compensated for hardship with freedom, adventure and romance—gold coinage, as it were. It's never dull."

"No," I agreed, "it's never dull. But I think that eventually we should need some form of intellectual stimulation to avoid becoming boat bums, concerned only with daily survival. Photography, writing, marine biology, anything so long as it stimulates the mind. The other ingredient for success as a walkabout is to renounce materialism. Possessions must be a means to an end, and no more. And that is not everybody's cup of tea."

Liz nodded. "Nearly everyone we have met has said how much they envy us. I wonder how many mean it? The desire to escape from the rat race is usually genuine, but they imagine escaping to a martinis-on-the-sundeck existence. The reality is a very low standard of living, not to mention the hardship and lack of security."

"Do you think the children have benefited?" I asked.

"Oh, enormously," she said at once. "They have learned so much, apart from boat work, which has given Kevin and Mark, at any rate, a sense of responsibility. At every new port they have had to find their way about, and without much help from us, handle new currencies, new languages, new peoples. We've never wrapped them in cotton wool, have we? I'm sure they have become more self-reliant than they would have in normal life, and they have, without perhaps knowing it, become aware that the world is a much wider place than just their home, their school or even their country. But perhaps the most important thing they have learned is how to get along with all types of people. They have had to make friends quickly."

"You don't think the continual change has made them feel insecure?"

"Not really. The boat itself is the fixed point in their lives, because it's a home. I think that is important."

"On the other hand," I said, "if we are entirely honest, we must admit that the children are too young to grasp the romance of sailing. They are prosaic little souls. An ocean crossing is simply thirty uncomfortable days."

We were silent for a while. Dawn was not far off and a chill mist could be seen stealing over the smooth sea.

"I never realised," I said, presently, "how much more difficult it is to end a voyage than to begin one. How well Tennyson understood.

> I cannot rest from travel: I will drink
> Life to the lees.

How does it go on?

> I am a part of all that I have met;
> Yet all experience is an arch wherethro'
> Gleams that untravell'd world, whose margin fades
> For ever and for ever when I move.
> How dull it is to pause, to make an end,
> To rust unburnish'd, not to shine in use!

"Then we must do what Ulysses did," said Liz, quietly. "The only way to end a voyage is to plan the next."

APPENDICES

APPENDIX I

WALKABOUT

The Boat

Walkabout is the sister ship to W. A. Robinson's *Svaap*, designed by the celebrated naval architect from Boston, John Alden. She was built in 1954 by the Driscoll brothers in Fremantle, Australia. Her principal dimensions are:

l.o.a.	33ft 2ins
l.w.l.	28ft
beam	9ft 6ins
draught	5ft 10ins
nett tonnage	11·98 tons

Walkabout carries approximately 3½ tons of lead in the keel and ½ ton as internal ballast, and she is heavily constructed of jarrah, a dense Australian timber. By modern standards, therefore, she is a heavy vessel, but this does give her the advantage of being able, through sheer momentum, to carry through a choppy head sea, and the long, deep keel grips the water well in heavy weather. She could be sailed very hard without anxiety. Despite the keel and the weight, however, the underwater lines are sweet and the hull is easily driven. Except in very light winds, where we suffered from lack of large light weather sails, we made good passage times. *Walkabout* is sea-kindly and well balanced and proved to be free of all handling vices, except that she shipped rather more water than was comfortable. Perhaps the fact that we were usually 9 inches deeper than the design water-line was partly to blame.

An elevation of the boat together with a glossary of the more common items is given in Fig. 1.

The Rig

The rig is an unusual one and quite different from *Svaap*. It could be called a gaff schooner-ketch; the masts are the same height but the bigger sail is carried on the main not the mizzen mast. The masts, at 30ft, are a trifle on the stubby side, but while this was a disadvantage in light conditions we were grateful for it in rough weather. With plain canvas (i.e. headsail, main and mizzen) we could spread 550 sq. ft., but this could easily be pushed up to over

GLOSSARY OF COMMON TERMS

SPARS

1. Main mast
2. Mizzen mast
3. Main boom
4. Gaff

4a. Gaff, eased to belly main sail

5. Mizzen boom
6. Bowsprit

RIGGING

7. Forestay
8. Running forestay
9. Inner forestay (normally stowed along shroud)
10. Main shrouds
11. Mizzen shrouds
12. Bowsprit shrouds
13. Bobstay
14. Rigging screws
15. Chainplates
16. Bowsprit ring
17. Outhaul
18. Sheets
19. Halyards
20. Vang
21. Belaying pins

SAILS

22. Headsails (jib and genoa)
23. Staysail
24. Mainsail
25. Mizzen
26. Mizzen staysail

GEAR

37. Liferaft
38. Dinghy
39. Self-steering
40. Stanchions and safety lines
41. Safety line between masts
42. Dodgers
43. Radar reflector

THE BOAT

27. Keel
28. Rudder
29. Tiller
30. Coachwork
31. Cockpit
32. Main hatch
33. Forehatch
34. Stemhead
35. Samson post
36. Transom

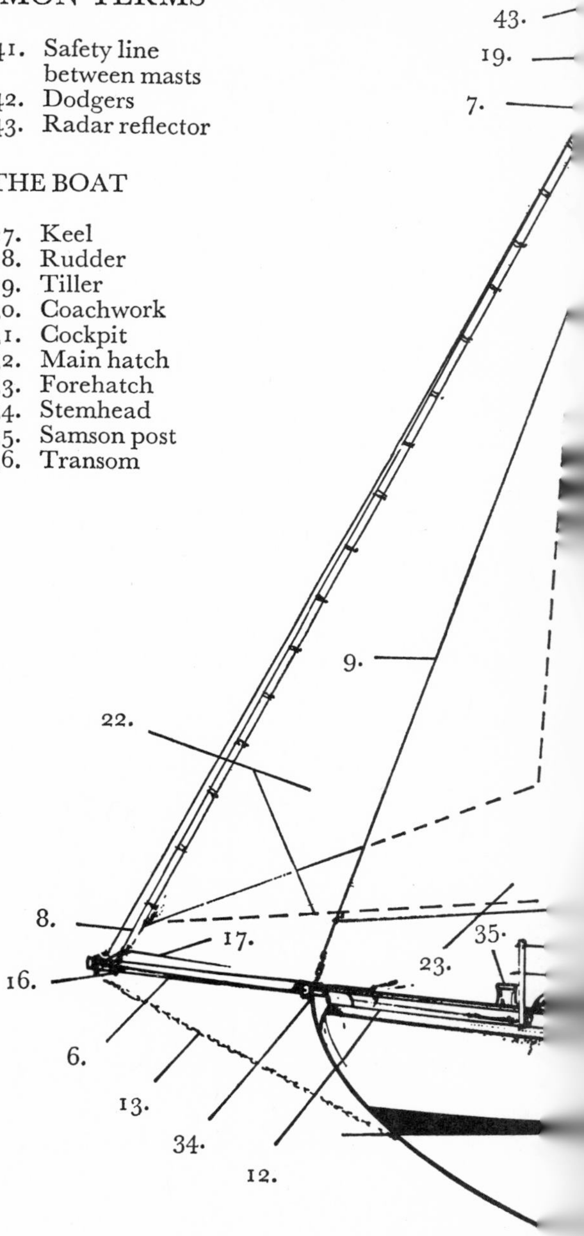

FIG. 1: *WALKABOUT*

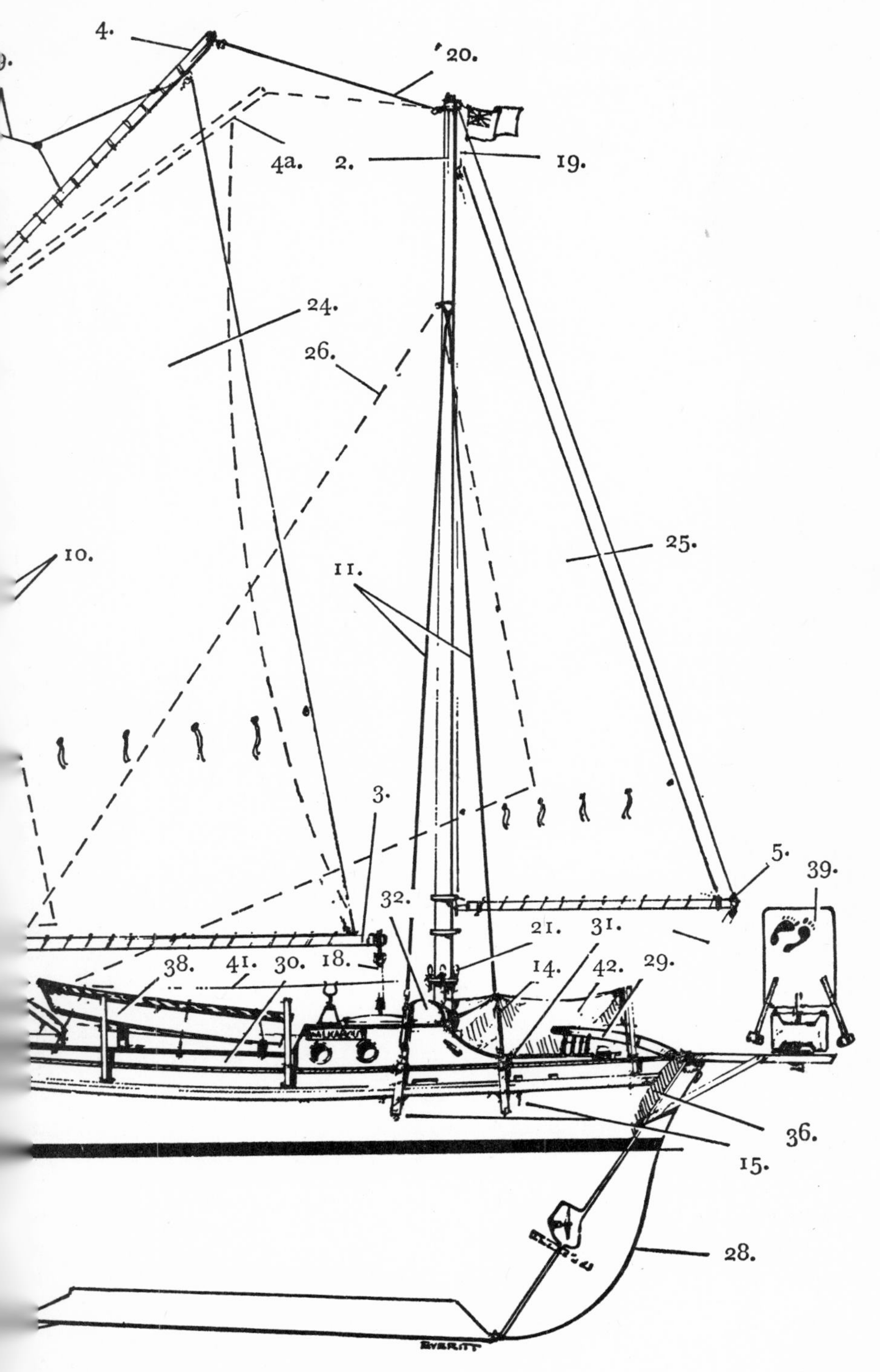

4.
20.
4a.
2.
19.
24.
26.
25.
10.
11.
3.
5.
39.
32.
21.
31.
38.
41.
30.
18.
14.
42.
29.
36.
15.
28.
EVERITT

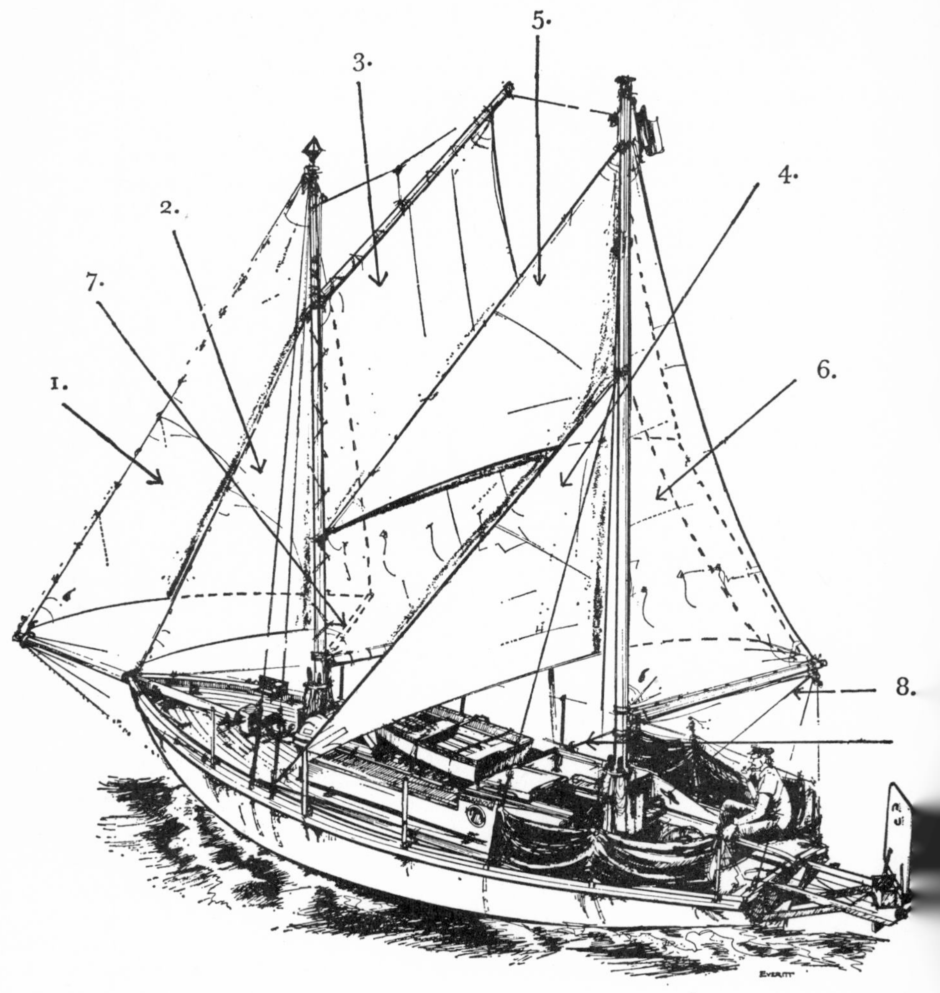

FIG 2: ALL SAILS FLYING ON A BROAD REACH

1. Main headsail—genoa
2. Staysail—inner forestay removed to facilitate tacking when this sail is not used.
3. Main
4. Mizzen staysail
5. Occasional mizzen staysail
6. Mizzen
7. Genoa boom—bamboo pole lashed to gooseneck
8. Mizzen staysail sheet
9. Mizzen boom forward guy.

800 sq. ft. with the addition of staysails and about 1,000 sq. ft. with the squaresail.

The staysail set on the inner forestay was a nuisance of a sail, difficult to tack and prone to disrupt smooth wind-flow between headsail and main; it was used only in very light windward work and to help balance the boat on a reach. The mizzen staysail, on the other hand, was a very powerful sail with the wind aft, or across. Sometimes a third staysail was set, as shown in Fig. 2. The running rig has been described in Chapter XI.

Gaff rigs have fallen out of fashion, but for a cruising boat there is much to commend them. The masts are shorter and failure is less likely, for the stresses are less and there are fewer vital bits of metal to break. Off-wind the gaff sail is more powerful than its Bermudan counterpart, and I have found it quicker and easier to handle, except in light following breezes when the gaff slams about. As for windward performance, this depends more on the size and the height of the headsails than on the design of the mainsail.

But to get the best out of a gaff sail it should be controlled by a vang at the top as well as a sheet at the bottom, as shown in Fig. 1. Using the vang as an upper sheet, one can control the twist in the sail, and by hardening the peak halyard the sail can be flattened for beating, or conversely, by slackening the halyard the sail can be ballooned for running. In this way the gaff becomes a sensitive and flexible piece of canvas.

The rigging gear was robust and simple—too simple, I often swore to myself, struggling at night in a rising wind. I consoled myself with the thought that Columbus never needed a two-speed winch. We had in fact no winches at all; running rigging was what we could get. Standing rigging was galvanised wire rope protected with plastic piping filled with fish oil. Jib booms were usually bamboo poles. There was, however, roller reefing on the main and that was worth its weight in gold.

Self-steering

The self-steering, dubbed Muncher, was of the horizontally hinged wind vane type, home-made of wood and various bits of metal. Its construction is shown in Fig. 3, which is self-explanatory. The main feature is that the tiller lines are led through a hollow vertical pivot so that they need never be unhooked and crossed over. To facilitate rapid and accurate adjustment of tiller line length (essential for satisfactory course-keeping) the adjusting system shown in Fig. 3 was devised.

Muncher was a vital piece of gear, and although a water servo blade would have been more powerful it worked well in all weathers, sometimes assisted by shock cords in strong reaching winds. The

FIG 3: 'MUNCHER'

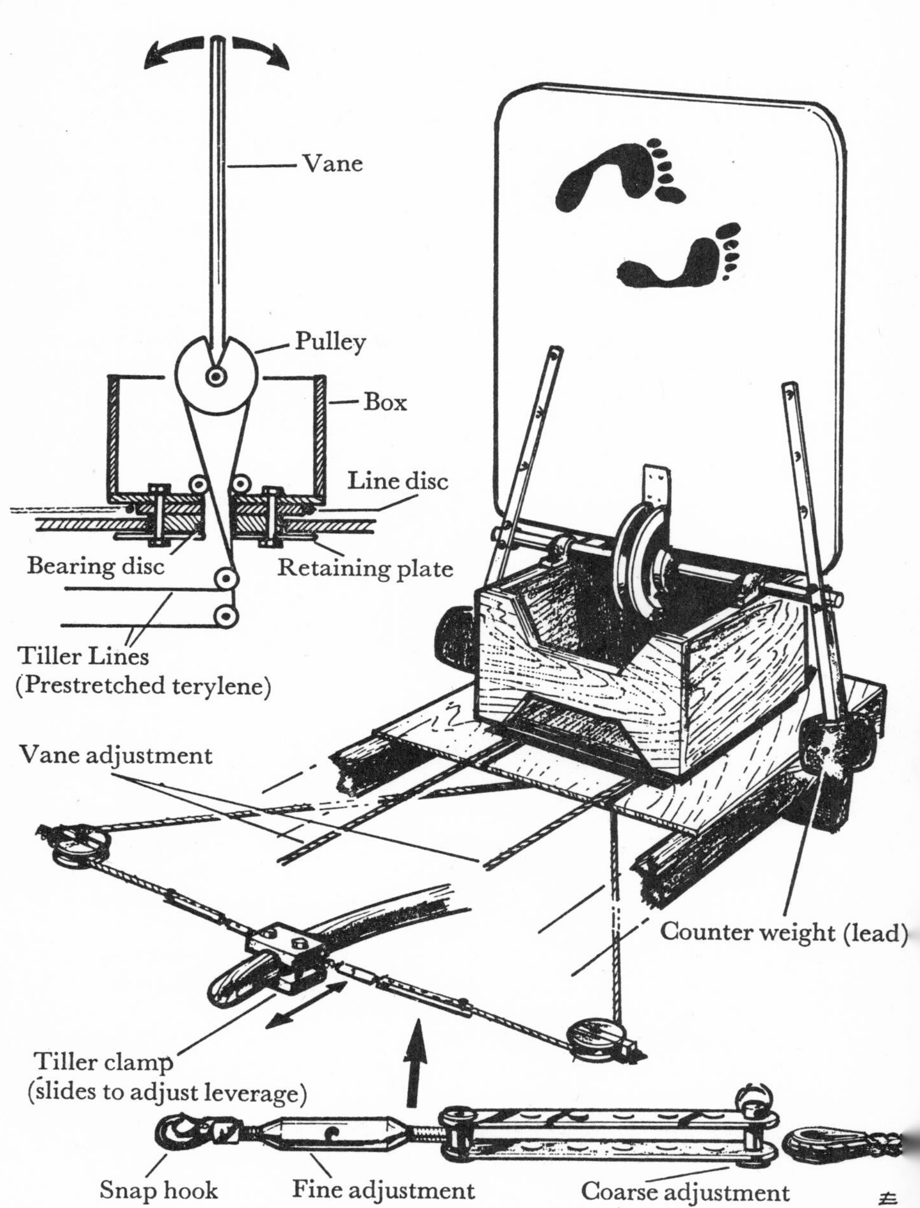

essential requirement, however, for any self-steering system is a balanced boat. If the sails are balanced first most steering gears can attend to the small corrections.

Dinghy and other gear

Crawlabout was handmaid of all work, only slightly less important than *Walkabout* herself. The first task on reaching port was to swing the dinghy over the side, and she was in continual demand as ferry boat, fishing boat, children's play boat and our only means of transport. Rather like the family car, except that she could be driven by anyone over the age of six. Even at sea she served as a sail locker and playpen.

Rubber dinghies are poor machines for this sort of work because they handle so badly, particularly with children. *Crawlabout* is a very sturdy plywood pram, just under 8ft long. I fitted her with leeboard and lateen sail for the children and they used an oar as a rudder. What other modifications they made I cannot remember, but they were many and complex, and the children had a great deal of fun.

They used life-jackets in the dinghy, but on board only safety harnesses were used. These were stowed in a special box next to the main hatch and a steel rope safety line was strung between the two masts.

We found that various covers were essential to comfort, if not safety. A main hatch cover, shown in Fig. 4, was devised to keep the weather out of the cabin and admit light, a job it did surprisingly well in all conditions, bar a direct hit by a wave. Spray covers were used for the same reason on the forehatch, and in tropical ports we found that sun awnings were absolutely essential.

All gear was simple; not so much a virtue as a financial necessity, but it did at least do its job.

The Cabin

The layout of the cabin, shown in Fig. 5, could be termed open-plan living. Except for a curtain across the heads there was no privacy, but squeamishness is a luxury on a small boat, and modesty is more a state of mind than a state of reality.

Bunks were laid along either side with separate seats lower down. Although this reduces the feeling of spaciousness, it provides extra locker space and one never has far to fall in a seaway.

Great attention was paid to stowage, and not a single cubic inch was wasted. Clothes were stored in individual nets, as were some perishable food and other stores; there were even nets inside locker lids. Everything had a place, and tools, for example, were filed in hanging bags, while the Tilley lamp was gripped on a special shelf.

FIG 4: MAIN HATCH COVER

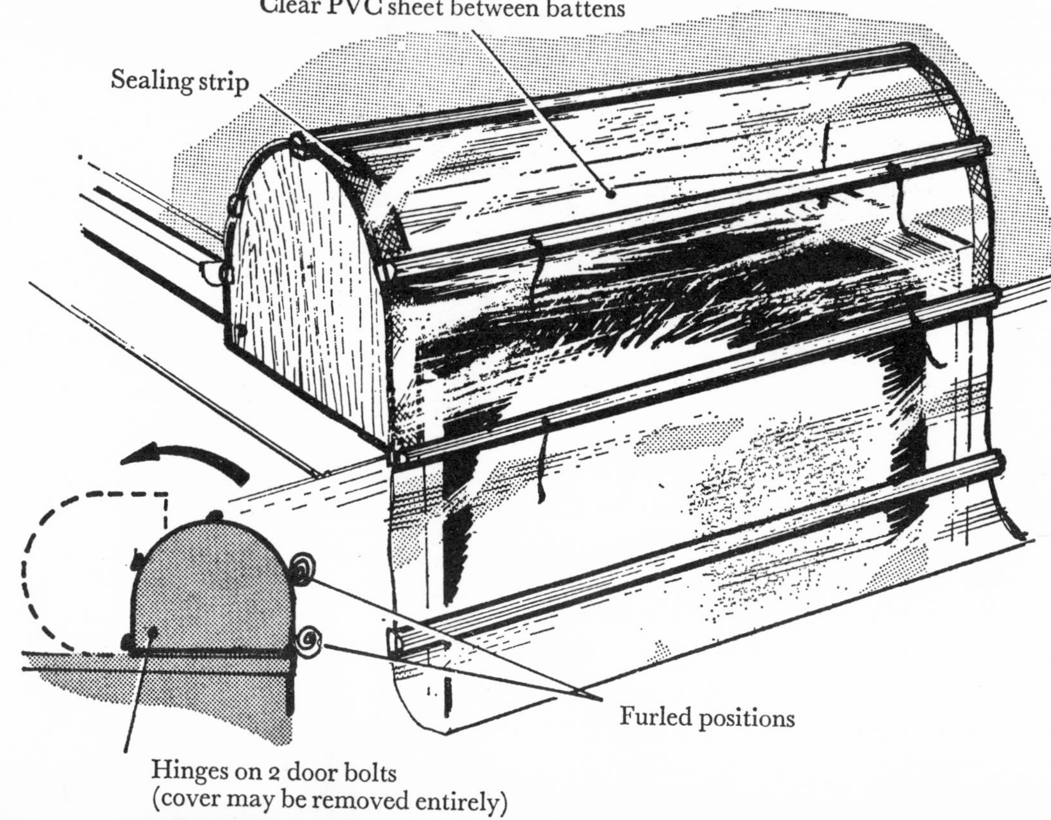

The vital areas on a boat are the galley and the chart table. The galley was relatively spacious with large working surfaces, a very deep sink, and shelving with high fiddles. The stove was a home-made steel framework holding two primus stoves with a deep spillage tray under; it was gimballed with pivots fore and aft and had adjustable steel pegs to grip the pots. A tin oven sat on a primus when needed. Kerosene was piped from the main 14-gallon tank to avoid pouring at sea. Both fresh and salt water were piped to the sink, the latter for washing up. The fresh water ran from a 3-gallon head tank, which was in turn pumped from a 30-gallon main tank. The balance of the 140 gallons was carried in plastic bags.

Navigation

The chart table was fitted with a parallel rule and opened like a travelling trunk to store charts. Immediately to the right were the radio receiver, the chronometer (a Smith's clock with electronic tuning fork mechanism), the barometer and all the navigational books to hand. The area was designed to be easy to work in.

The radio receiver was an ordinary portable transistor with four wave bands covering 0·5 to 22 MHz. It carried out satisfactorily its main function of picking up time signals from B.B.C. and W.W.V.

The only other instruments were a sextant, with a spare plastic one for emergencies, ship's compass, hand-bearing compass, an old R.D.F. which occasionally worked and the only luxury—a trailing log.

Mechanics

The engine, rarely used, was a 1·5l. Newage Captain B.M.C. diesel with a straight-through gearbox. 49 gallons of fuel were carried in two tanks.

Two 12 v. batteries had a total capacity of 150 ampère hours and were charged by a 15 amp., gasoline-driven, Honda generator. Electric lights were fitted throughout the cabin and over each bunk.

FIG 5: CABIN LAYOUT

SECTION AT GALLEY

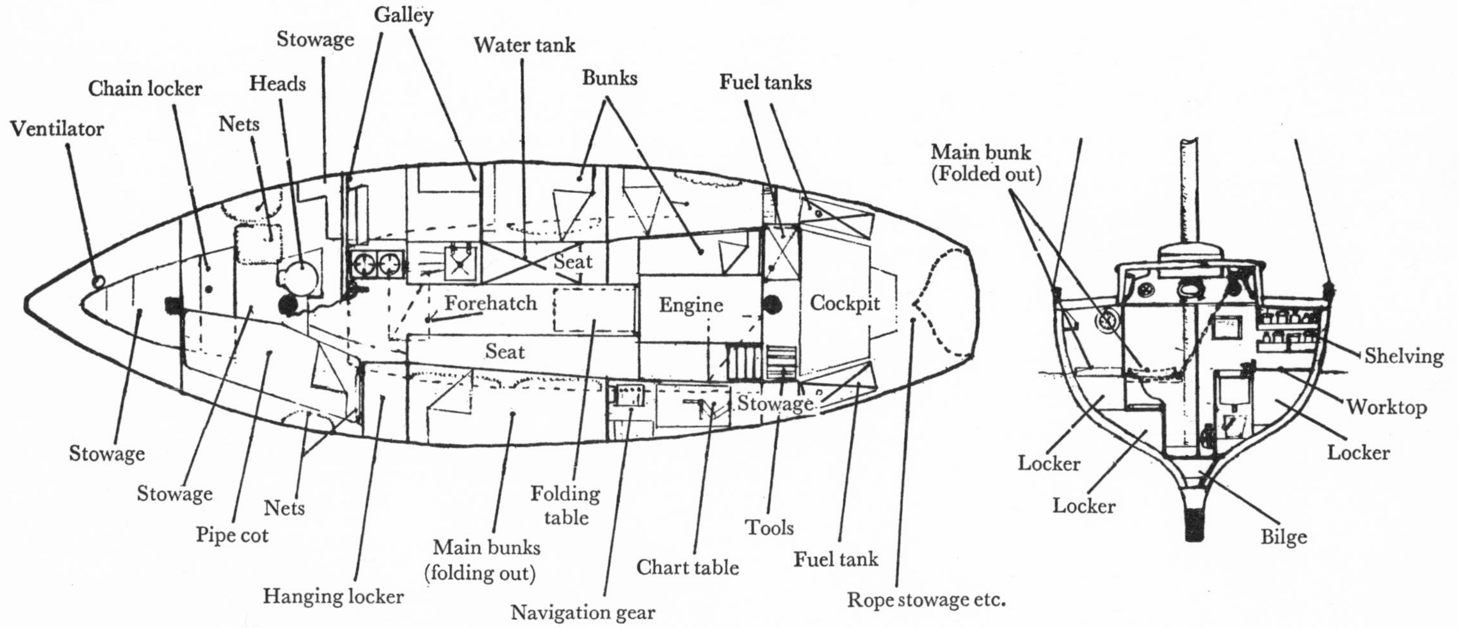

APPENDIX II

THE WALKABOUTS

As I have already explained, a walkabout is a person who, like the Australian aborigine, suddenly chucks in his job, abandons the security of a rigid roof and mortar walls, and takes to wandering. The nomadic life is as old as the hills, but its modern expression in small pleasure craft is relatively new. One day a man refuses to catch the 8.45, stamps on his bowler hat and takes to a small sailing boat. How many are doing this I do not know, but one indication is that, of the forty-odd walkabouts we met, all but six were new to the game.

An even better indication of the increasing popularity of cruising is provided by the number of yachts calling at Horta in the Azores, a port that can only be reached after crossing at least half an ocean. "Peter" and his father at Café Sport have kept records of every cruising yacht in port since 1929, when four yachts put in. An average of three or four a year continued to call until 1962, when ten put in, and by 1968 the number had risen into the twenties. Then there was a dramatic increase—sixty in 1970 and well over a hundred by 1973! The number of nationalities increased, too. Before 1960 nearly all the yachts were either British or American, with an occasional Norwegian or Frenchman or some such. In 1972 there were sixteen nationalities, including Japanese, Finnish and Chilean.

Most of those that call at Horta are not true walkabouts, i.e. they retain their land homes and are indulging in a long cruise. But they are a sign of the times.

The main reason, I believe, for the increasing number of walkabouts is a general disillusionment with modern materialistic life, coupled perhaps with the inability to cope with everything that is implied by "the rat race". At the same time the increased level of prosperity makes it easier for the average man to become a walkabout, though oddly enough you will very rarely find a wealthy walkabout—that is, someone who can really afford to be one.

Most are quite hard up, though they come from all walks of life; just over half of those we met were professional people, a third were tradesfolk, and the balance businessmen and others. They covered all ages, though the majority were between thirty and forty and about a third had children aboard.

As for their boats and gear, the main features are best summarised in the following tables, which refer to forty walkabouts.

Age of boat	
10 years or less	57%
11–20 years	22%
21–30 years	16%
Over 30 years	5%

Hull size		*Hull material*		*Keel*	
Under 23ft	3%	Wood	56%	Long	67%
23–29ft	18%	G.R.P.	26%	Medium or fin	30%
30–40ft	45%	Steel	13%	Centre-board	3%
Over 40ft	34%	Ferrocement & aluminium	5%	Bilge	0%

Rig		
Ketch	45% (average size 41ft)	i.e. the larger boats tend to have two masts and the smaller one
Sloop	42% (average size 30ft)	
Yawl	5%	
Cutter	5%	
Schooner	3%	
Gaff rigs	14% of total	

Self-steering		*Tenders*		
Horizontally hinged vane	16%	Wood	27%	51% solid
Vertically hinged vane	5%	G.R.P.	14%	
Vane and trim tab	16%	Aluminium	10%	
Pendulum servo	21%	Inflatable	45%	
Staysail sheets	3%	Folding	4%	
Electric	5%			
None	34%			

Cooking fuel		*Engine fuel*		*Radio transmitter*
Kerosene	45%	Diesel	78%	55%
Gas	45%	Gasoline	22%	
Alcohol	5%			
Diesel (with gas)	5%			

The gear was as varied as the people themselves, and tended to be what they could afford rather than what they would like. None the less it was generally very practical, for the sea quickly sorts out the frivolous from the functional. A third of the yachts, for example, had fridges, but less than half of these were functioning and only one man was satisfied with his unit. Radio transmitters were even worse. Over half had them, but only a fifth of those were working (to chat to each other), and not one was used for meaningful navigation purposes.

Maintenance is a most persistent problem, and the more complex the gear the worse the headache; consequently, walkabouts have a predilection for gear that is simple, and they are less influenced by fashion than other sailors. If you are permanently afloat you can expect to spend on average half your time in port on maintenance, which will also absorb a good deal of your cost of living; some figures are given in the last appendix.

The other main problem is a more nebulous one, and is simply the result of the increasing number of yachties—port facilities are becoming overstrained. Walkabouts are dependent on port facilities at some time or another for safe berths, provisions, water, maintenance work and jobs. Even a few years ago an ocean cruiser was sufficiently uncommon for yacht clubs to lavish hospitality on the voyager. Now, however, there are so many cruising yachts that clubs and ports are finding it increasingly difficult to cope, even when charges are levied, and locals tend to resent large numbers of water gypsies. One solution is to establish marinas which approach the matter in a purely commercial spirit, but that is only possible in the more intensive cruising areas. The other solution lies with the walkabouts themselves, who would be wise to make themselves as independent as it is possible to be, and at the same time remember they have chosen a way of life that makes them strangers in any land, even to some extent their own.

APPENDIX III

A TENDER/LIFEBOAT

In the ordinary way a yacht's lifeboat is an inflatable life-raft. Inflatable life-rafts are specifically designed to keep the crew afloat, to shield them from exposure, and to remain near the scene of the disaster until help arrives. Being constructed of flexible material and generally round in shape, they cannot be propelled for any distance by any means.

While such a life-raft is ideal for coastal and frequented waters, it is less than satisfactory in the more remote seas. What is needed is a life-raft that can actually sail. And can sail, moreover, over long distances, surviving the combined assault of sea, sun and fish which led, in the case of the Robertson family's ordeal,* to the disintegration of their life-raft.

The two requirements of sailing ability and toughness point to a craft made of solid rather than of flexible material. Which means in turn that the lifeboat will have to double as a tender, for there is only space on most yachts for one solid dinghy, and a dinghy/lifeboat could not in any case be accommodated on yachts below about 35ft. As mentioned in Appendix I, the dinghy is also a vital piece of cruising gear, serving both as a workboat and as a playboat.

To fulfil these various functions the dinghy must be strong, relatively large and yet light. I feel that aluminium is the best material of construction, but one has to accept that after a time it will look like an old saucepan. However, nearly all the well-used fibreglass and moulded ply dinghies I have seen were suffering badly from the battering that a cruiser's dinghy always receives, whereas none of the aluminium dinghies were seriously affected. A stout plywood or wooden construction is usually robust, but tends to be heavy.

The size of the dinghy should be the largest that can be conveniently carried, but a tender that is too heavy is not only difficult to take aboard but difficult to drag ashore. Much depends on the size of the parent yacht and the method of hoisting and stowing. On a large yacht with many crew, each wishing to row off in different directions, there is a good case for a large dinghy and a small tender. On yachts larger than 40ft a dinghy of 10ft can usually be accommodated.

* *Survive the Savage Sea*, by Dougal Robertson.

FIG 6: TENDER/LIFEBOAT

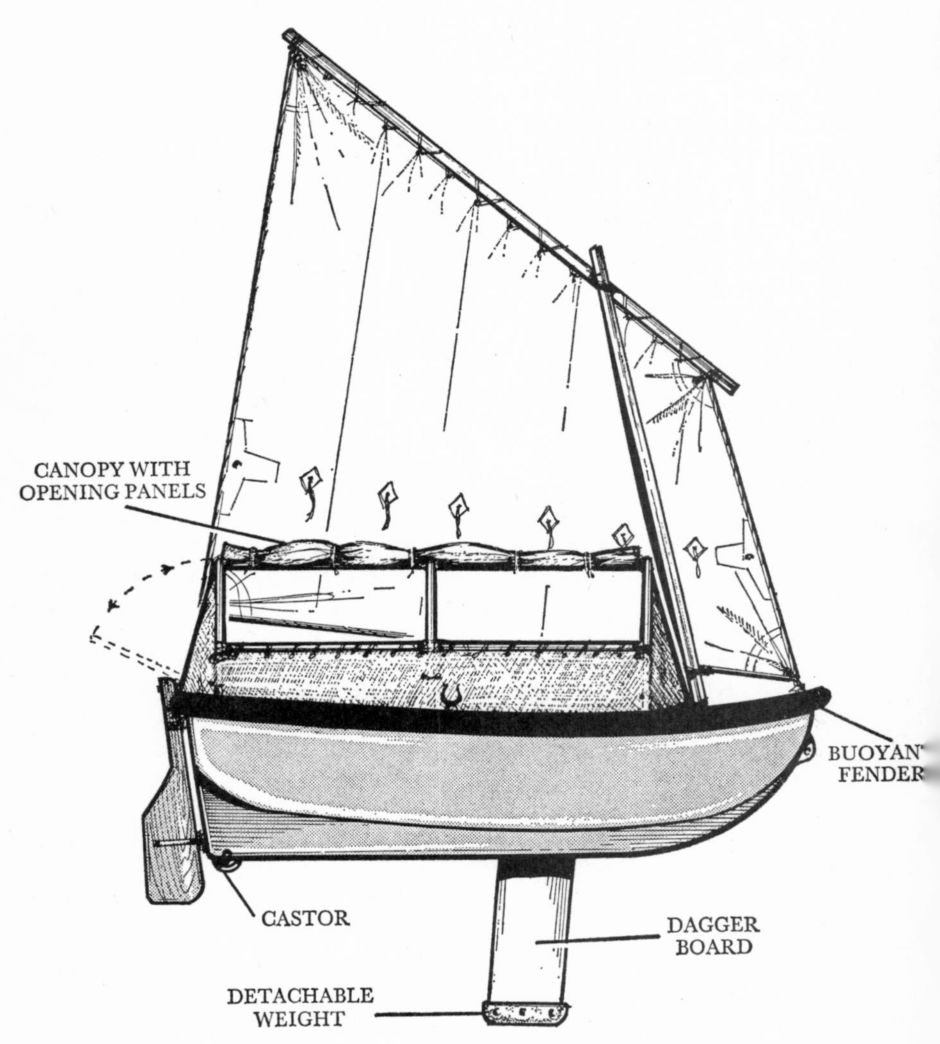

The dinghy shown in Fig. 6 can best be described by summarising the main features:

(*a*) Adequate buoyancy is required of two sorts, for two different functions. The first is buoyancy at high level to assist self-righting tendencies, and this can best be provided by a buoyant fender running right round the boat. The second is buoyancy at low level to lift the gunwales above the surface if the boat founders, and this would be built into the boat at stem and stern and possibly under the thwarts.

(*b*) For stability, and to assist self-righting tendencies, a hollow keel would be built which would fill automatically with water through neoprene non-return flaps along the bottom. These flaps would normally be shut off for tender work. To increase stability a keel weight could be clamped on to the foot of the centreboard, but again this would only normally be used for lifeboat work. The dinghy used as a lifeboat should, therefore, be unsinkable and self-righting.

(*c*) A flexible cover, mounted on curved frames, for protection of the crew, is essential; the lower section would, in effect, raise the freeboard, while the upper section would be fitted with panels which can be removed for access or in fine weather. With the yacht under way the material would be fixed in position, but the frames would hinge down flat until needed; a single movement would then erect the cover. In port the whole affair would be removed.

(*d*) For the sail I should choose a single lug sail, providing balanced off-wind performance, with modest spars and simple rigging. There are doubtless many other possible arrangements which would be satisfactory.

(*e*) Emergency rations in sealed canisters would be fastened in while under way and removed in port.

(*f*) For use in port the dinghy should have good oars with captive rowlocks, a castor on the keel for dragging her ashore, suspended canvas stowage bags and a little folding anchor, to discourage her from escaping. An outboard motor of 2–4 h.p. is of great use, though not essential.

Many remarkable voyages have been accomplished in tiny craft, and there is no good reason why this lifeboat should not achieve at least 1,000 miles a month in trade wind regions.

It will be a costly little boat, but will probably not exceed the combined cost of a conventional tender and a life-raft, which, it should be remembered, is an expensive item that usually lies rotting on deck year in and year out.

APPENDIX IV

COMMISSIONING LISTS

While several excellent commissioning lists have been published, it is hoped that the following lists will be of some assistance to those planning voyages with children.

The quantities are based on the needs of two adults and four children at sea for sixty days, with a margin of safety. Equipment lists tend to the minimal. The lists are based on personal experience, however, and should be used only as a guide; every boat, every crew and every voyage are different.

In the following lists and in particular the Medicine Chest, the U.S. equivalents of what we actually carried are given wherever possible.

1. *Food*

Average consumption was about 11 lb. a day, but we laid in roughly 15 lb. a day, not only for safety, but also to provide variety up to the last day. Assuming 2 children equal to 1 adult, these figures are equivalent to $2\frac{3}{4}$ lb. and $3\frac{3}{4}$ lb. per adult per day.

		lb.
citrus fruits		60
other fruits		50
tomatoes and vegetables		20
onions		15
potatoes		30
eggs	doz.	16
butter		10
cheese		2
bacon		2
smoked cheese (lasts indefinitely)		4
Parmesan cheese	pkts	4
brown flour		50
white flour		60
yeast, dried	3 × 4 oz. tins	
breakfast cereals		25
rice		10
spaghetti (pasta)		10
powdered milk (skim)		30
cooking oil	gals	3
margarine		20
sugar		20
jams, honey, etc.		30
peanut butter		3
tea		2
coffee, fresh		2
coffee, instant		4
cocoa		2
cookies		15
crisp breads		18
nuts		12
dried fruit		40
dried beans		5
salt		4
pepper		$\frac{1}{4}$
mustard		$\frac{1}{2}$
garlic		2
spices and herbs		
sauces, chutneys, etc.	bottles	10
salad dressing and sandwich spread	bottles	4
Marmite	jars	3
pickles, olives, etc.	jars	17

Food that is really fresh, and is stored well, will last in hot weather roughly as follows:

potatoes, onions, eggs (sealed with vaseline) 2–2½ months
citrus fruits 1½–2 months
apples 5–6 weeks
butter, open salami, cabbage 2 weeks
soft fruit, tomatoes, bacon, cheese 7–10 days
carrots, green vegetables 3–4 days

Cans

beef stew, etc.	20 × 1 lb.
ham	6 × 2 lb.
chicken	6 × 2 lb.
pâté	10 × 4 oz.
sardines	10
other fish	20 × 1 lb.
soups (condensed)	50 × 1 lb.
baked beans	10 × 1 lb.
spaghetti	10 × 1 lb.
sweet corn	3 × 1 lb.
tomatoes	15 × 1 lb.
tomato puree	20 × 2 oz.
vegetables	40 × 1 lb
fruits	60 × 1 lb.
soup cubes	12 pkts
beer	12 cans
wine	3 bottles
spirits	2 bottles
fruit juice (concentrate)	10 bottles
soft drinks	6 bottles
sweets	12 lb.
chocolate	5 lb.
popcorn	1 lb.
pudding mix	1 lb.
cornstarch	1 lb.
baking powder	2 tins
desiccated coconut	2 lb.
cigarettes	2,500

2. *Water and fuel* (*volumes in U.S. gallons*)

water, 3½ gals per day consumed
kerosene (paraffin), 1¼ gal. per week consumed for cooking only
alcohol (methylated spirit), 1½ pt per week consumed
gasoline (petrol), 1¾ gal. per week consumed (equivalent to 50 ampere hours per week for lighting)
diesel, 49 gals (300 mile range)
engine oil, 2 gals
selection of oils and freeing agents, 3 pts
selection of greases, 3 lb.
standby gas cylinder, 7 lb.
lighter fuel, 1 tube

3. *Consumable stores*

tissues	4 boxes
paper towels	8 rolls
toilet paper	8 rolls
toilet soap	8 cakes
shampoo	4 bottles
various toilet consumables (toothpaste, etc.)	
aluminum foil	1 roll

steel wool	2 lb.
liquid detergent	$3\frac{1}{2}$ gals
soap powder	2 lb.
various cleaning agents (Ajax, polishes, disinfectant, etc.)	11 containers
rags	10 lb.
matches	10 large packets
candles	1 packet
dry cell batteries for flashlights and all other appliances approx.	20 batteries in 60 days
mosquito coils (port only)	3 packets

4. *Household and personal items*

There were eighty items on the list, ranging from sleeping bags (6) through spectacles (spare) to string (2 balls). It would be of little help to list them all, but here are some notes:

Cooking and eating containers should be robust, reasonably sized and as high as they are wide. Mugs with lids are useful, and a pressure cooker essential. Mild steel utensils should be avoided if they have to be washed in sea-water.

Plastic containers, from buckets to Tupperware, should be small for compact stowage. A selection of 100–200 heavy-duty (500 ml) polythene bags is really useful.

A gas cylinder with an emergency cooking ring and light also served an iron, a soldering iron and a blowtorch.

A good selection of sewing gear is needed, and if space permits a sewing-machine will save hundreds of stitching hours.

5. *Clothes*

This again is a personal matter, but remember that every type of weather conditions may be encountered. One usually, however, takes too much fancy gear which just rots in the lockers. Ordinary zips are hopeless at sea: they must be completely corrosion-proof, as must studs and buckles. In clothes worn next to the skin, synthetic fibres are best avoided.

6. *Medicine chest*

The following guide should be supplemented with expert advice. A doctor will in any case be needed for those items on prescription.

Literature

A good reference book, such as *First Aid Afloat*, by Paul B. Sheldon (Yachting Publishing Corp.).

A list of every drug carried, with dose and application.

Surgical supplies

scissors	1 lb. absorbent cotton
razor blades	1 pkt surgical gauze
tweezers	3 rolls ½″ adhesive tape
thermometer	4 × 90 cm. Band-Aids
2 disposable syringes	3 × 3″ Ace bandages
1 pkt safety pins	
1 large tin Vaseline	

Wounds

Children are continually getting small wounds, and ordinary dressings are washed or worked off too quickly. An antiseptic and sealing spray that overcomes this problem is Izodine

85 g. Izodine	minor wounds
1 large bottle antiseptic, e.g. Zephirin	wounds and general
1 tube Neosporin	antiseptic cream
1 tube Furacin	antiseptic cream and antibiotic
4 butterfly sutures	large wounds instead of stitches
36 petrolatum gauze dressings	large wounds

Burns and skin afflictions

Children are also continually getting minor burns, and it seems that a paste of bicarbonate of soda and water applied immediately is as good as the various patent medicines that we have tried.

1 lb. bicarbonate of soda	burns
1 tin 10 Sofra Tulle dressings	severe burns
1 bottle Caladryl	sunburn and skin irritation
2 tubes Uval	prevention of sunburn
1 bottle Surfadil	irritation

Analgesic and pain relief

One of the most used drugs in the chest is an effective yet safe analgesic that will give relief from pain or fever and allow the body to heal itself. Ponstel proved to be the best of those we tried.

200 ml. Ponstel suspension	analgesic, children
25 Ponstel capsules (cheaper)	analgesic, adults
20 tablets Sonalgin	pain relief and sleep
Numorphan suppositories	very severe pain
10 ml. oil of cloves	toothache
20 tablets Coricidin	cold suppressant
20 tablets throat lozenges (SpecT)	sore throat

Intestinal

60 tablets preferred sea sickness tablets (e.g. Bonine, Dramamine, Marezine

1 bottle Maalox	antacid (also helps prolonged seasickness)
1 bottle Kaopectate	diarrhoea
20 tablets Lomotil c. neomycin	diarrhoea, adults
1 pkt Tigan suppositories	severe vomiting, children
48 Sennakot tablets	laxative
1 bottle Sedadrops	colic

Eye, ear and lung

2 tubes Achromycin ointment	eye and ear infections
1 Neosynephrine spray	nasal dilatant
1 eye lotion	eye strain
12·5 ml. Auralgan	earache
4 oz. Phensedyl	cough mixture

Infections

Broad spectrum antibiotics are required for severer infections, internal and external.

6 bottles (courses) Achromycin suspension (children)
100 tablets Terramycin (adults)

Various

1,000 tablets multivitamin	diet deficiency
1,000 tablets ascorbic acid (vitamin C)	diet deficiency
Daraprim (prophylactic)	malaria areas
Camoquin (treatment)	malaria areas
300 tablets chlorine	purification of bad water
25 tablets Vallium	sleeping pills
50 tablets benzedrine	stimulant for emergencies

Any special medicines needed by individual members of the crew.

7. *Entertainment*

This is another personal list, including books and music. For the children we had in addition a wide variety of board games, plastic bricks and musical instruments, and a great deal of stationery, glues and paints for drawing and construction. We also took such things as a sewing kit and rags for collage. Unwieldy or fragile toys were avoided.

8. *Safety gear*

Survival

6-man life-raft with the following attached:

$2\frac{1}{2}$ gal. water-can

sealed bag with 15 lb. survival rations
12 fish-hooks
30 yd heavy fishing-line
plankton net
stainless knife
3 pkts cigarettes and matches
paper and pencils
2 large plastic bags
30 ft light rope

2 canvas and wood hull tingles (repair strips)
essential documents and money (in plastic wallet)

General
safety harnesses
life-jackets
flares, red and white
foghorn
radar reflector
3 fire extinguishers
life-belt
emergency knife

It is only fair to say that many yachts have a more extensive inventory.

9. *Navigational gear*

Documents: The British Admiralty publishes all necessary charts, routeing charts, sailing directions, lists of lights, etc., for every part of the world. It is best to purchase their catalogue and make a selection. In addition to about 150 charts and twenty Admiralty publications we carried:

The Nautical Almanac (Nautical Almanac Office, U.S. Naval Observatory)
The Mariners' Handbook N.P. 100 (Hydrographer of the Royal Navy)
Sight Reduction Tables for Air Navigation, Vols. 2 and 3, H.O. Pub No. 249 (U.S. Navy Hydrographic Office)
Burton's Nautical Tables (The Maritime Press)
Navigation book (e.g. *Sextant Observations for the Seafarer,* by Graeme Richards, Nautical Publishing Co.)
Cruising Under Sail, by Eric C. Hiscock (Oxford University Press)
Brown's Signalling (Brown, Son and Ferguson)
Ship's log
Provisions log
Deck log
Calculation forms (home-made)

Instruments

ship's compass and spare
hand-bearing compass
sextant and plastic spare
patent log
echo-sounder
lead and line
stop-watch
thermometer
barometer
radio receiver (short wave up to 20 MHz min.)
chronometer (e.g. tuning fork clock)
small R.D.F.
dividers
Douglas protractor
parallel rules
pencils
rubber
1 pad graph paper
slide rule

Signalling

Ensign and national courtesy flags
Set of international code flags or at least N, C, Q, G, D, K, V
Signalling lamp/spotlight

10. *Deck gear*

ground tackle: at least 2 anchors, warp and chain
boat hook
fenders
dodgers
sun awnings
cockpit cushions
bosun's chair
dinghy and gear
battery generator (if engine not hand-start)
mooring lines
navigation lights
2 buckets and cleaning gear
water and fuel containers
2 funnels
2 bilge pumps

11. *Spares and repairs*

Tools

Wrenches

adjustable 2 × 15″, 8″, 4″
pipe 2 × 12″, 6″
set of socket wrenches
selection of flat and box-end wrenches
Allen keys

Drills

½″ hand
⅜″ electric
ratchet brace
generous selection twist bits $\frac{1}{16}$″–½″
selection of wood bits ¼″–1″
expandable bit ¾″–3″
rose bits

Clamps

1 × 8″, 2 × 6″, 4 × 3″
3½″ clamp-on vice

Saws

hacksaw and 20 blades
wood, tenon, keyhole and coping

Pliers, etc.
1 large, 2 medium
long nose
vice-grips
tin snips
wire cutter

Screwdrivers, etc.
set of 4, including Philips
1 heavy levering
2 screwdriver bits
bradawl

Percussion
hammers: 4 lb., 1½ lb., ½ lb.
punches: blunt, centre, circular

Files, etc.
plane
rasps: round and half-round
files: generous selection from minifiles to 14″
paint scrapers
putty knife
wire brush

Bosun's locker
2 hollow marline spikes
peening punch and brass eyelets
sewing gear, palm and twine
spare rope, good selection
waxed whipping twine
hambro line
shockcord and hooks
black tape
spare wire rope—selection
copper and galvanised wire—selection
polythene piping antichafe
spare sailcloth
spare canvas
sail tape
shackles—selection
slides—selection

Chisels and cutters
selection of wood ¼″–1¼″
selection of cold ¼″–¾″
plane
spokeshave
Stanley knife

Various
pop riveter
battery hydrometer
grease gun and oilcan
set-square
feeler gauges
lamp circuit tester
steel tape
oil stone
caulking iron
kerosene lamp and soldering iron

hanks—selection
thimbles—selection
blocks—selection
bulldog grips—selection
rigging screws—selection
cleats—selection

Engine spares
handbook
filter elements
water-pump kits
dynamo and starter kits
hydraulic cylinder kits
belts
similar to above for battery generator
distilled water
hydraulic oil
asbestos string
selection of rubber hose and clips
selection of copper and nylon tubing and fittings

Electrical spares
bulbs for every light
P.V.C. insulation cable and clips
selection of switches, connectors, etc.
insulation tape
fuse wire
solder wire

Appliance spares
Complete set of spares for bilge pumps, toilet, galley stove, etc.
Kerosene pressure appliances need at least two sets of spares for burning parts

Fastenings
Wide selection of wood and metal fastenings, especially bronze gripfast nails, brass screws and stainless threaded rod with nuts and washers
split-pins and rivets

Paints and glues
primers, wood and metal
surface paints and varnish
thinners
antifouling
selection of paint brushes
selection of sanding papers
linseed oil
anhydrous lanoline
paint remover
epoxy glue } metal
epoxy putty } metal
resorcinal glue—wood
contact glue—sails and general
filler putty
caulking compounds
caulking cotton
specialist glues, e.g. for waterproof clothing

12. *Fishing tackle*
200 yd heavy hand-line
selection of hooks, feathered lures, tracers, swivels, weights, rods and reels
gaff
masks and flippers
underwater gun
gill nets

APPENDIX V

COSTS

The following figures are intended to give a rough idea of the cost of extended cruising in a frugal style.

The figures are approximate, partly because of the continuous fluctuation in exchange rates of the eight currencies we handled and partly because of high rates of inflation everywhere. Allowance should be made for the fact that costs refer to 1971–73.

Fitting out

In our case this cost about $3360 in materials and included actual fitting out, instruments, charts, bedding, life raft, re-rigging—everything, in fact, apart from the boat herself and the simple gear that accompanied her.

Running costs—33ft boat, 2 adults and 4 children

Food, fuel and all other provisions	$155·00 per month
General maintenance and repairs averaged over 1½ years	$130·00 per month
Miscellaneous, e.g. harbour dues and shore transport	$25·00 per month
Total	$310·00 per month

Shore entertainment and drink, which can be expensive, are not included.

The thing to note about the above figures is the high cost of maintenance (materials only), confirmed by many yachties we met. Yet in our case the money was just enough to keep the boat and gear in sound and seaworthy condition and no more. Sails and rigging, which provided thousands of horsepower hours, demanded a good proportion of this. Contrary to popular supposition, the wind is not free.